BLACK SHEEP, SCOUNDRELS AND WEIRDOS, PETER QUILL, A.K.A. STAR-LORD, DRAX THE DESTROYER, GAMORA, ROCKET RACCOON AND GROOT LEARNED TO LOOK AFTER THEIR OWN INTERESTS, THEN DISCOVERED THEY COULD NOT STAND BY WHEN THE UNIVERSE WAS IN PERIL. THEY HAVE N̶ ... ...'RE IN TROUBLE (OR YOU'VE GOT A ... ... YOU CAN CALL THE...

All New GUARDIANS of the GALAXY

All-New GUA of the G

BEFORE EMBARKING ON THEIR BOLD QUEST FOR THE INFINITY STONES (ALL OFF THE MAP
SINCE THE MULTIVERSE CHANGED INDISCERNIBLY), THE GUARDIANS STOPPED ON EARTH
TO SEE IF ANYONE THERE COULD HELP.

NOT ONLY WAS THERE A DEARTH OF HELPFULNESS, THERE WERE A BUNCH OF BOZOS ASKING FOR
FAVORS. ONE, SCOTT LANG, A.K.A. *ANT-MA*, HAD MADE A BAD MISTAKE — BETRAYING HIS FELLOW
HEROES WHILE THINKING HE WAS PROTECTING HIS DAUGHTER — AND WAS LOOKING FOR A PLACE
TO LIE LOW. THE GUARDIANS (THEMSELVES SEASONED MISTAKE-MAKERS) AGREED TO LET HIM TAG
ALONG OFF-PLANET...RIGHT BEFORE A FEW NOVA CORPSMEN (INTERGALACTIC COPS) SHOWED UP.

WHAT DO THEY *WANT?!*

ALL-NEW GUARDIANS OF THE GALAXY VOL. 3: INFINITY QUEST. Contains material originally published in magazine form as GUARDIANS OF THE GALAXY #146-150. First
printing 2018. ISBN 978-1-302-90546-0. Published by MARVEL WORLDWIDE, INC., a subsidiary of MARVEL ENTERTAINMENT, LLC. OFFICE OF PUBLICATION: 135 West 50th
Street, New York, NY 10020. Copyright © 2018 MARVEL. No similarity between any of the names, characters, persons, and/or institutions in this magazine with those of
any living or dead person or institution is intended, and any such similarity which may exist is purely coincidental. **Printed in Canada.** DAN BUCKLEY, President, Marvel
Entertainment; JOE QUESADA, Chief Creative Officer; TOM BREVOORT, SVP of Publishing; DAVID BOGART, SVP of Business Affairs & Operations, Publishing & Partnership;
DAVID GABRIEL, SVP of Sales & Marketing, Publishing; JEFF YOUNGQUIST, VP of Production & Special Projects; DAN CARR, Executive Director of Publishing Technology; ALEX
MORALES, Director of Publishing Operations; SUSAN CRESPI, Production Manager; STAN LEE, Chairman Emeritus. For information regarding advertising in Marvel Comics
or on Marvel.com, please contact Vit DeBellis, Custom Solutions & Integrated Advertising Manager, at vdebellis@marvel.com. For Marvel subscription inquiries, please call
888-511-5480. **Manufactured between 1/19/2018 and 2/20/2018 by SOLISCO PRINTERS, SCOTT, QC, CANADA.**

10 9 8 7 6 5 4 3 2 1

RDIANS ALAXY

INFINITY QUEST

WRITER **GERRY DUGGAN**

ARTISTS **MARCUS TO** WITH **AARON KUDER** [#150]

COLOR ARTIST **IAN HERRING** LETTERER **VC'S CORY PETIT**

COVER ART **AARON KUDER & IVE SVORCINA** [#146-148],
AARON KUDER & JORDIE BELLAIRE [#149] AND **ALEX ROSS** [#150]

ASSISTANT EDITORS **ANNALISE BISSA, KATHLEEN WISNESKI & CHARLES BEACHAM**

ASSOCIATE EDITOR **DARREN SHAN** EDITOR **JORDAN D. WHITE**

COLLECTION EDITOR **JENNIFER GRÜNWALD** ASSISTANT EDITOR **CAITLIN O'CONNELL** ASSOCIATE MANAGING EDITOR **KATERI WOODY**
EDITOR, SPECIAL PROJECTS **MARK D. BEAZLEY** VP PRODUCTION & SPECIAL PROJECTS **JEFF YOUNGQUIST** SVP PRINT, SALES & MARKETING **DAVID GABRIEL**
BOOK DESIGNERS **JAY BOWEN & MANNY MEDEROS**

EDITOR IN CHIEF **C.B. CEBULSKI** CHIEF CREATIVE OFFICER **JOE QUESADA** PRESIDENT **DAN BUCKLEY** EXECUTIVE PRODUCER **ALAN FINE**

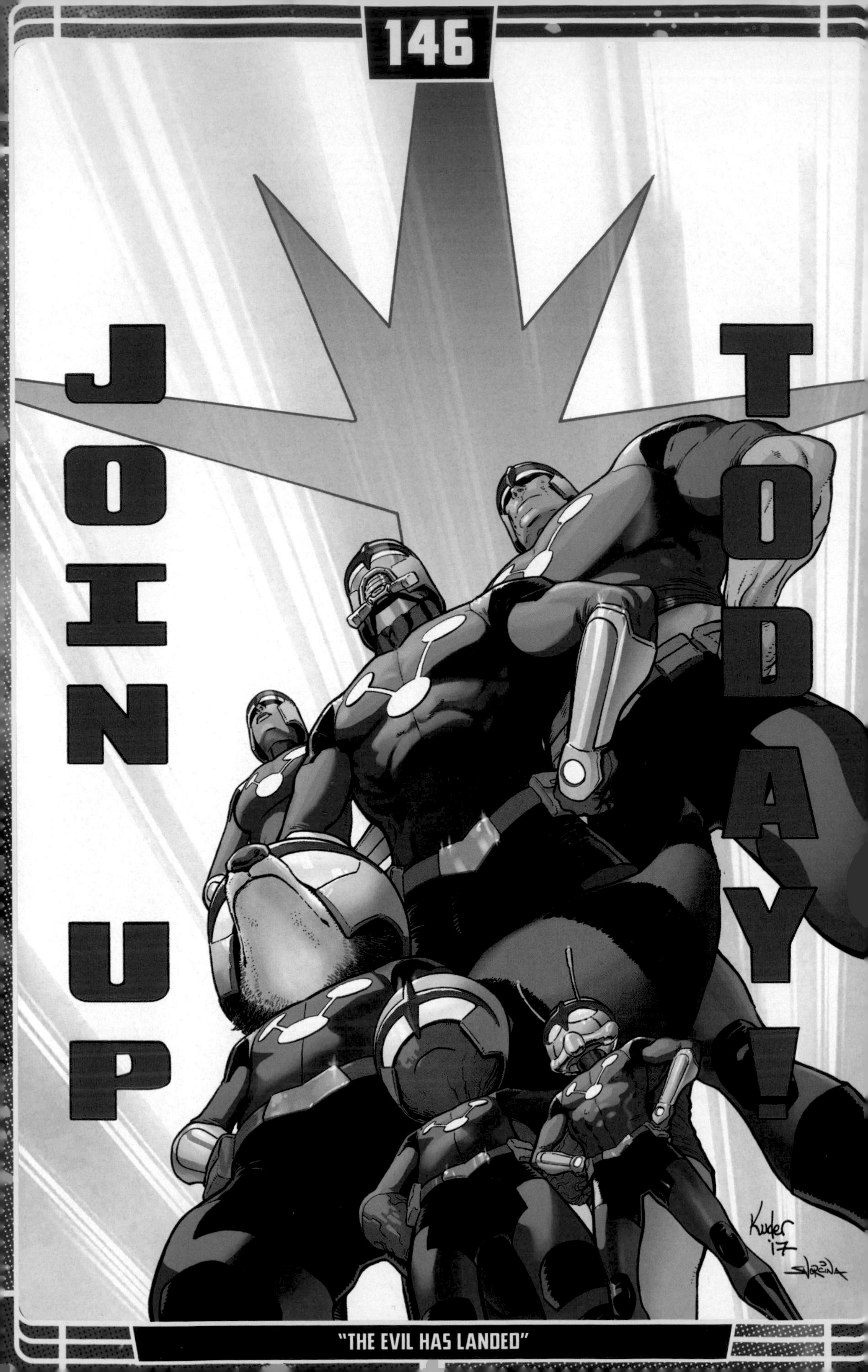
146
JOIN UP
TODAY!
Kuder '17
"THE EVIL HAS LANDED"

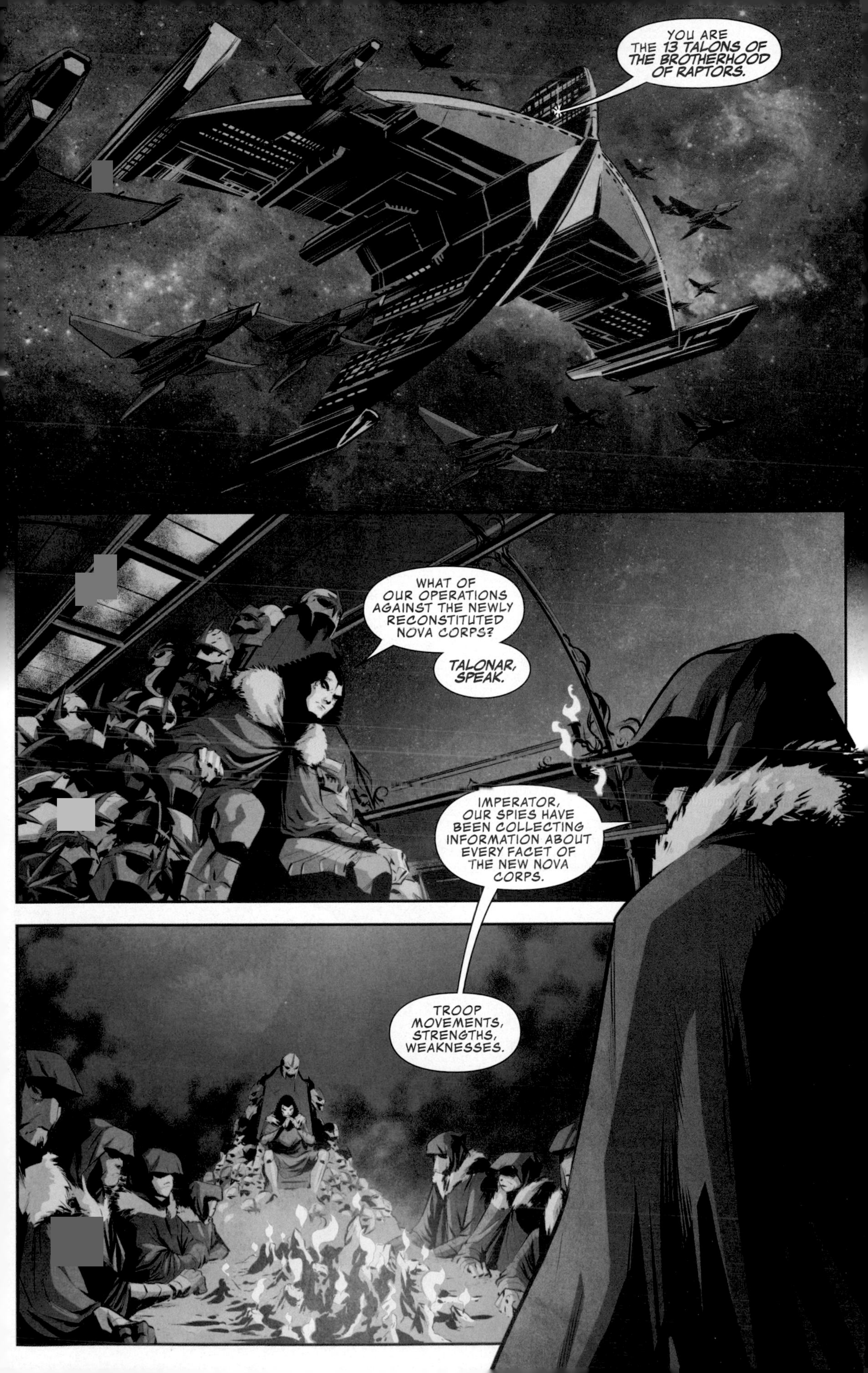
YOU ARE THE 13 TALONS OF THE BROTHERHOOD OF RAPTORS.
WHAT OF OUR OPERATIONS AGAINST THE NEWLY RECONSTITUTED NOVA CORPS?
TALONAR, SPEAK.
IMPERATOR, OUR SPIES HAVE BEEN COLLECTING INFORMATION ABOUT EVERY FACET OF THE NEW NOVA CORPS.
TROOP MOVEMENTS, STRENGTHS, WEAKNESSES.

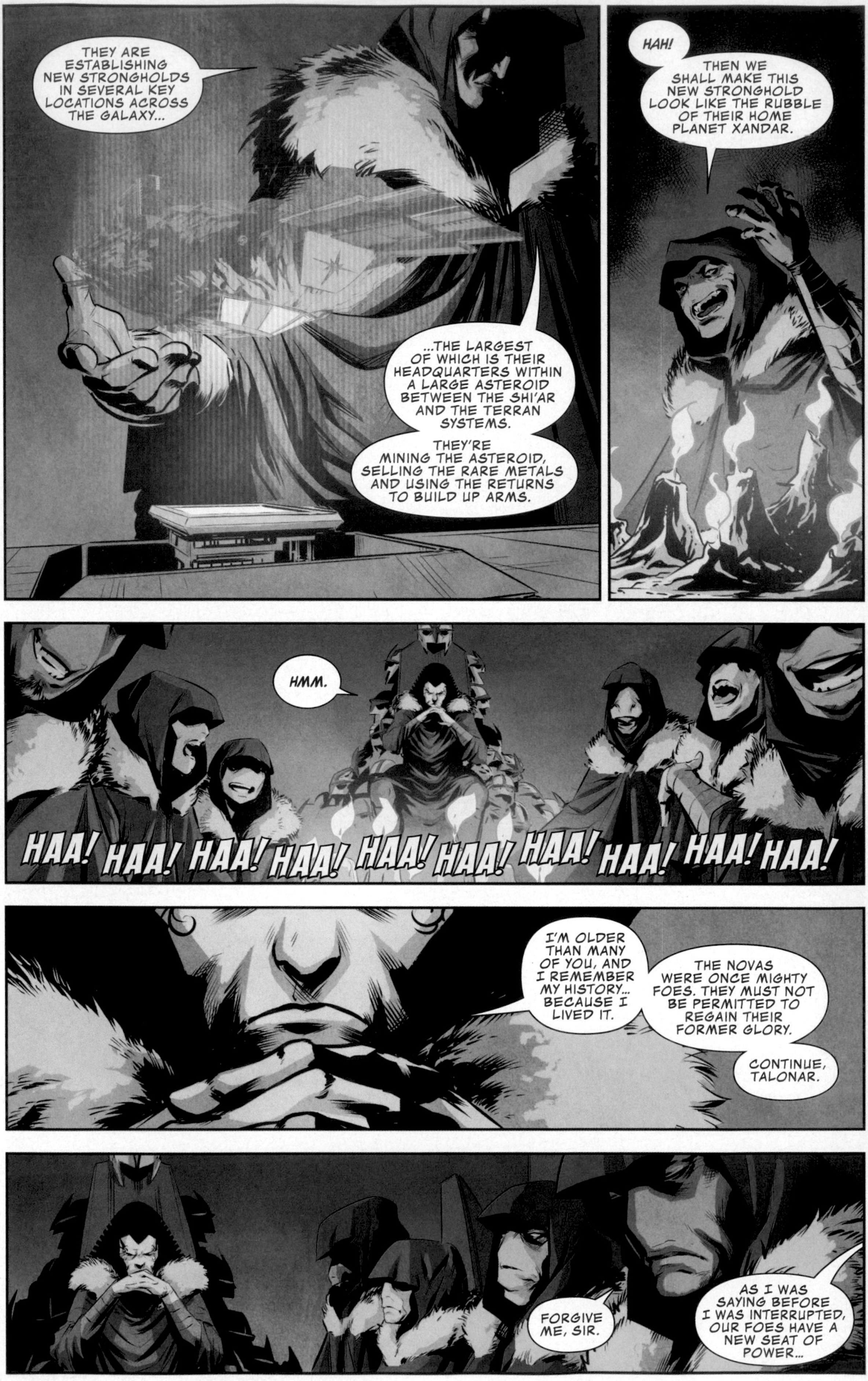
THEY ARE ESTABLISHING NEW STRONGHOLDS IN SEVERAL KEY LOCATIONS ACROSS THE GALAXY...
...THE LARGEST OF WHICH IS THEIR HEADQUARTERS WITHIN A LARGE ASTEROID BETWEEN THE SHI'AR AND THE TERRAN SYSTEMS.
THEY'RE MINING THE ASTEROID, SELLING THE RARE METALS AND USING THE RETURNS TO BUILD UP ARMS.
HAH!
THEN WE SHALL MAKE THIS NEW STRONGHOLD LOOK LIKE THE RUBBLE OF THEIR HOME PLANET XANDAR.
HMM.
HAA! HAA! HAA! HAA! HAA! HAA! HAA! HAA! HAA! HAA!
I'M OLDER THAN MANY OF YOU, AND I REMEMBER MY HISTORY... BECAUSE I LIVED IT.
THE NOVAS WERE ONCE MIGHTY FOES. THEY MUST NOT BE PERMITTED TO REGAIN THEIR FORMER GLORY.
CONTINUE, TALONAR.
FORGIVE ME, SIR.
AS I WAS SAYING BEFORE I WAS INTERRUPTED, OUR FOES HAVE A NEW SEAT OF POWER...

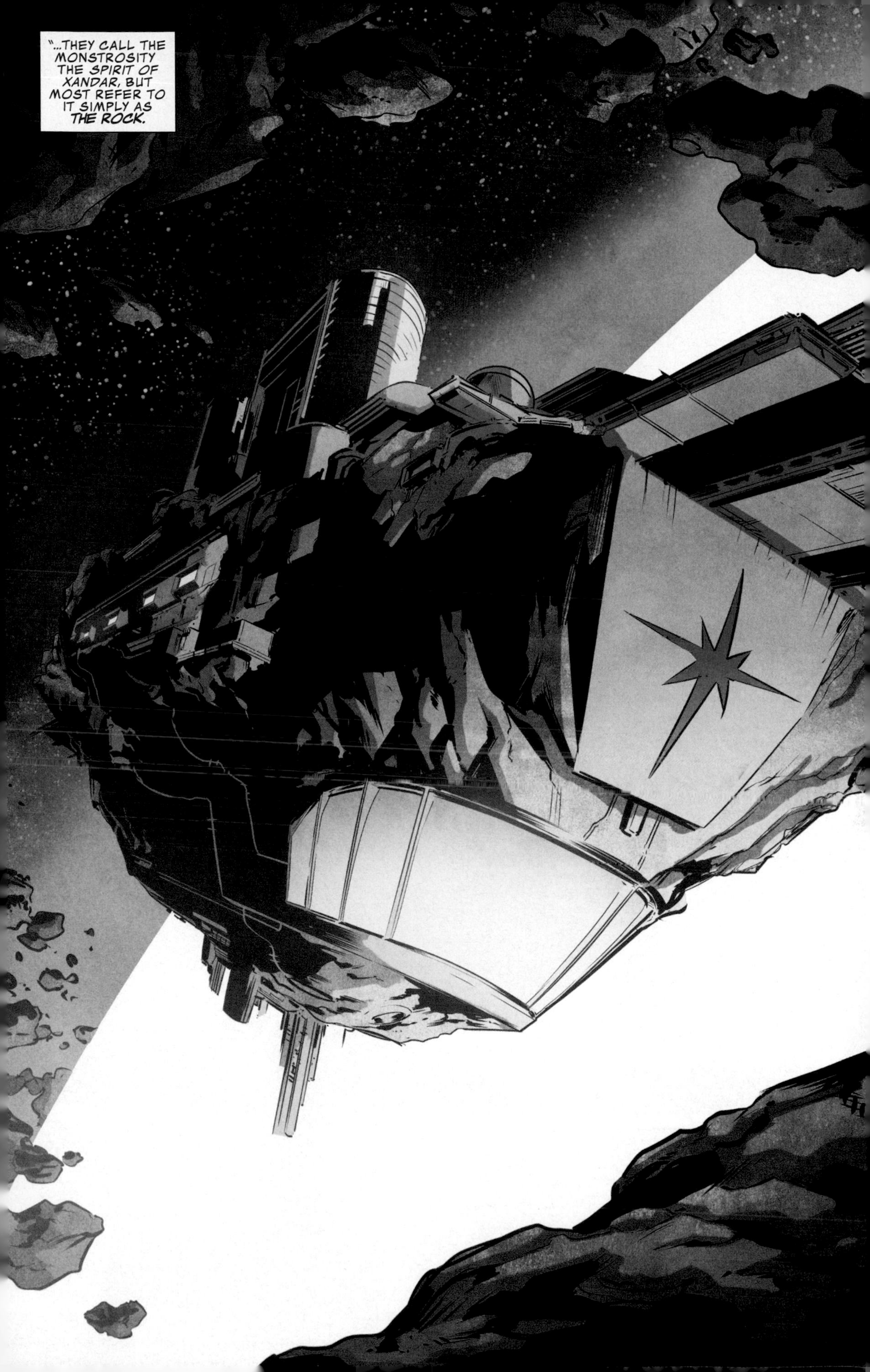
"...THEY CALL THE MONSTROSITY THE *SPIRIT OF XANDAR*, BUT MOST REFER TO IT SIMPLY AS ***THE ROCK.***

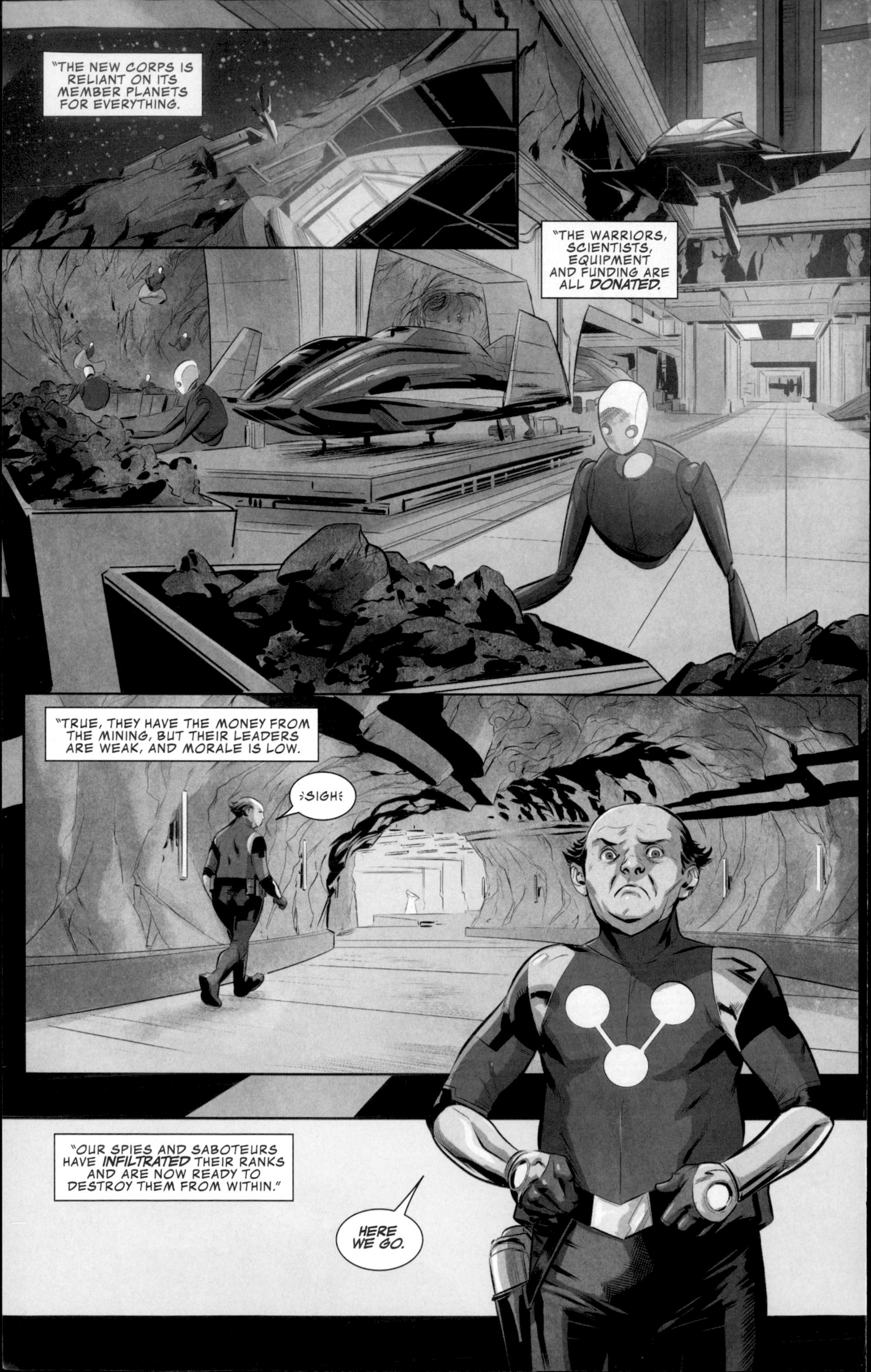
"THE NEW CORPS IS RELIANT ON ITS MEMBER PLANETS FOR EVERYTHING.
"THE WARRIORS, SCIENTISTS, EQUIPMENT AND FUNDING ARE ALL DONATED.
"TRUE, THEY HAVE THE MONEY FROM THE MINING, BUT THEIR LEADERS ARE WEAK, AND MORALE IS LOW.
SIGH
"OUR SPIES AND SABOTEURS HAVE INFILTRATED THEIR RANKS AND ARE NOW READY TO DESTROY THEM FROM WITHIN."
HERE WE GO.

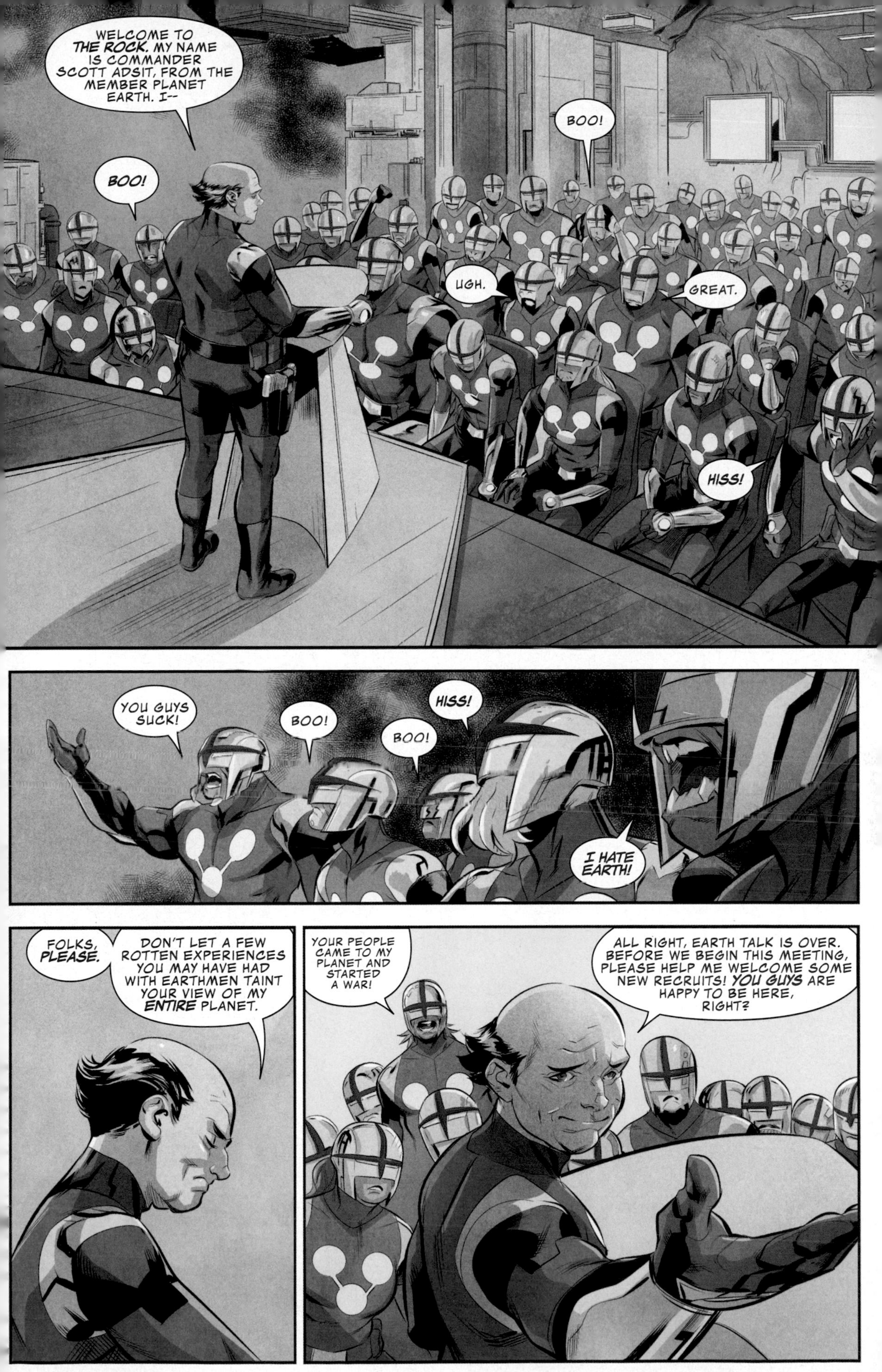
WELCOME TO THE ROCK. MY NAME IS COMMANDER SCOTT ADSIT, FROM THE MEMBER PLANET EARTH. I--
BOO!
BOO!
UGH.
GREAT.
HISS!
YOU GUYS SUCK!
BOO!
BOO!
HISS!
I HATE EARTH!
FOLKS, PLEASE.
DON'T LET A FEW ROTTEN EXPERIENCES YOU MAY HAVE HAD WITH EARTHMEN TAINT YOUR VIEW OF MY ENTIRE PLANET.
YOUR PEOPLE CAME TO MY PLANET AND STARTED A WAR!
ALL RIGHT, EARTH TALK IS OVER. BEFORE WE BEGIN THIS MEETING, PLEASE HELP ME WELCOME SOME NEW RECRUITS! YOU GUYS ARE HAPPY TO BE HERE, RIGHT?

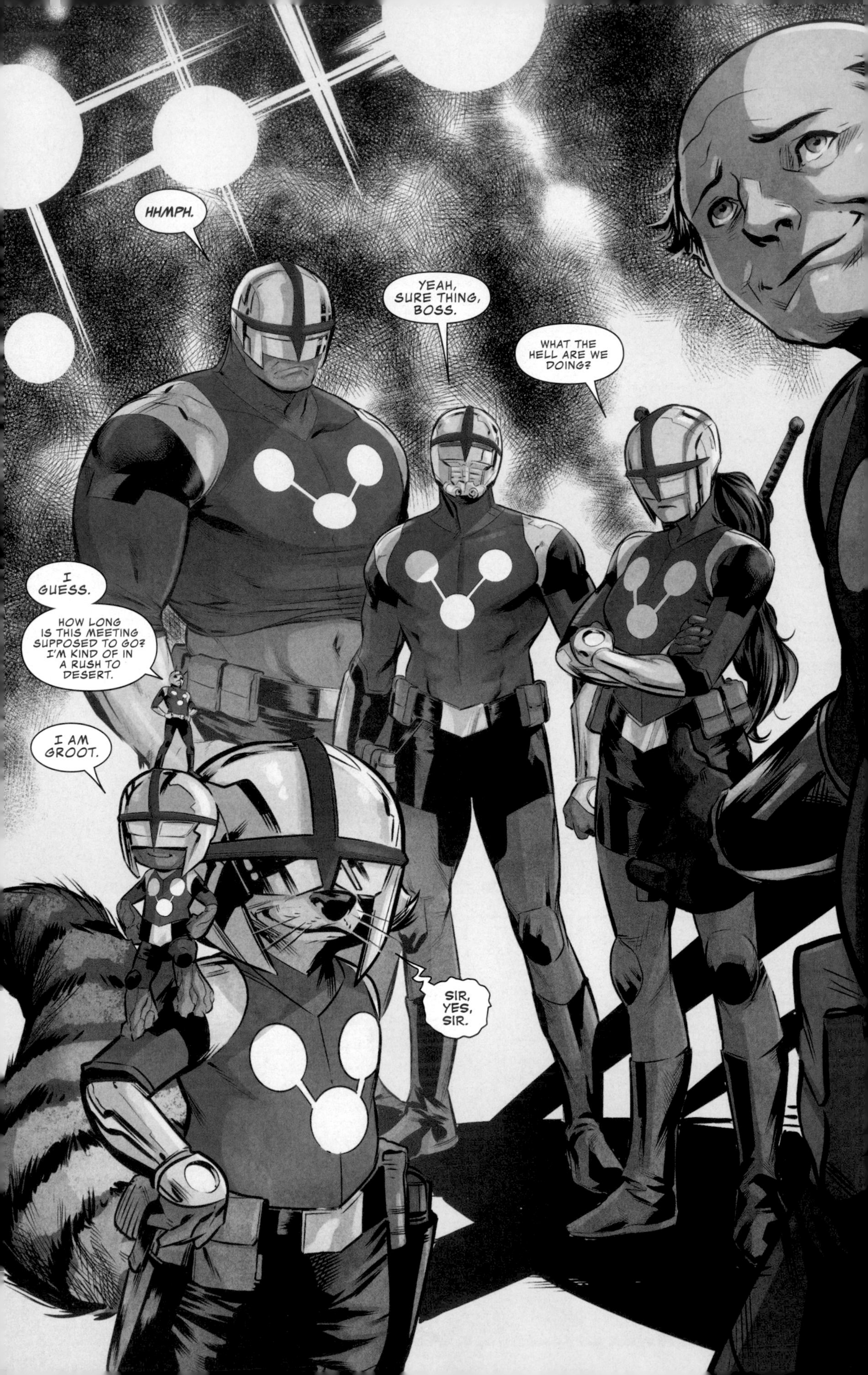
HHMPH.
YEAH, SURE THING, BOSS.
WHAT THE HELL ARE WE DOING?
I GUESS.
HOW LONG IS THIS MEETING SUPPOSED TO GO? I'M KIND OF IN A RUSH TO DESERT.
I AM GROOT.
SIR, YES, SIR.

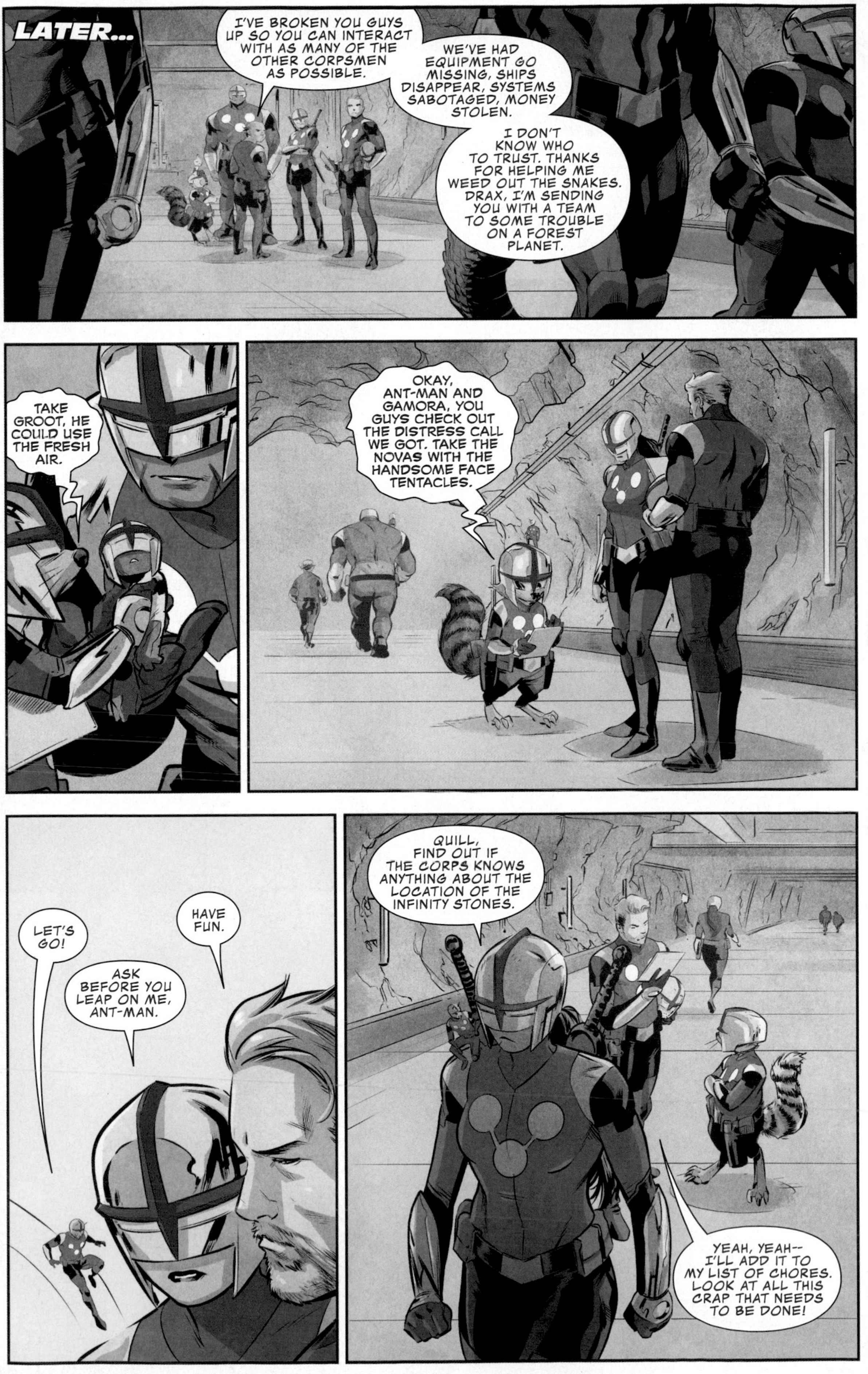
LATER...
I'VE BROKEN YOU GUYS UP SO YOU CAN INTERACT WITH AS MANY OF THE OTHER CORPSMEN AS POSSIBLE.
WE'VE HAD EQUIPMENT GO MISSING, SHIPS DISAPPEAR, SYSTEMS SABOTAGED, MONEY STOLEN.
I DON'T KNOW WHO TO TRUST. THANKS FOR HELPING ME WEED OUT THE SNAKES. DRAX, I'M SENDING YOU WITH A TEAM TO SOME TROUBLE ON A FOREST PLANET.
TAKE GROOT, HE COULD USE THE FRESH AIR.
OKAY, ANT-MAN AND GAMORA, YOU GUYS CHECK OUT THE DISTRESS CALL WE GOT. TAKE THE NOVAS WITH THE HANDSOME FACE TENTACLES.
LET'S GO!
HAVE FUN.
ASK BEFORE YOU LEAP ON ME, ANT-MAN.
QUILL, FIND OUT IF THE CORPS KNOWS ANYTHING ABOUT THE LOCATION OF THE INFINITY STONES.
YEAH, YEAH-- I'LL ADD IT TO MY LIST OF CHORES. LOOK AT ALL THIS CRAP THAT NEEDS TO BE DONE!

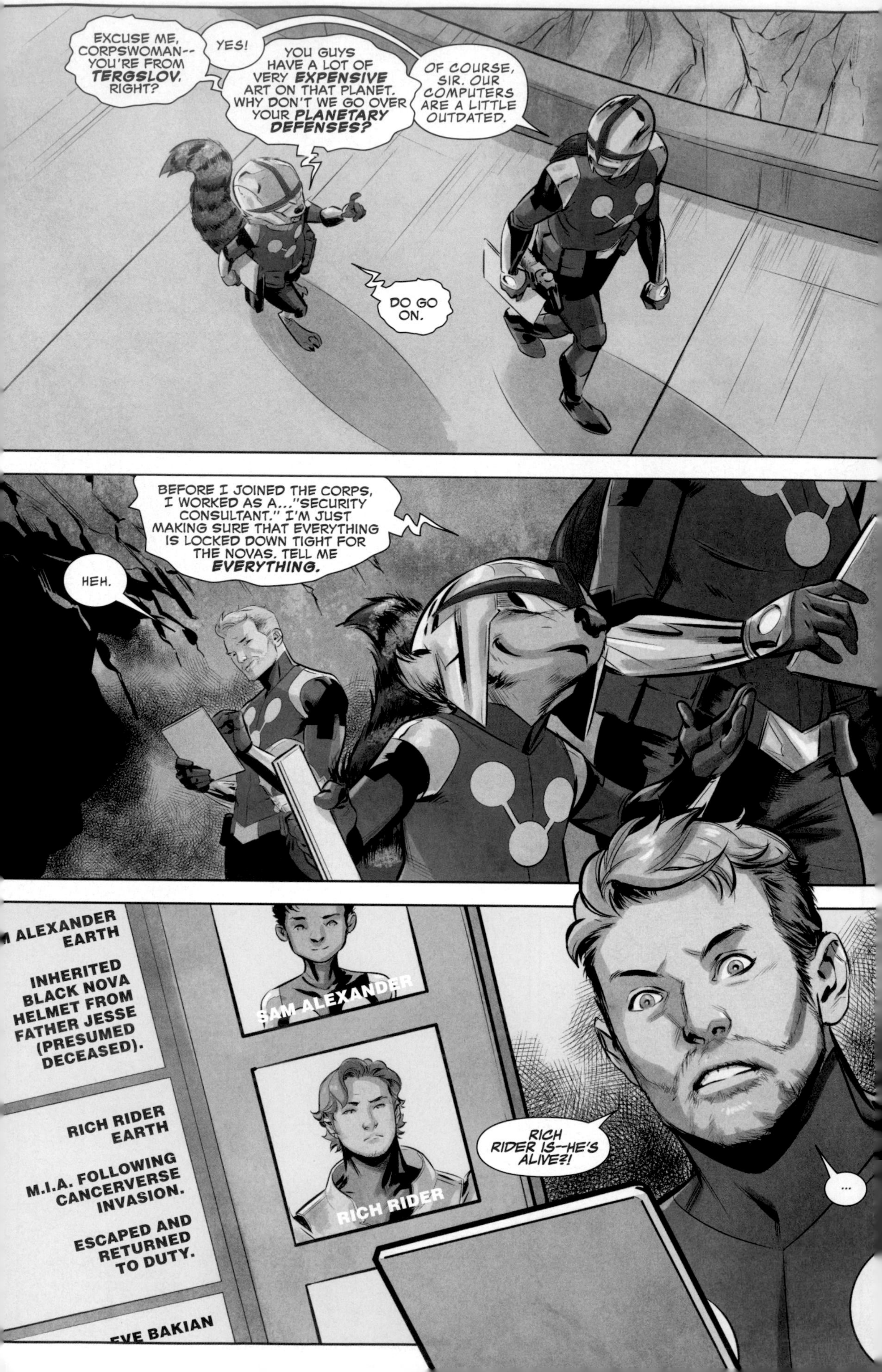
EXCUSE ME, CORPSWOMAN-- YOU'RE FROM TERGSLOV, RIGHT?
YES!
YOU GUYS HAVE A LOT OF VERY EXPENSIVE ART ON THAT PLANET. WHY DON'T WE GO OVER YOUR PLANETARY DEFENSES?
OF COURSE, SIR. OUR COMPUTERS ARE A LITTLE OUTDATED.
DO GO ON.
BEFORE I JOINED THE CORPS, I WORKED AS A..."SECURITY CONSULTANT." I'M JUST MAKING SURE THAT EVERYTHING IS LOCKED DOWN TIGHT FOR THE NOVAS. TELL ME EVERYTHING.
HEH.
M ALEXANDER EARTH
INHERITED BLACK NOVA HELMET FROM FATHER JESSE (PRESUMED DECEASED).
SAM ALEXANDER
RICH RIDER EARTH
M.I.A. FOLLOWING CANCERVERSE INVASION.
ESCAPED AND RETURNED TO DUTY.
RICH RIDER
EVE BAKIAN
RICH RIDER IS--HE'S ALIVE?!
...

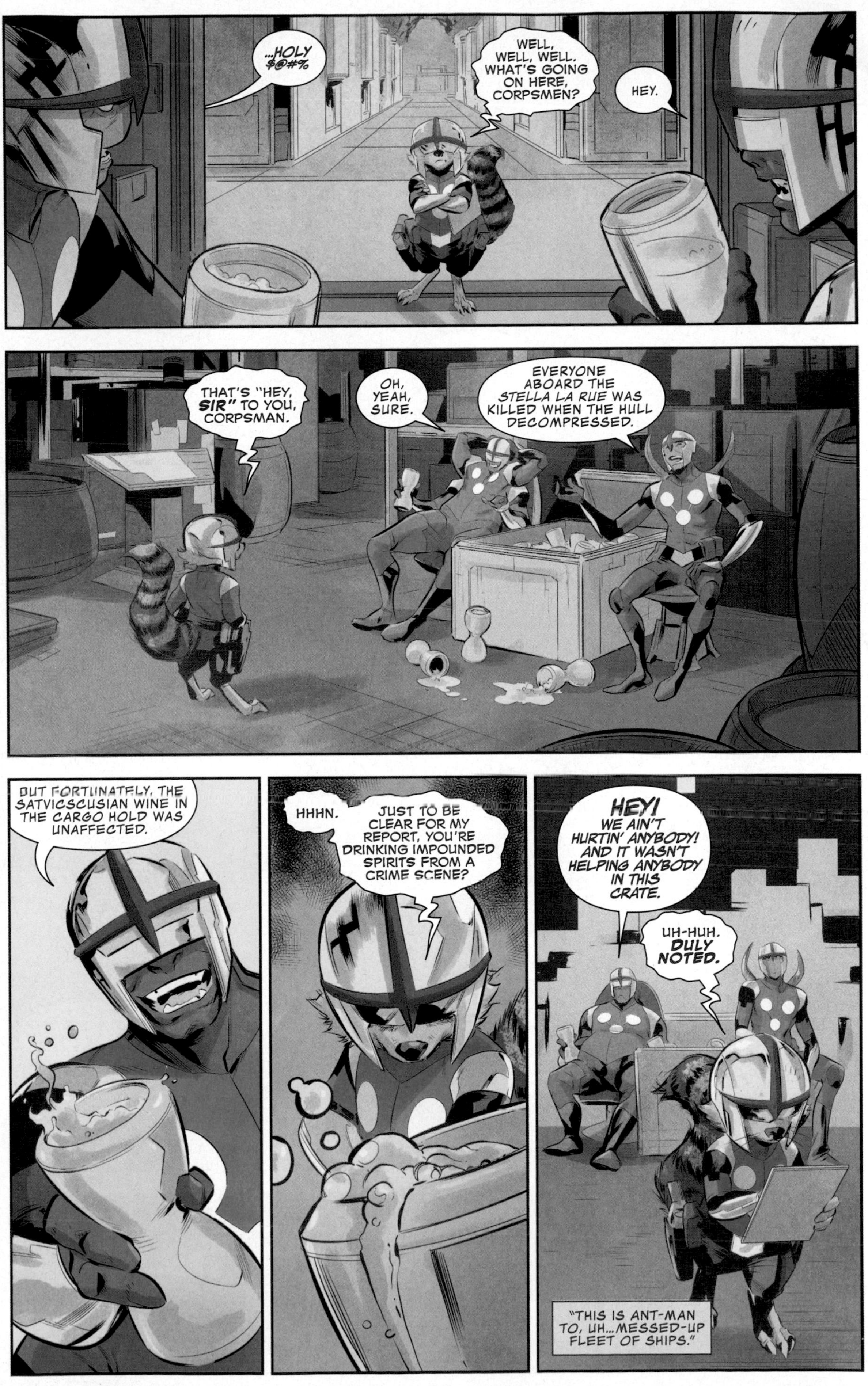
...HOLY $@#%
WELL, WELL, WELL. WHAT'S GOING ON HERE, CORPSMEN?
HEY.
THAT'S "HEY, SIR" TO YOU, CORPSMAN.
OH, YEAH, SURE.
EVERYONE ABOARD THE STELLA LA RUE WAS KILLED WHEN THE HULL DECOMPRESSED.
BUT FORTUNATELY, THE SATVICSCUSIAN WINE IN THE CARGO HOLD WAS UNAFFECTED.
HHHN.
JUST TO BE CLEAR FOR MY REPORT, YOU'RE DRINKING IMPOUNDED SPIRITS FROM A CRIME SCENE?
HEY! WE AIN'T HURTIN' ANYBODY! AND IT WASN'T HELPING ANYBODY IN THIS CRATE.
UH-HUH. DULY NOTED.
"THIS IS ANT-MAN TO, UH...MESSED-UP FLEET OF SHIPS."

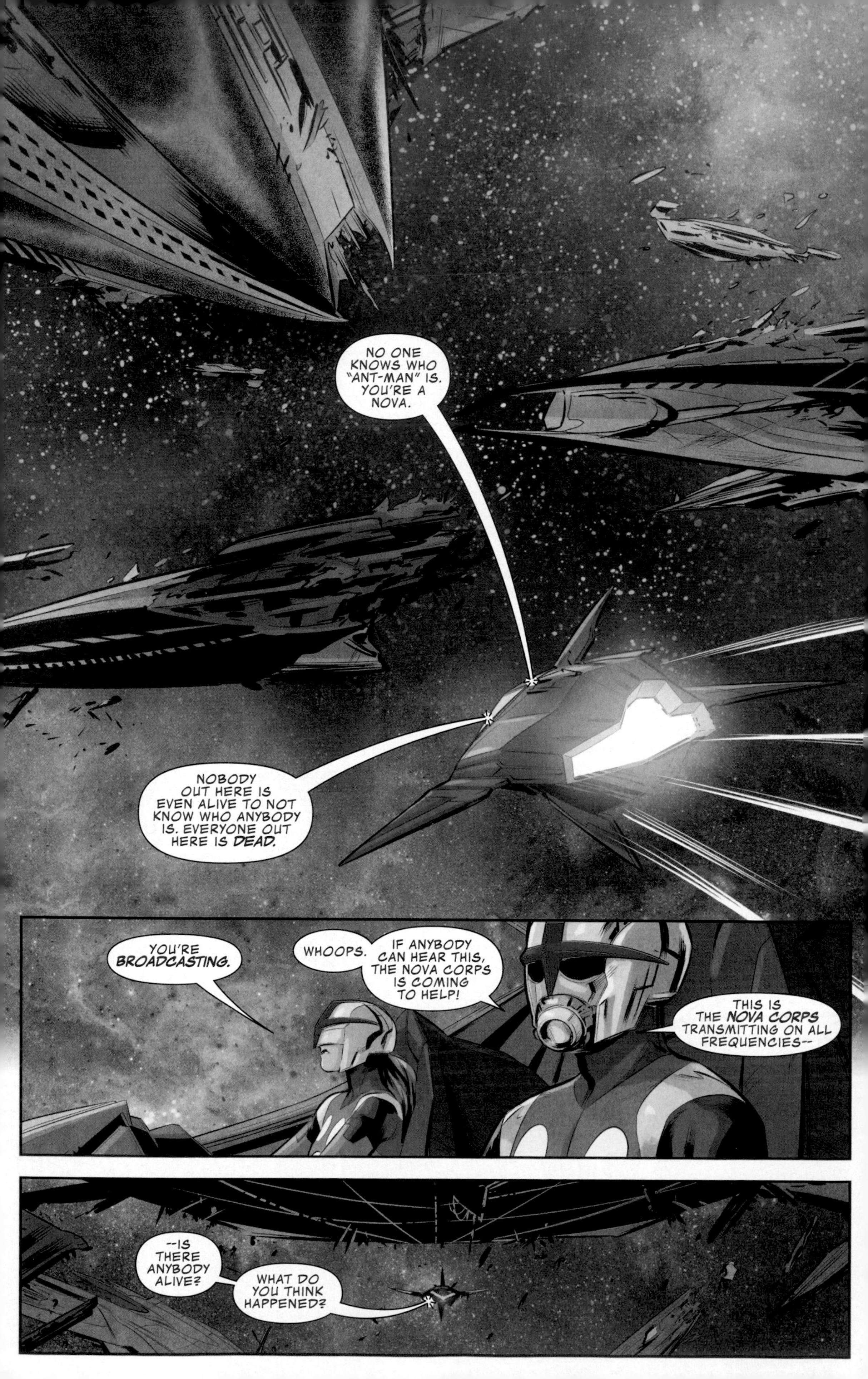
NO ONE KNOWS WHO "ANT-MAN" IS. YOU'RE A NOVA.
NOBODY OUT HERE IS EVEN ALIVE TO NOT KNOW WHO ANYBODY IS. EVERYONE OUT HERE IS DEAD.
THIS IS THE NOVA CORPS TRANSMITTING ON ALL FREQUENCIES--
YOU'RE BROADCASTING.
WHOOPS.
IF ANYBODY CAN HEAR THIS, THE NOVA CORPS IS COMING TO HELP!
--IS THERE ANYBODY ALIVE?
WHAT DO YOU THINK HAPPENED?

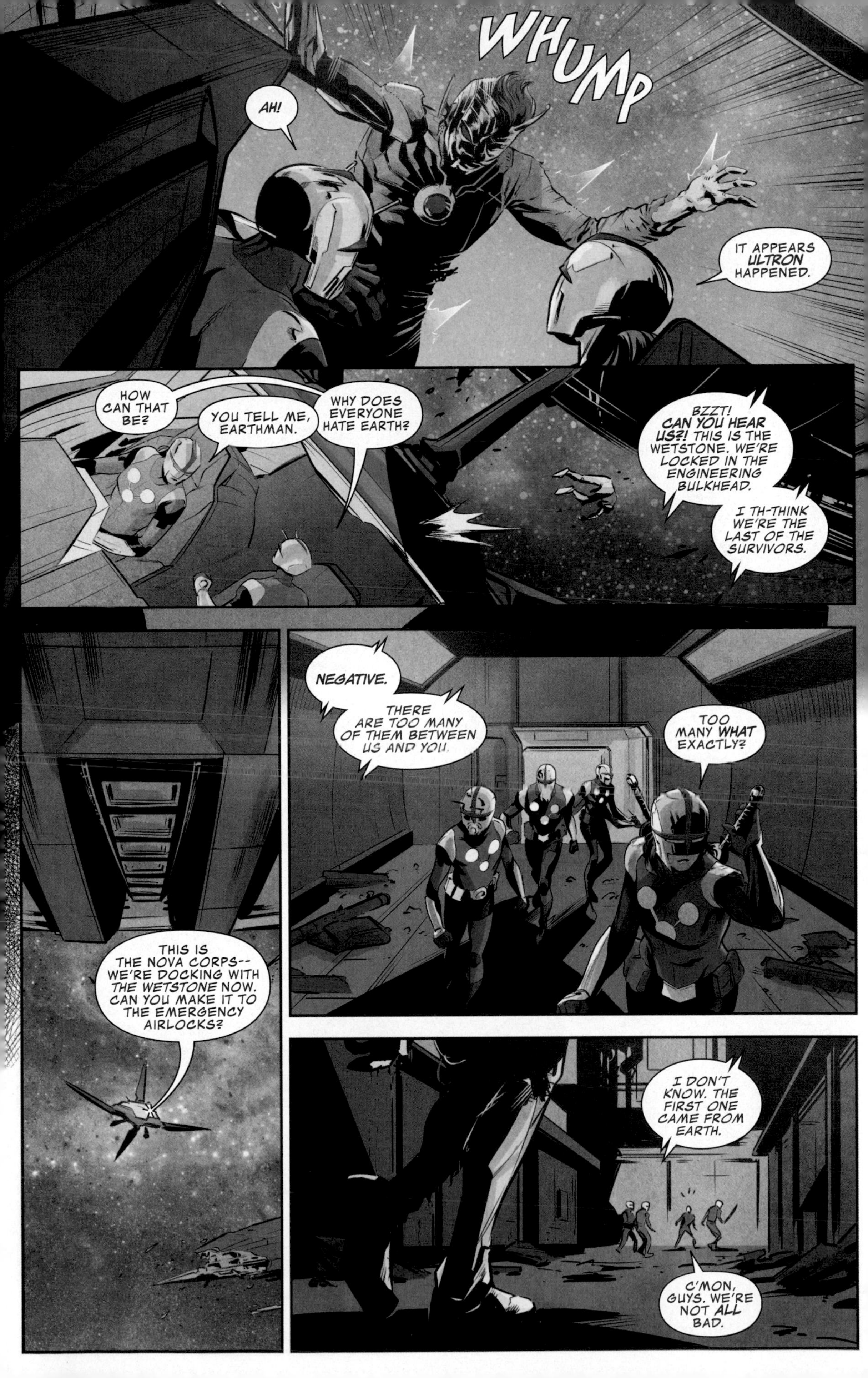
WHUMP
AH!
IT APPEARS ULTRON HAPPENED.
HOW CAN THAT BE?
YOU TELL ME, EARTHMAN.
WHY DOES EVERYONE HATE EARTH?
BZZT! CAN YOU HEAR US?! THIS IS THE WETSTONE. WE'RE LOCKED IN THE ENGINEERING BULKHEAD.
I TH-THINK WE'RE THE LAST OF THE SURVIVORS.
THIS IS THE NOVA CORPS-- WE'RE DOCKING WITH THE WETSTONE NOW. CAN YOU MAKE IT TO THE EMERGENCY AIRLOCKS?
NEGATIVE.
THERE ARE TOO MANY OF THEM BETWEEN US AND YOU.
TOO MANY WHAT EXACTLY?
I DON'T KNOW. THE FIRST ONE CAME FROM EARTH.
C'MON, GUYS. WE'RE NOT ALL BAD.

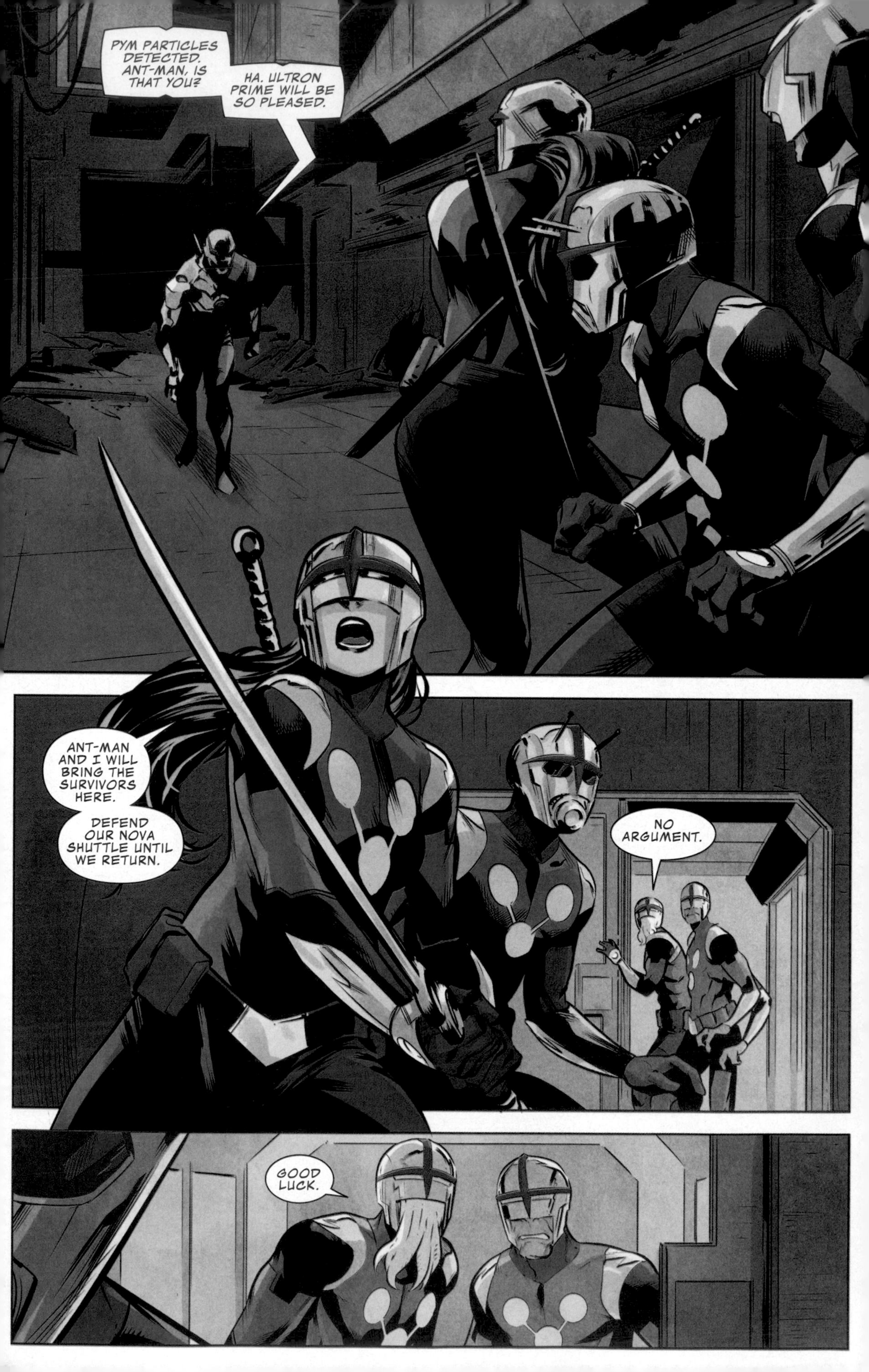
PYM PARTICLES DETECTED. ANT-MAN, IS THAT YOU?
HA. ULTRON PRIME WILL BE SO PLEASED.
ANT-MAN AND I WILL BRING THE SURVIVORS HERE.
DEFEND OUR NOVA SHUTTLE UNTIL WE RETURN.
NO ARGUMENT.
GOOD LUCK.

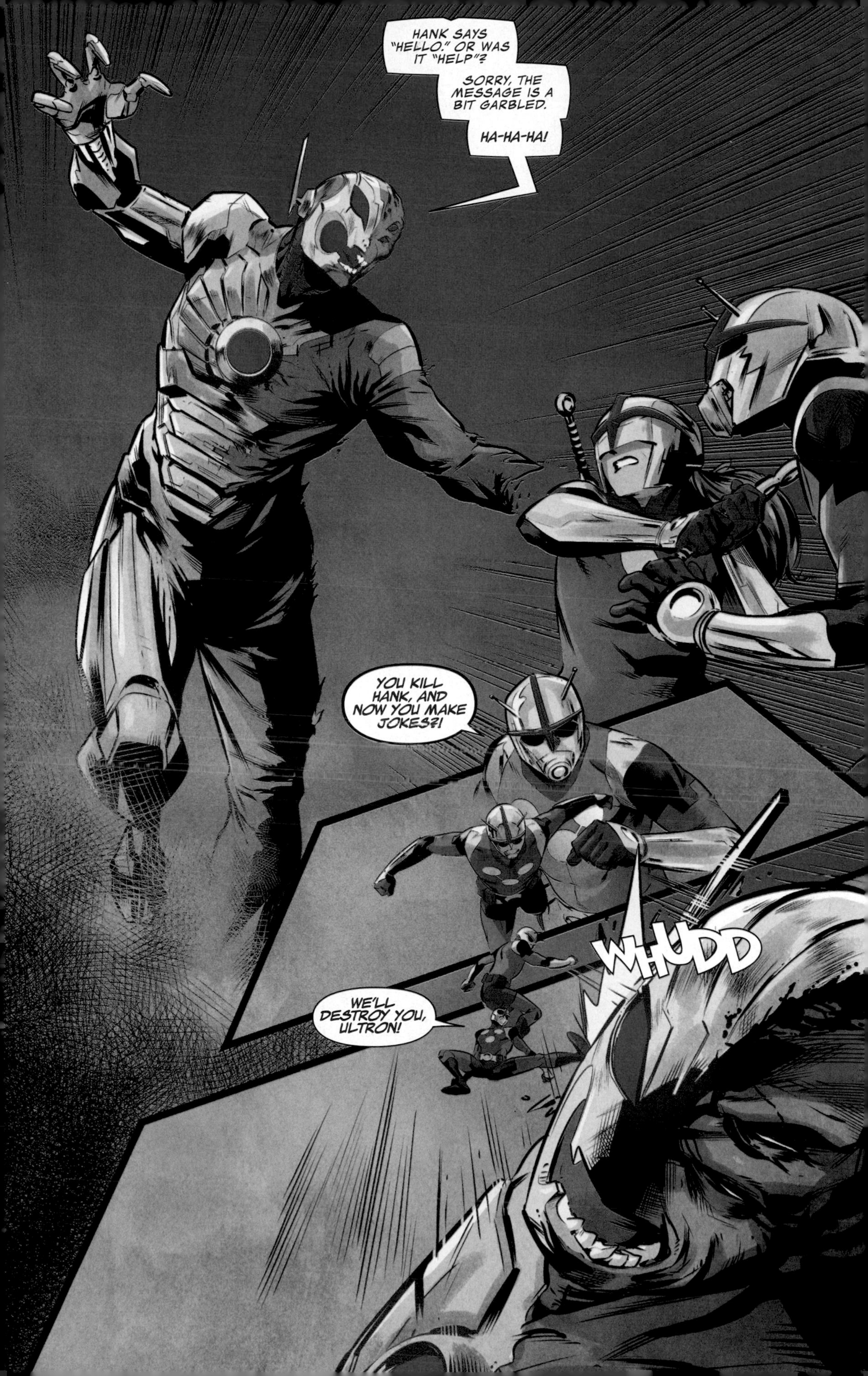
HANK SAYS "HELLO." OR WAS IT "HELP"?
SORRY, THE MESSAGE IS A BIT GARBLED.
HA-HA-HA!
YOU KILL HANK, AND NOW YOU MAKE JOKES?!
WHUDD
WE'LL DESTROY YOU, ULTRON!

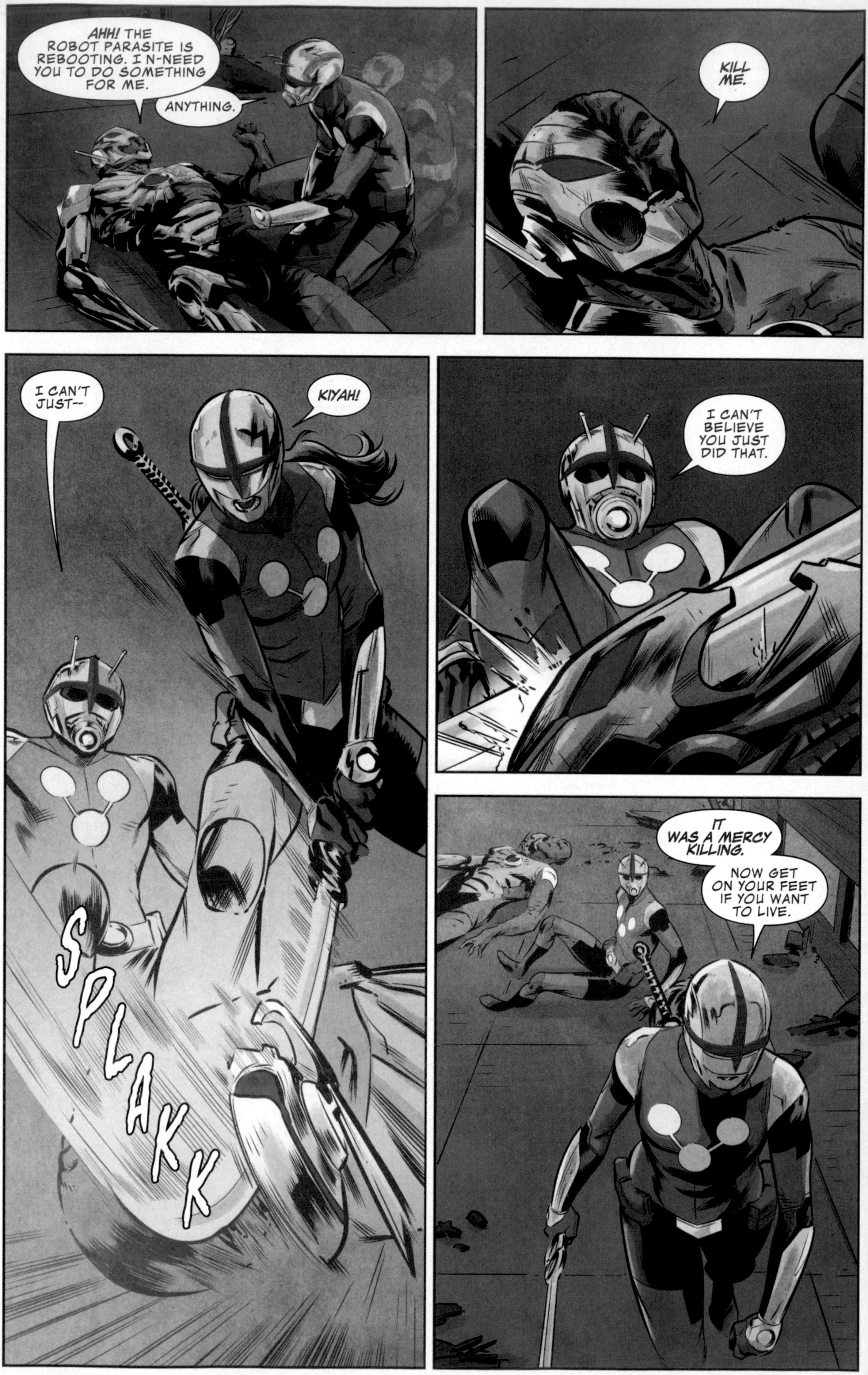
AHH! THE ROBOT PARASITE IS REBOOTING. I N-NEED YOU TO DO SOMETHING FOR ME.
ANYTHING.
KILL ME.
I CAN'T JUST--
KIYAH!
SPLAKK
I CAN'T BELIEVE YOU JUST DID THAT.
IT WAS A MERCY KILLING.
NOW GET ON YOUR FEET IF YOU WANT TO LIVE.

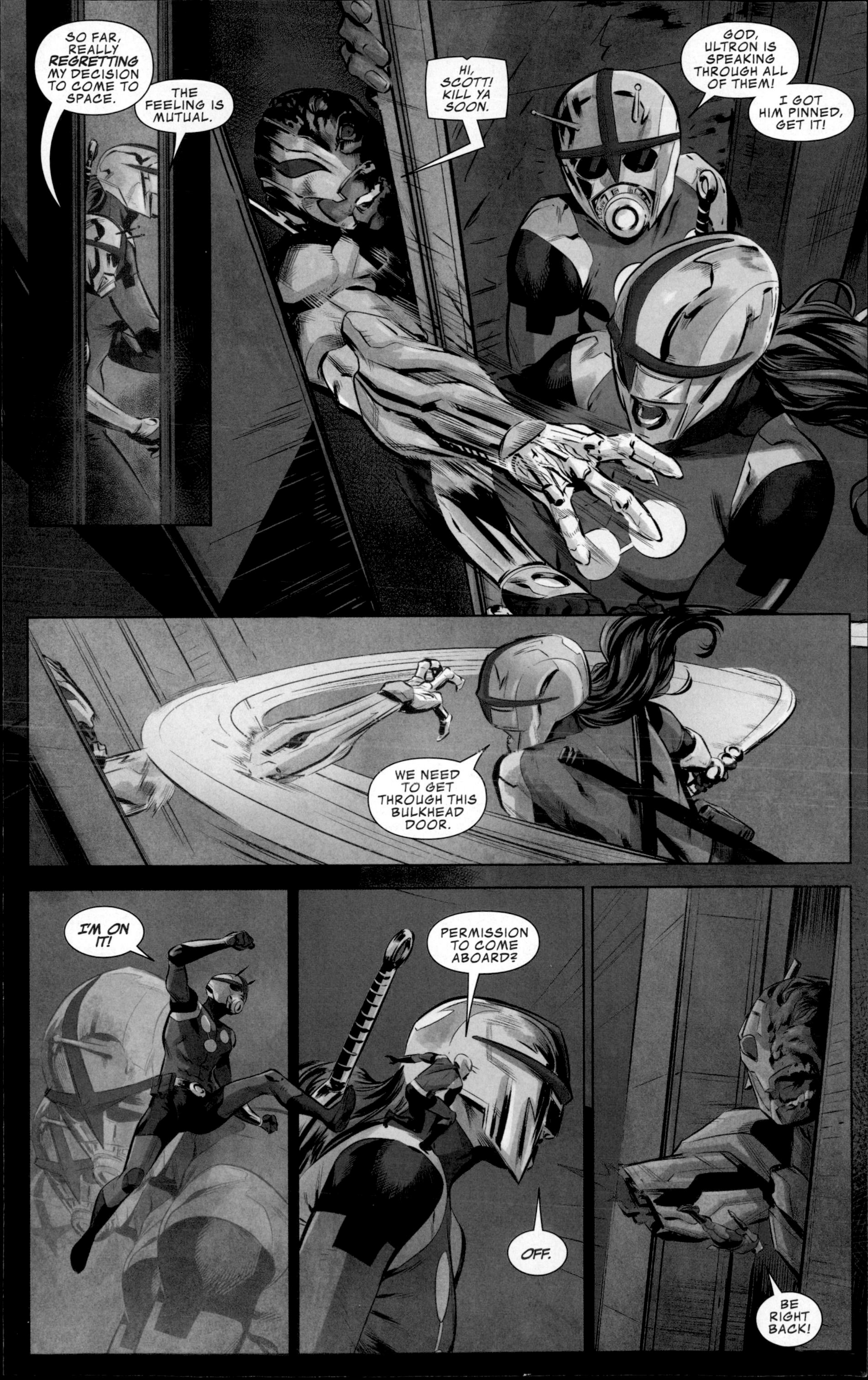
SO FAR, REALLY REGRETTING MY DECISION TO COME TO SPACE.
THE FEELING IS MUTUAL.
HI, SCOTT! KILL YA SOON.
GOD, ULTRON IS SPEAKING THROUGH ALL OF THEM!
I GOT HIM PINNED, GET IT!
WE NEED TO GET THROUGH THIS BULKHEAD DOOR.
I'M ON IT!
PERMISSION TO COME ABOARD?
OFF.
BE RIGHT BACK!

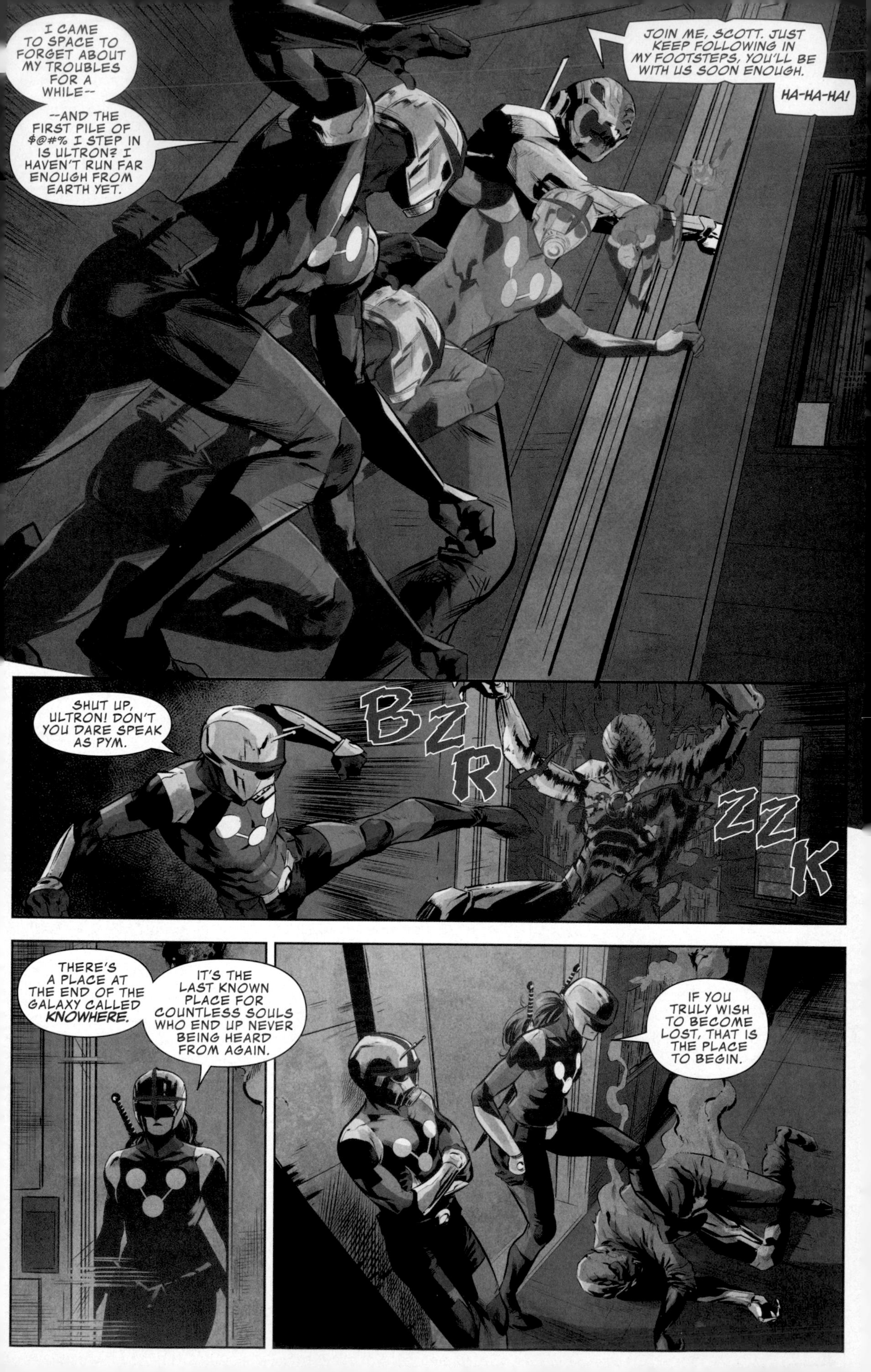
I CAME TO SPACE TO FORGET ABOUT MY TROUBLES FOR A WHILE--
--AND THE FIRST PILE OF $@#% I STEP IN IS ULTRON? I HAVEN'T RUN FAR ENOUGH FROM EARTH YET.
JOIN ME, SCOTT. JUST KEEP FOLLOWING IN MY FOOTSTEPS, YOU'LL BE WITH US SOON ENOUGH.
HA-HA-HA!
SHUT UP, ULTRON! DON'T YOU DARE SPEAK AS PYM.
BZR
ZZK
THERE'S A PLACE AT THE END OF THE GALAXY CALLED KNOWHERE.
IT'S THE LAST KNOWN PLACE FOR COUNTLESS SOULS WHO END UP NEVER BEING HEARD FROM AGAIN.
IF YOU TRULY WISH TO BECOME LOST, THAT IS THE PLACE TO BEGIN.

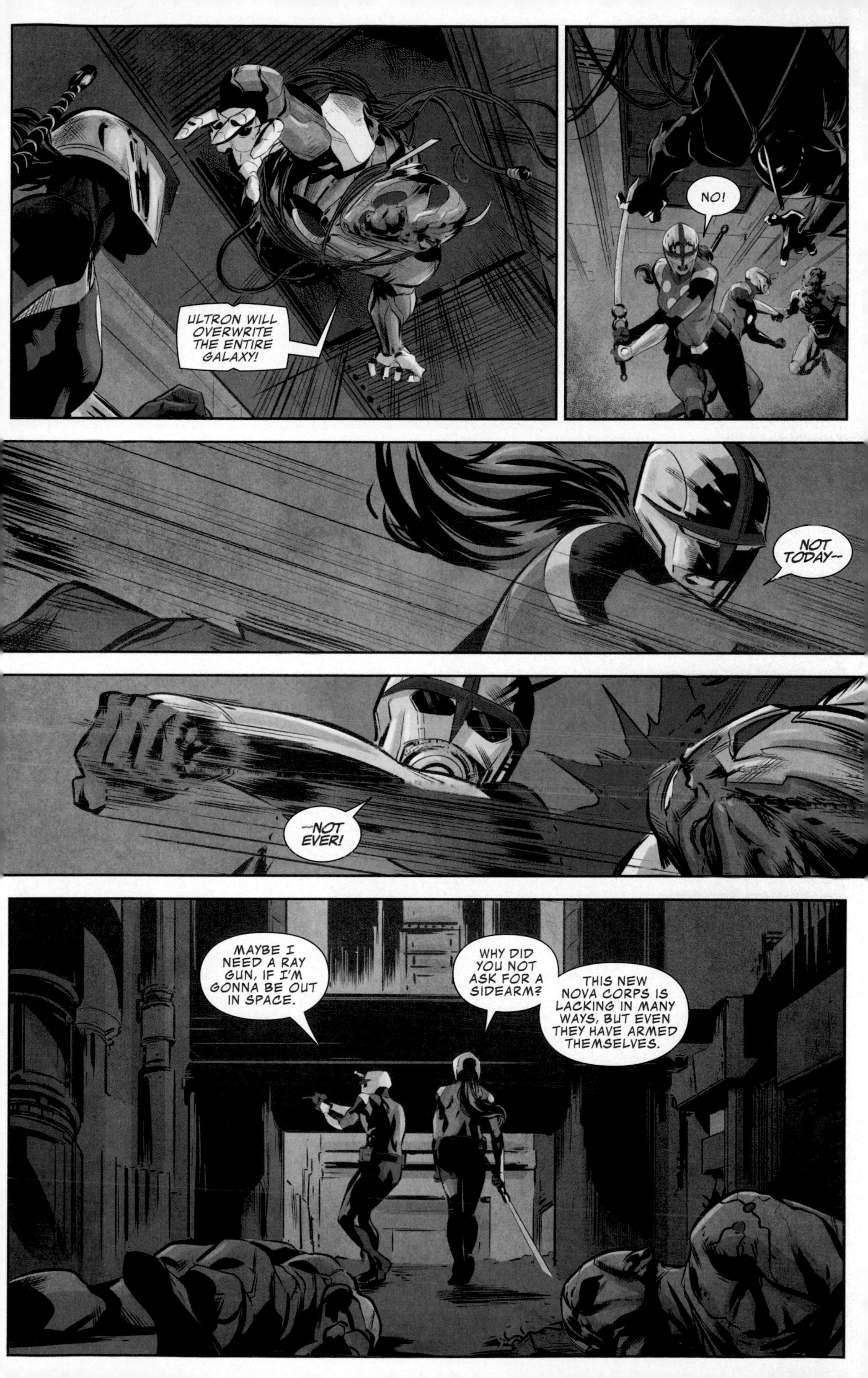
ULTRON WILL OVERWRITE THE ENTIRE GALAXY!
NO!
NOT TODAY--
--NOT EVER!
MAYBE I NEED A RAY GUN, IF I'M GONNA BE OUT IN SPACE.
WHY DID YOU NOT ASK FOR A SIDEARM?
THIS NEW NOVA CORPS IS LACKING IN MANY WAYS, BUT EVEN THEY HAVE ARMED THEMSELVES.

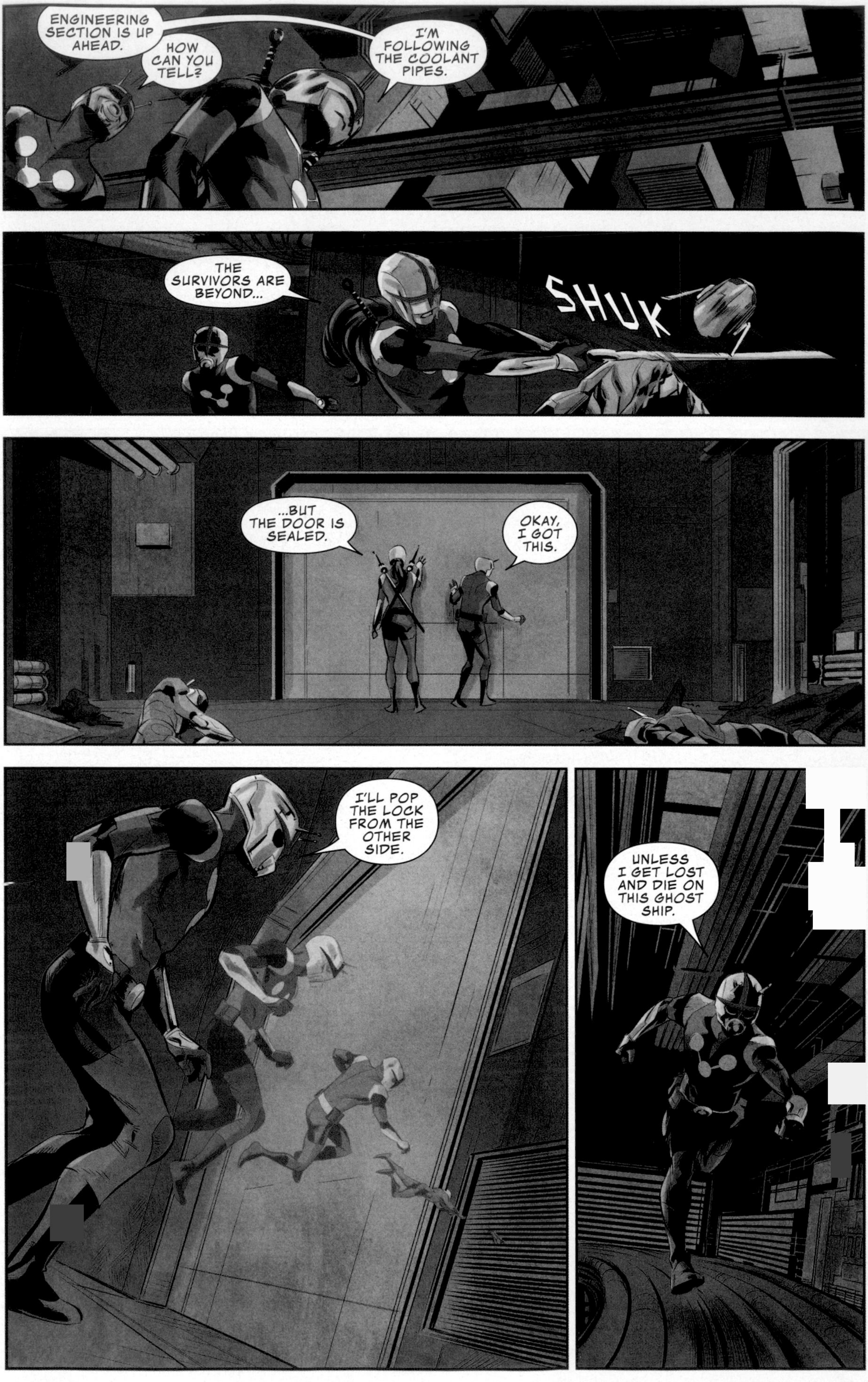
ENGINEERING SECTION IS UP AHEAD.
HOW CAN YOU TELL?
I'M FOLLOWING THE COOLANT PIPES.
THE SURVIVORS ARE BEYOND...
SHUK
...BUT THE DOOR IS SEALED.
OKAY, I GOT THIS.
I'LL POP THE LOCK FROM THE OTHER SIDE.
UNLESS I GET LOST AND DIE ON THIS GHOST SHIP.

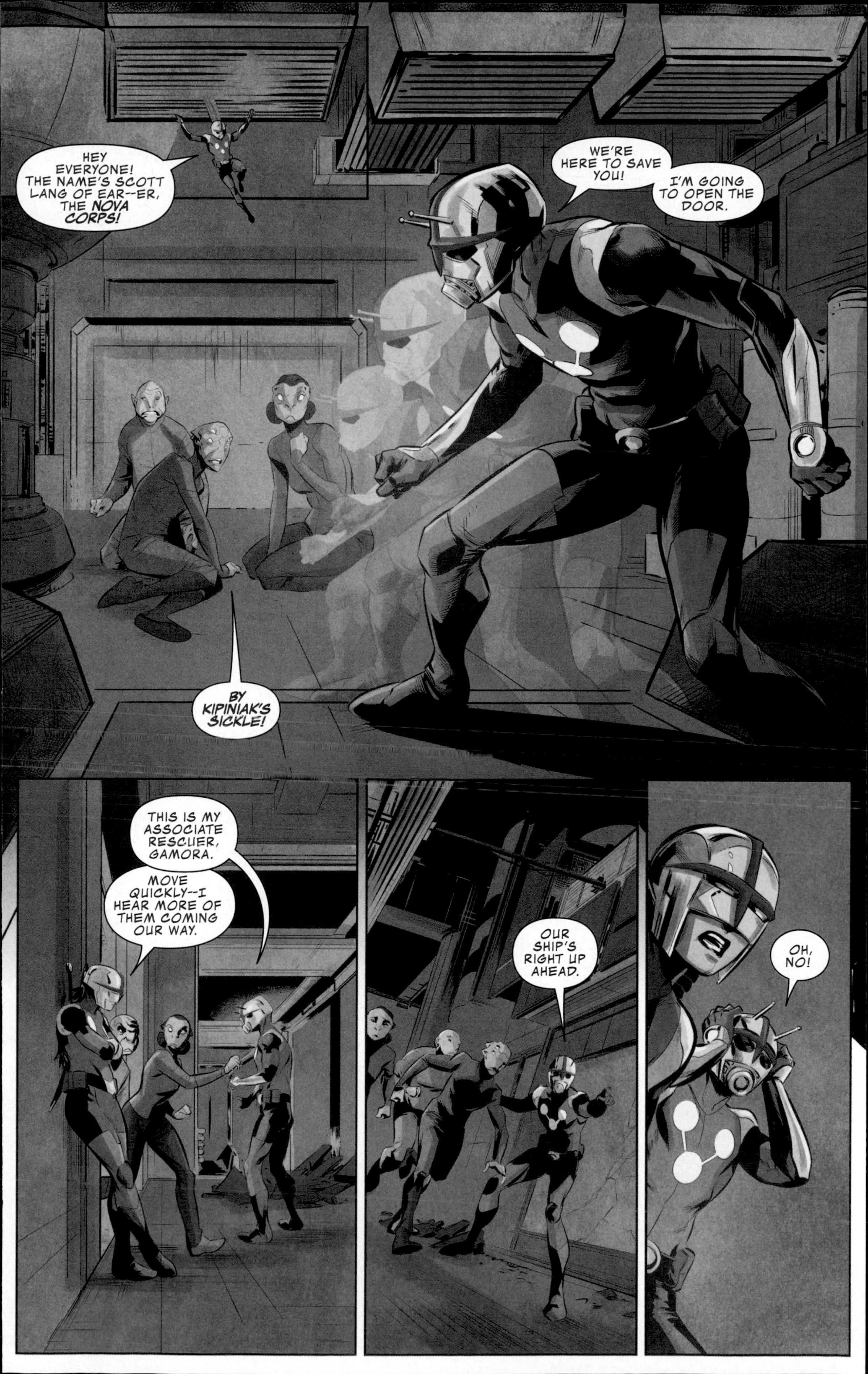
HEY EVERYONE! THE NAME'S SCOTT LANG OF EAR--ER, THE NOVA CORPS!
WE'RE HERE TO SAVE YOU!
I'M GOING TO OPEN THE DOOR.
BY KIPINIAK'S SICKLE!
THIS IS MY ASSOCIATE RESCUER, GAMORA.
MOVE QUICKLY--I HEAR MORE OF THEM COMING OUR WAY.
OUR SHIP'S RIGHT UP AHEAD.
OH, NO!

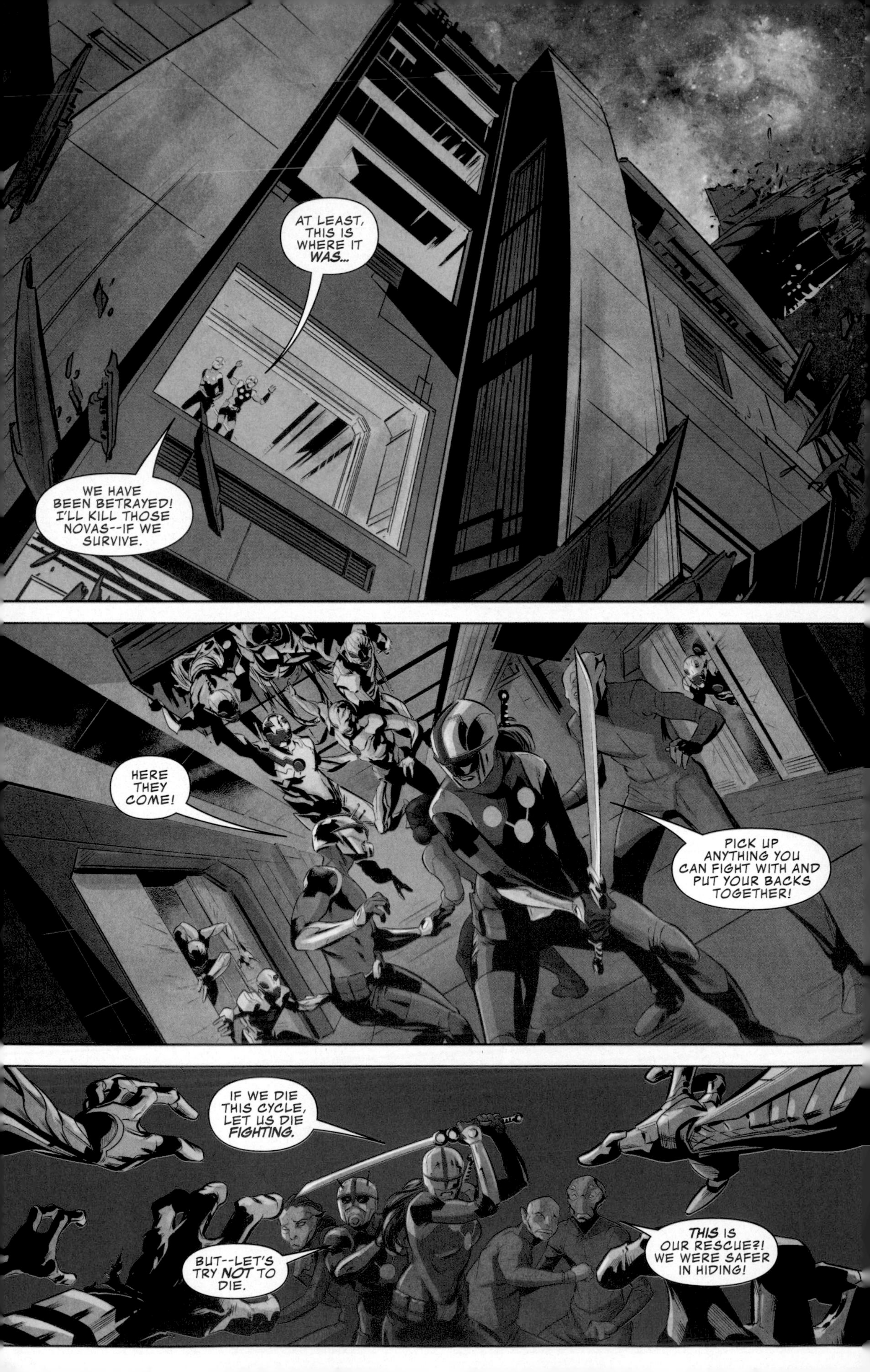
AT LEAST, THIS IS WHERE IT WAS...
WE HAVE BEEN BETRAYED! I'LL KILL THOSE NOVAS--IF WE SURVIVE.
HERE THEY COME!
PICK UP ANYTHING YOU CAN FIGHT WITH AND PUT YOUR BACKS TOGETHER!
IF WE DIE THIS CYCLE, LET US DIE FIGHTING.
BUT--LET'S TRY NOT TO DIE.
THIS IS OUR RESCUE?! WE WERE SAFER IN HIDING!

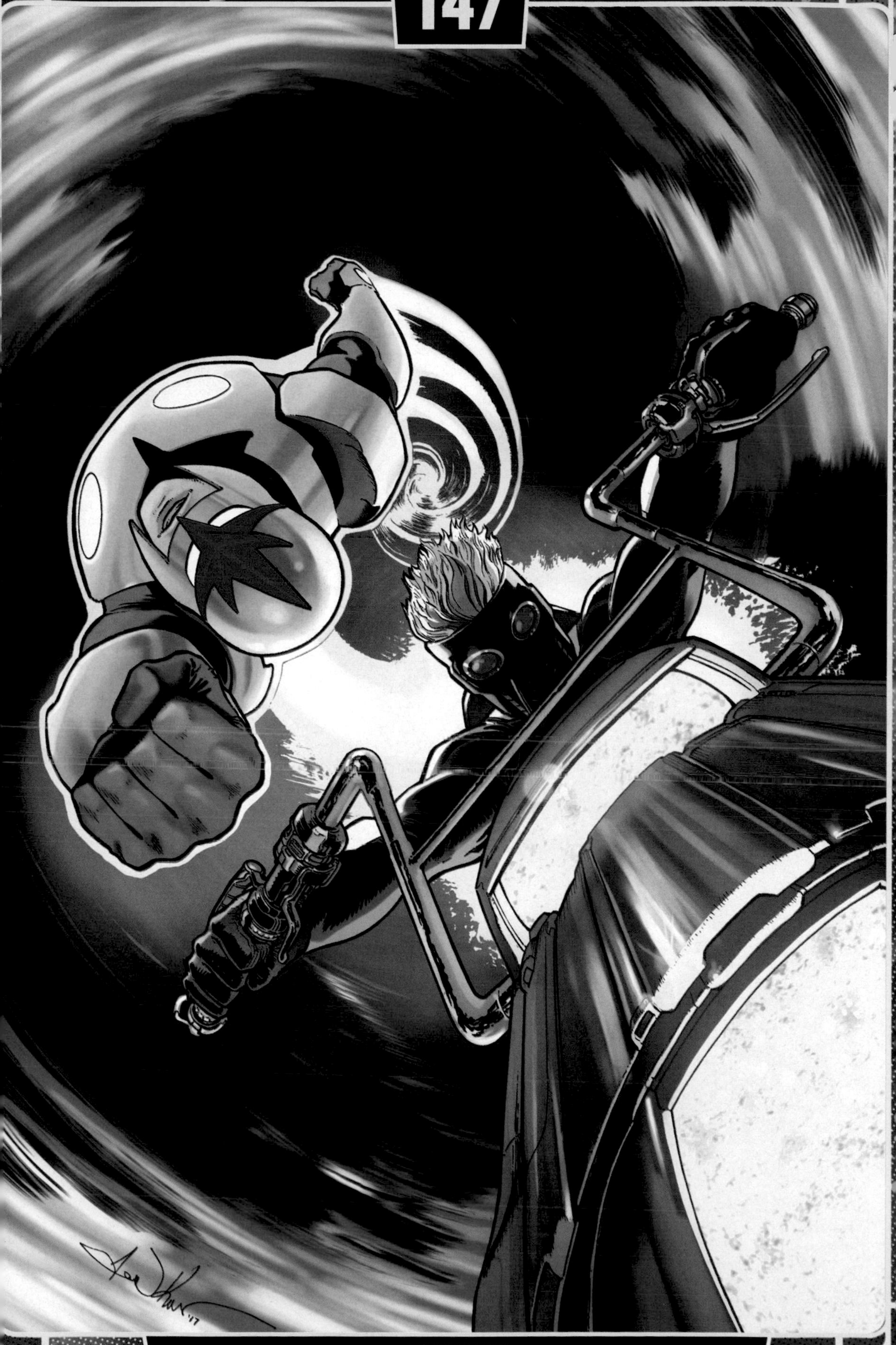

"FORTRESS"

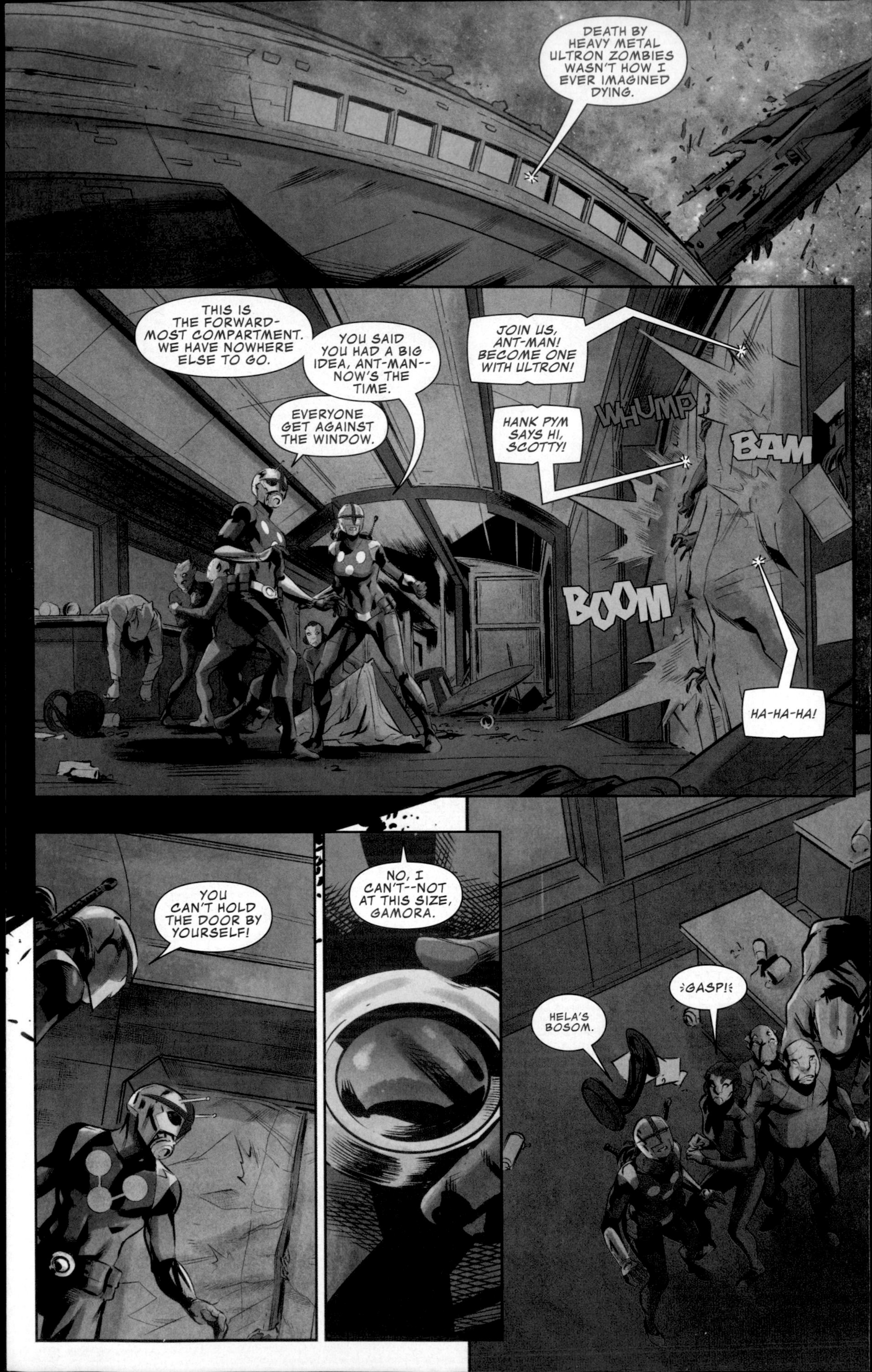
DEATH BY HEAVY METAL ULTRON ZOMBIES WASN'T HOW I EVER IMAGINED DYING.
THIS IS THE FORWARD-MOST COMPARTMENT. WE HAVE NOWHERE ELSE TO GO.
YOU SAID YOU HAD A BIG IDEA, ANT-MAN--NOW'S THE TIME.
EVERYONE GET AGAINST THE WINDOW.
JOIN US, ANT-MAN! BECOME ONE WITH ULTRON!
HANK PYM SAYS HI, SCOTTY!
WHUMP
BAM
BOOM
HA-HA-HA!
YOU CAN'T HOLD THE DOOR BY YOURSELF!
NO, I CAN'T--NOT AT THIS SIZE, GAMORA.
HELA'S BOSOM.
GASP!

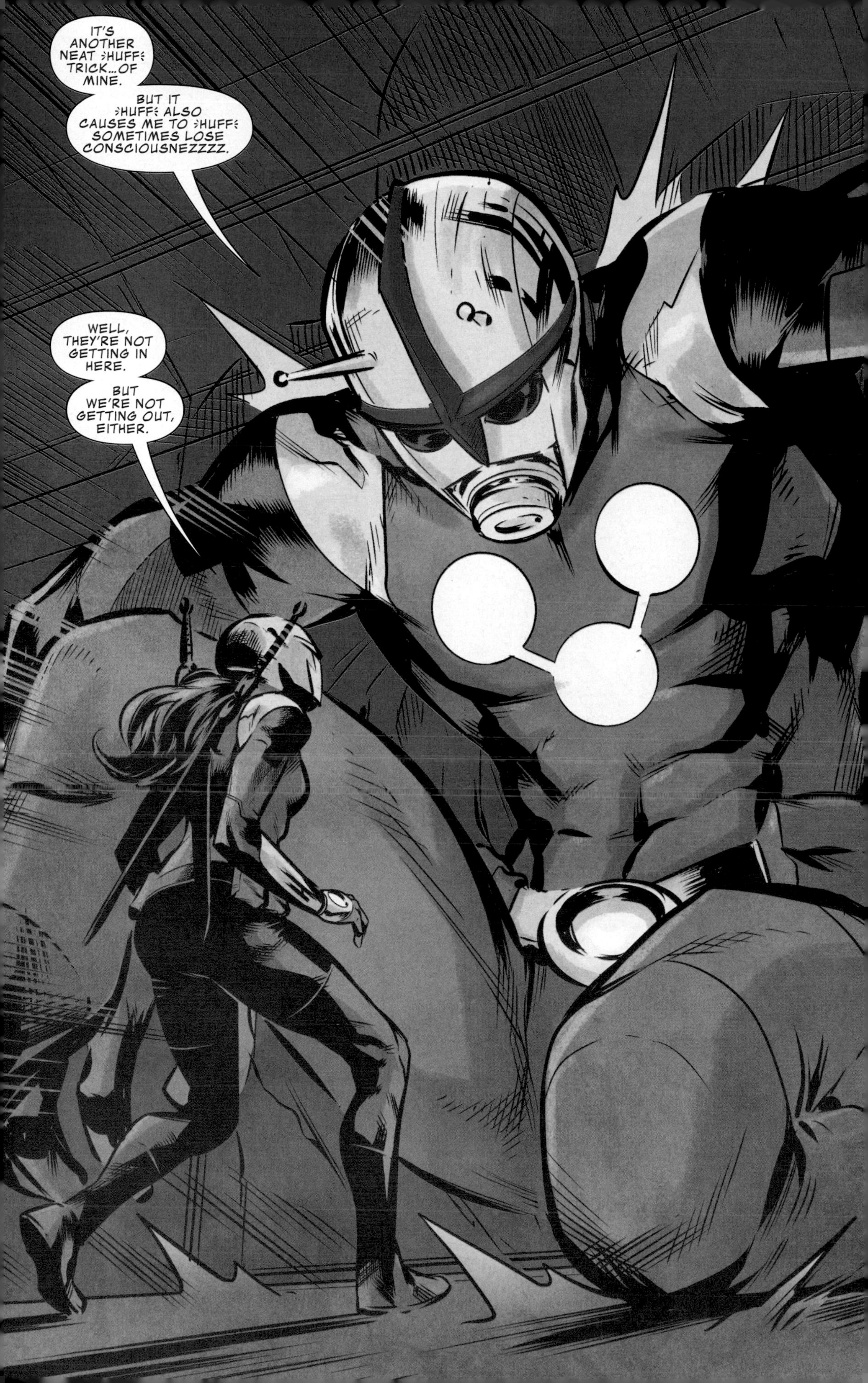
IT'S ANOTHER NEAT >HUFF< TRICK...OF MINE.
BUT IT >HUFF< ALSO CAUSES ME TO >HUFF< SOMETIMES LOSE CONSCIOUSNEZZZZ.
WELL, THEY'RE NOT GETTING IN HERE.
BUT WE'RE NOT GETTING OUT, EITHER.

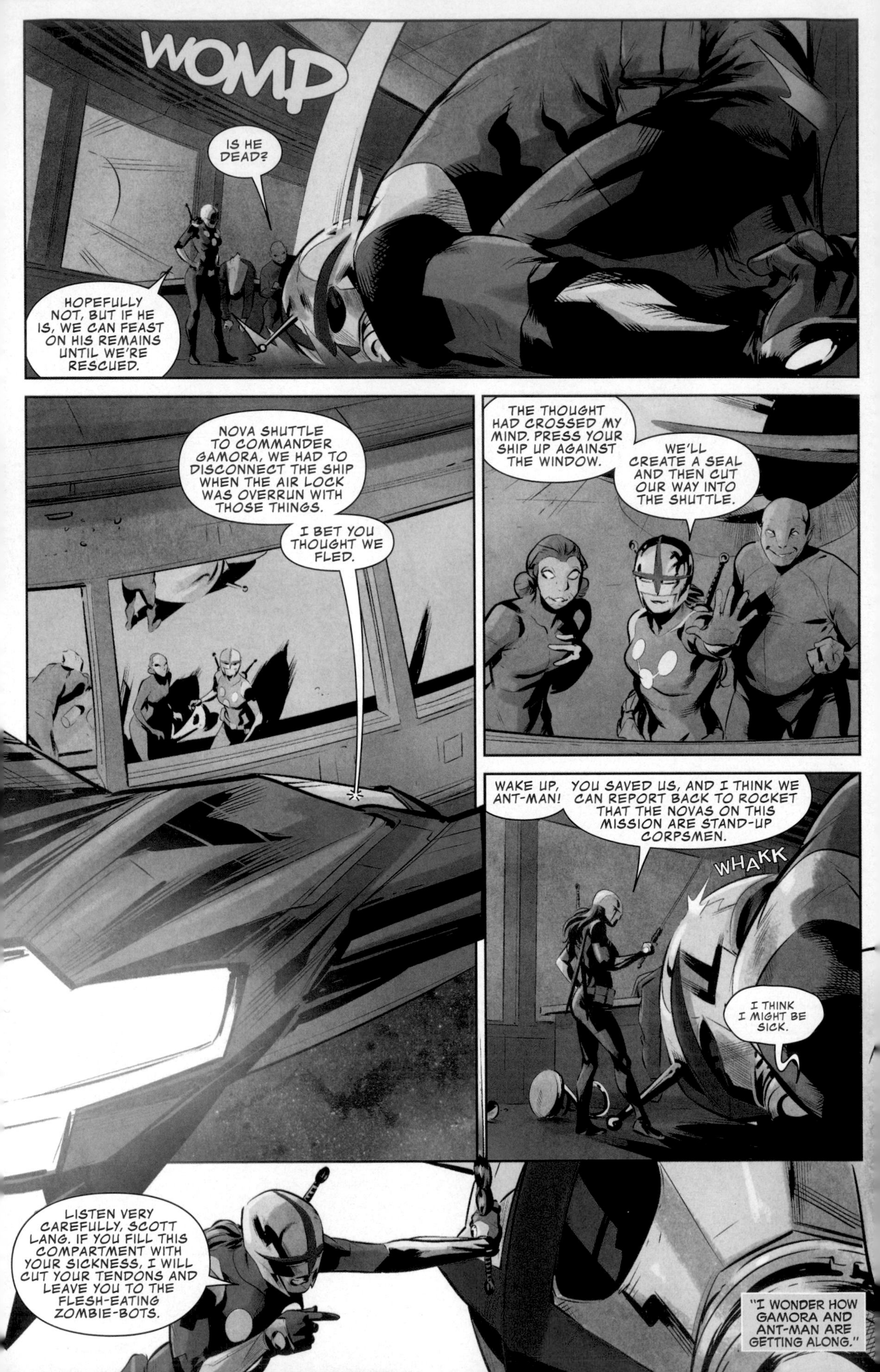
WOMP
IS HE DEAD?
HOPEFULLY NOT, BUT IF HE IS, WE CAN FEAST ON HIS REMAINS UNTIL WE'RE RESCUED.
NOVA SHUTTLE TO COMMANDER GAMORA, WE HAD TO DISCONNECT THE SHIP WHEN THE AIR LOCK WAS OVERRUN WITH THOSE THINGS.
I BET YOU THOUGHT WE FLED.
THE THOUGHT HAD CROSSED MY MIND. PRESS YOUR SHIP UP AGAINST THE WINDOW.
WE'LL CREATE A SEAL AND THEN CUT OUR WAY INTO THE SHUTTLE.
WAKE UP, ANT-MAN!
YOU SAVED US, AND I THINK WE CAN REPORT BACK TO ROCKET THAT THE NOVAS ON THIS MISSION ARE STAND-UP CORPSMEN.
WHAKK
I THINK I MIGHT BE SICK.
LISTEN VERY CAREFULLY, SCOTT LANG. IF YOU FILL THIS COMPARTMENT WITH YOUR SICKNESS, I WILL CUT YOUR TENDONS AND LEAVE YOU TO THE FLESH-EATING ZOMBIE-BOTS.
"I WONDER HOW GAMORA AND ANT-MAN ARE GETTING ALONG."

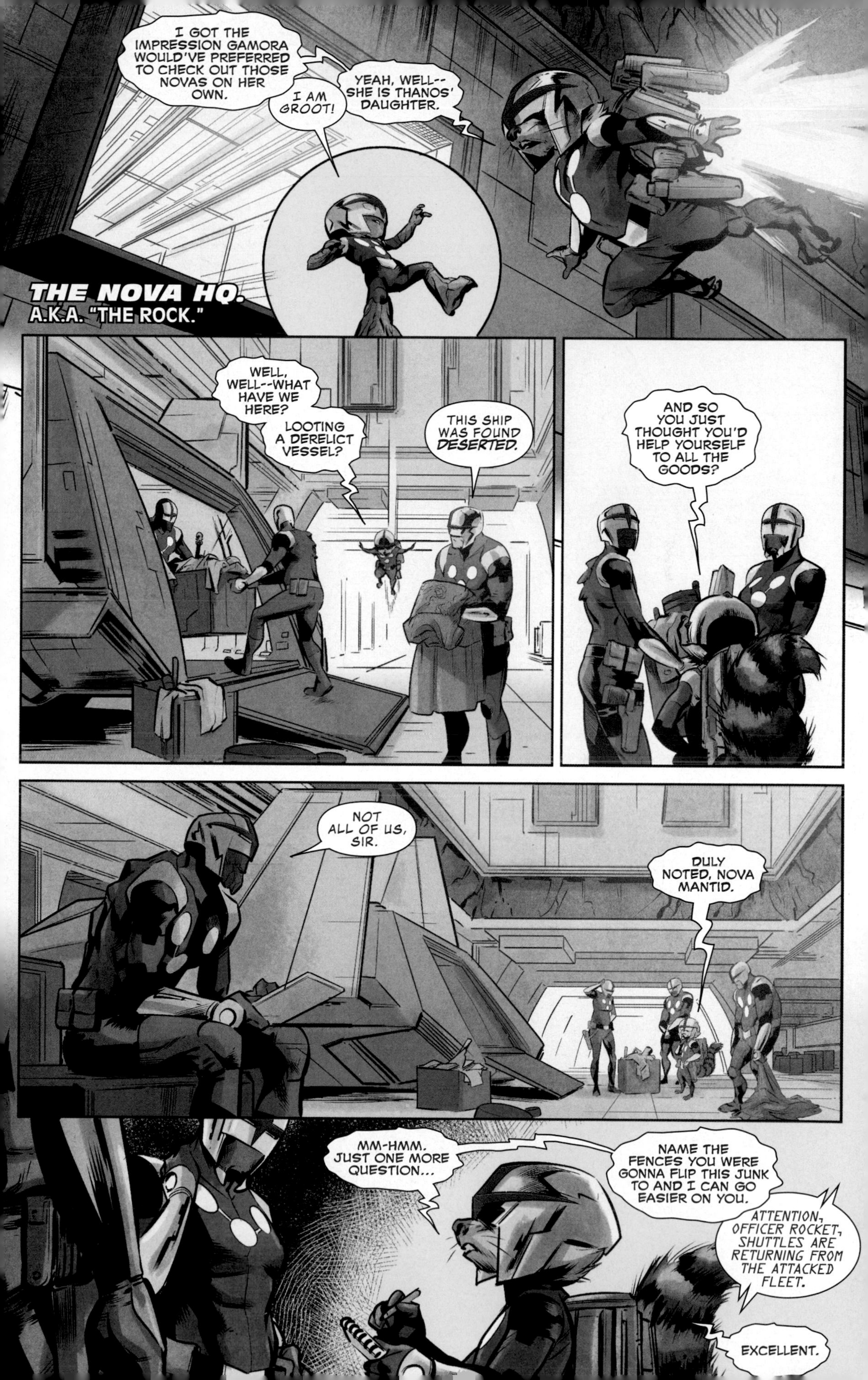
I GOT THE IMPRESSION GAMORA WOULD'VE PREFERRED TO CHECK OUT THOSE NOVAS ON HER OWN.
I AM GROOT!
YEAH, WELL-- SHE IS THANOS' DAUGHTER.
THE NOVA HQ.
A.K.A. "THE ROCK."
WELL, WELL--WHAT HAVE WE HERE?
LOOTING A DERELICT VESSEL?
THIS SHIP WAS FOUND DESERTED.
AND SO YOU JUST THOUGHT YOU'D HELP YOURSELF TO ALL THE GOODS?
NOT ALL OF US, SIR.
DULY NOTED, NOVA MANTID.
MM-HMM. JUST ONE MORE QUESTION...
NAME THE FENCES YOU WERE GONNA FLIP THIS JUNK TO AND I CAN GO EASIER ON YOU.
ATTENTION, OFFICER ROCKET, SHUTTLES ARE RETURNING FROM THE ATTACKED FLEET.
EXCELLENT.

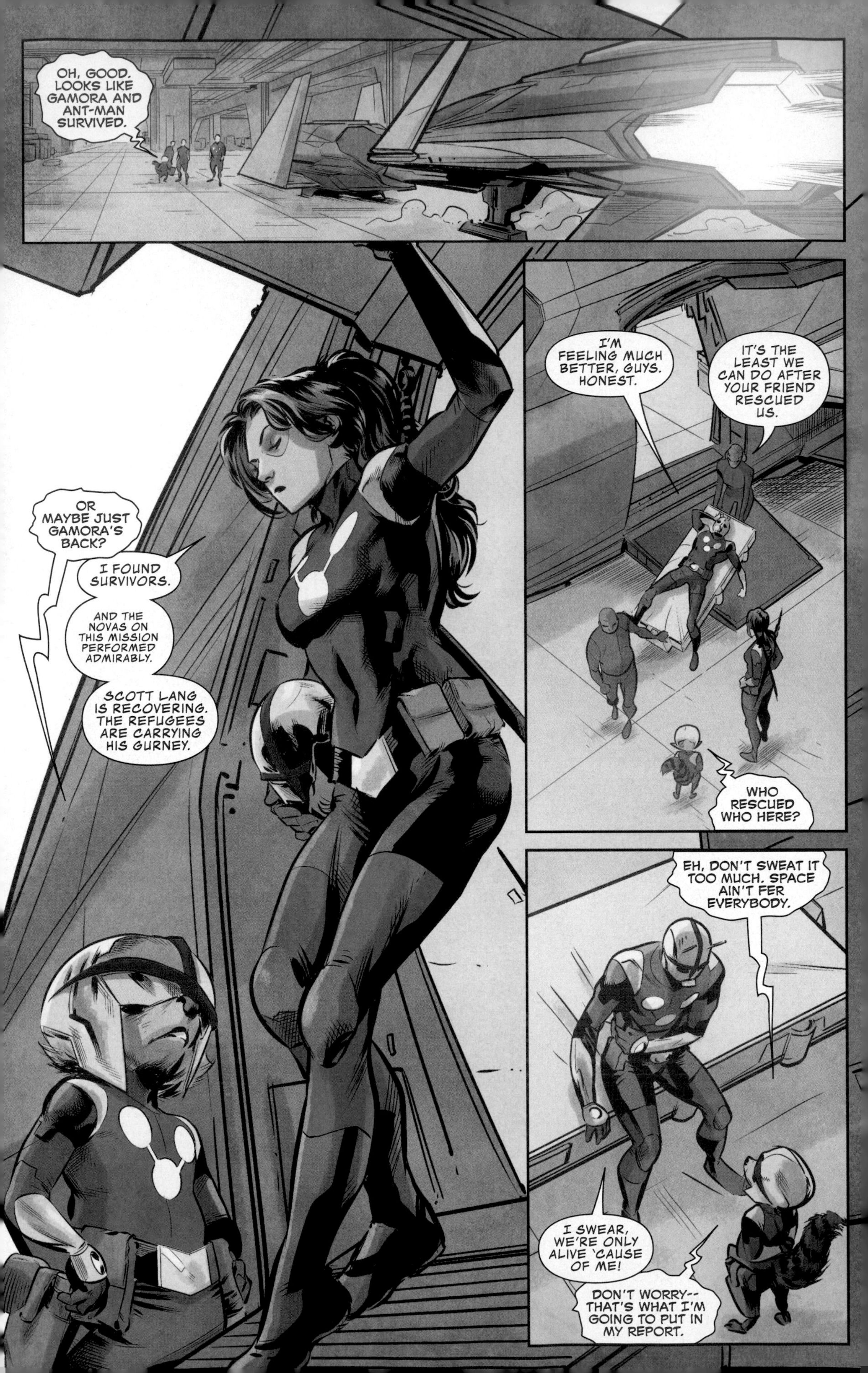
OH, GOOD. LOOKS LIKE GAMORA AND ANT-MAN SURVIVED.
OR MAYBE JUST GAMORA'S BACK?
I FOUND SURVIVORS.
AND THE NOVAS ON THIS MISSION PERFORMED ADMIRABLY.
SCOTT LANG IS RECOVERING. THE REFUGEES ARE CARRYING HIS GURNEY.
I'M FEELING MUCH BETTER, GUYS. HONEST.
IT'S THE LEAST WE CAN DO AFTER YOUR FRIEND RESCUED US.
WHO RESCUED WHO HERE?
EH, DON'T SWEAT IT TOO MUCH. SPACE AIN'T FER EVERYBODY.
I SWEAR, WE'RE ONLY ALIVE 'CAUSE OF ME!
DON'T WORRY-- THAT'S WHAT I'M GOING TO PUT IN MY REPORT.

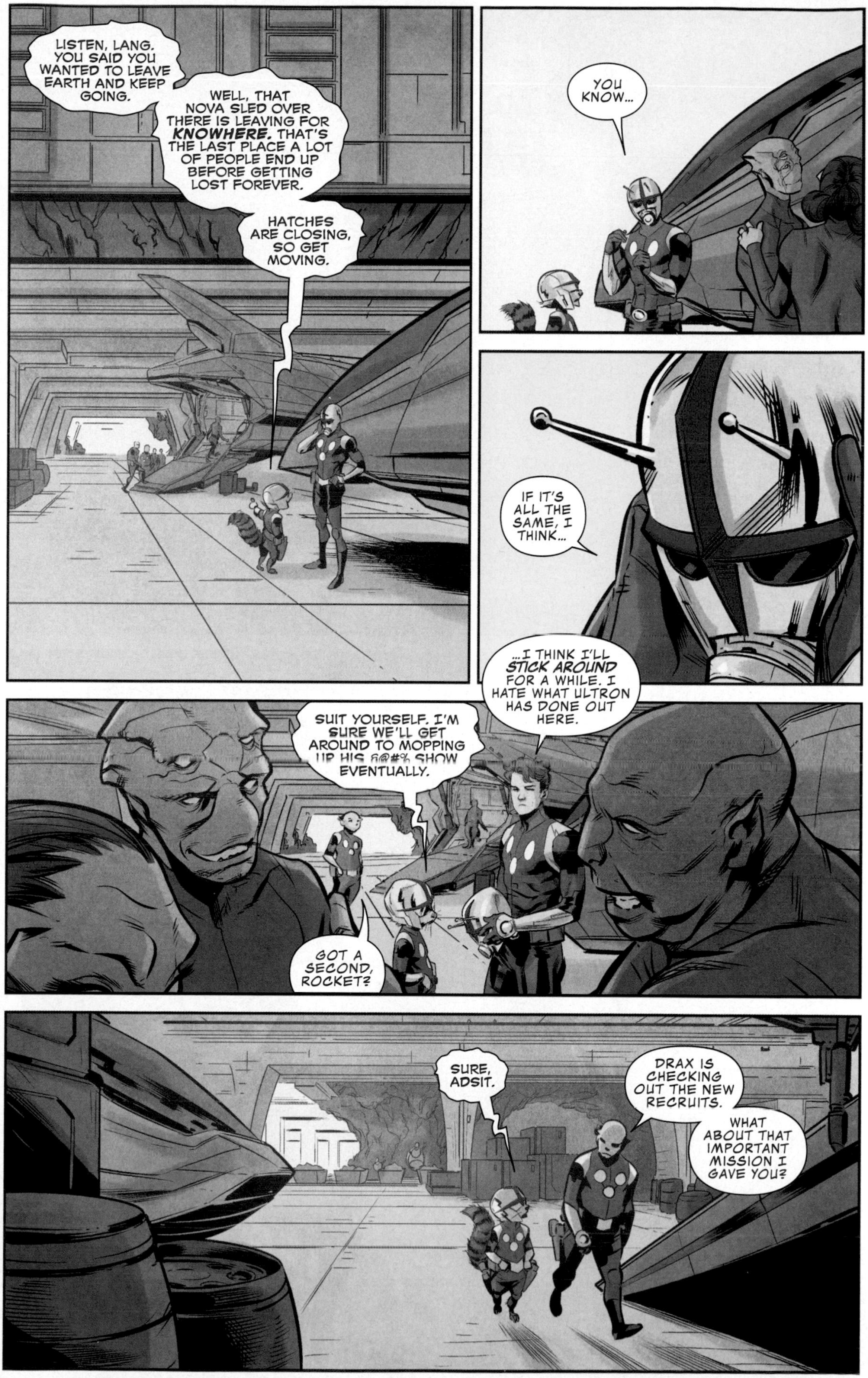
LISTEN, LANG. YOU SAID YOU WANTED TO LEAVE EARTH AND KEEP GOING.
WELL, THAT NOVA SLED OVER THERE IS LEAVING FOR KNOWHERE. THAT'S THE LAST PLACE A LOT OF PEOPLE END UP BEFORE GETTING LOST FOREVER.
HATCHES ARE CLOSING, SO GET MOVING.
YOU KNOW...
IF IT'S ALL THE SAME, I THINK...
...I THINK I'LL STICK AROUND FOR A WHILE. I HATE WHAT ULTRON HAS DONE OUT HERE.
SUIT YOURSELF. I'M SURE WE'LL GET AROUND TO MOPPING UP HIS &@#% SHOW EVENTUALLY.
GOT A SECOND, ROCKET?
SURE, ADSIT.
DRAX IS CHECKING OUT THE NEW RECRUITS.
WHAT ABOUT THAT IMPORTANT MISSION I GAVE YOU?

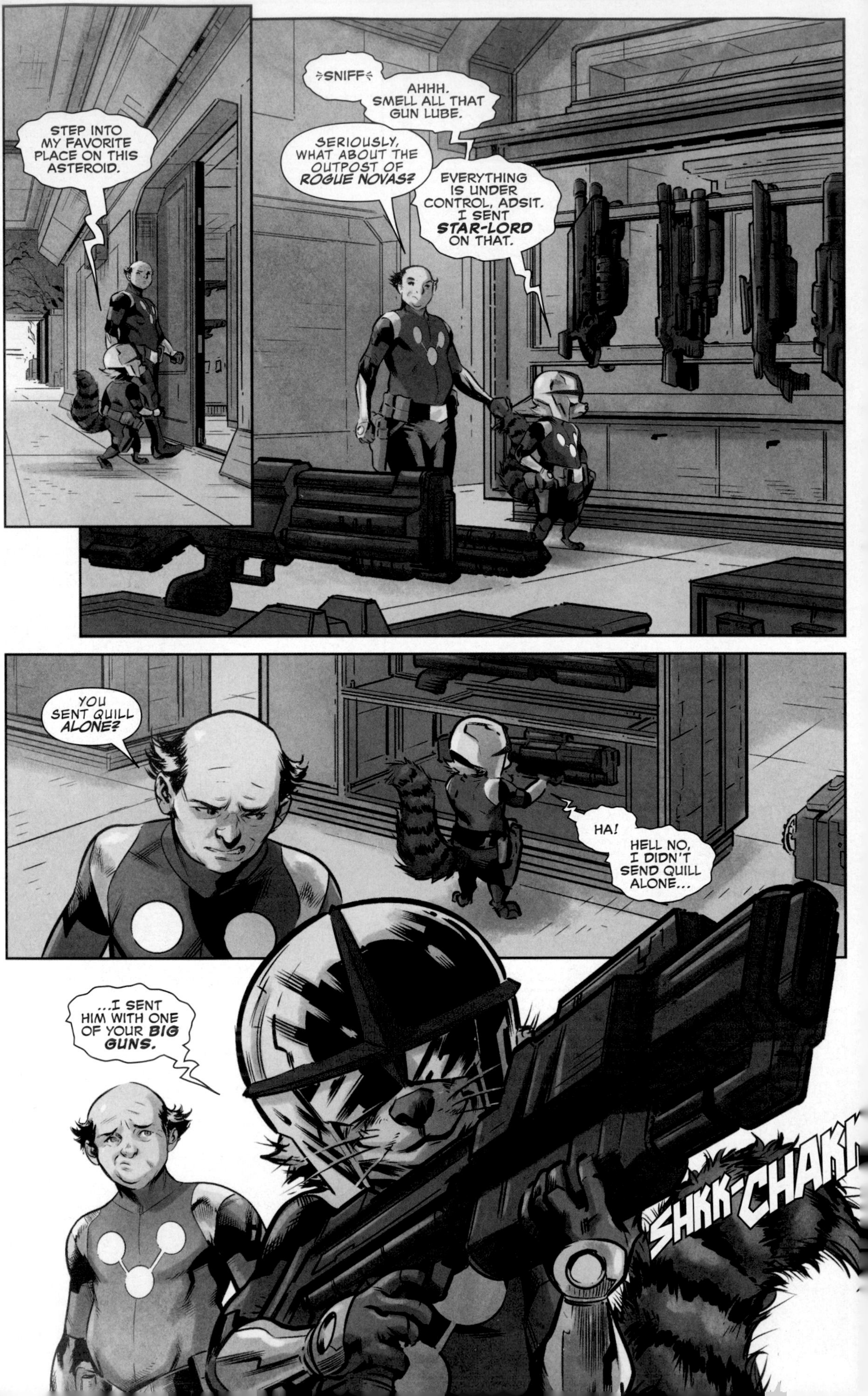
STEP INTO MY FAVORITE PLACE ON THIS ASTEROID.
≈SNIFF≈
AHHH. SMELL ALL THAT GUN LUBE.
SERIOUSLY, WHAT ABOUT THE OUTPOST OF ROGUE NOVAS?
EVERYTHING IS UNDER CONTROL, ADSIT. I SENT STAR-LORD ON THAT.
YOU SENT QUILL ALONE?
HA!
HELL NO, I DIDN'T SEND QUILL ALONE...
...I SENT HIM WITH ONE OF YOUR BIG GUNS.
SHKK-CHAK

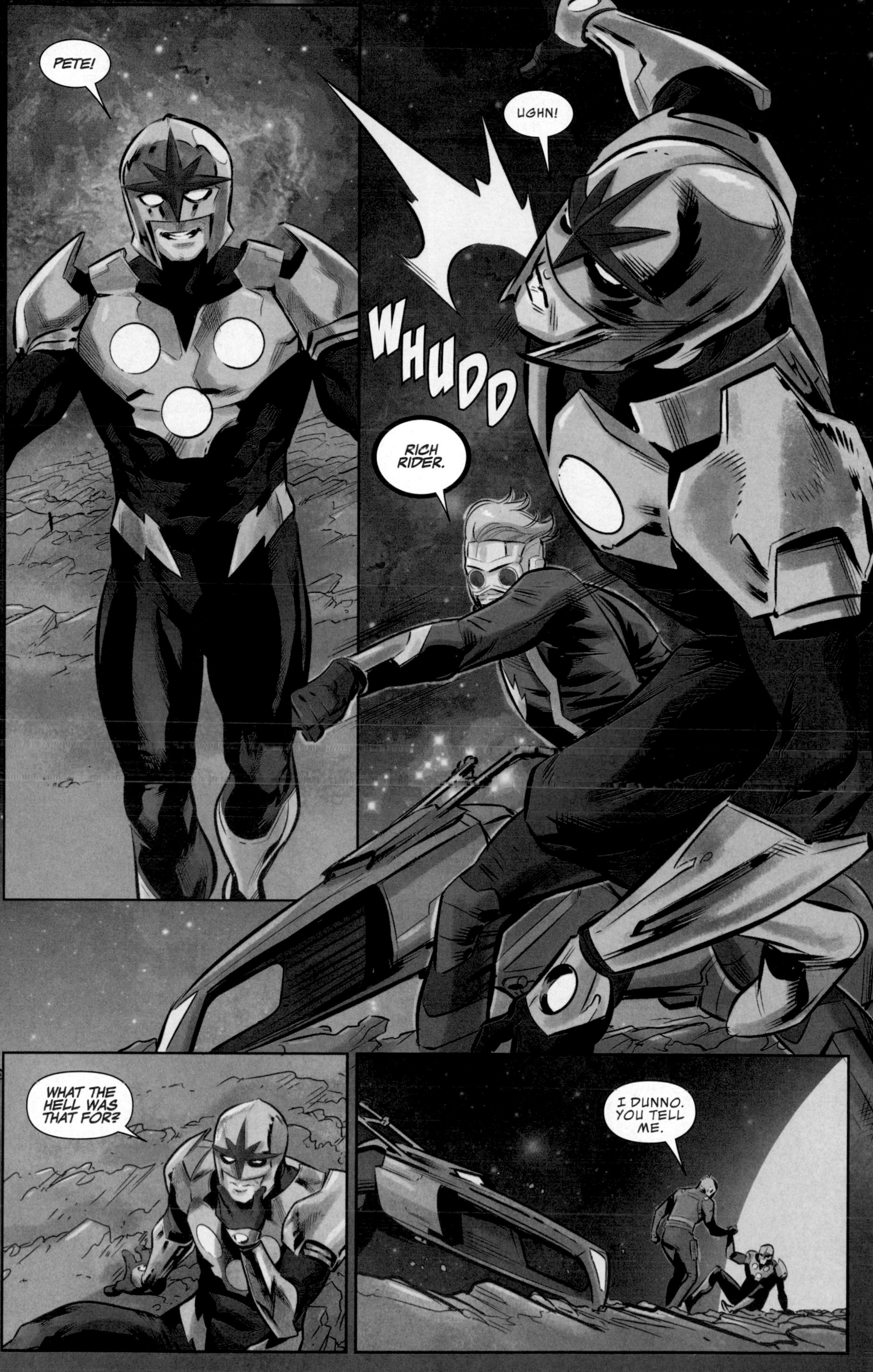
PETE!
UGHN!
WHUDD
RICH RIDER.
WHAT THE HELL WAS THAT FOR?
I DUNNO. YOU TELL ME.

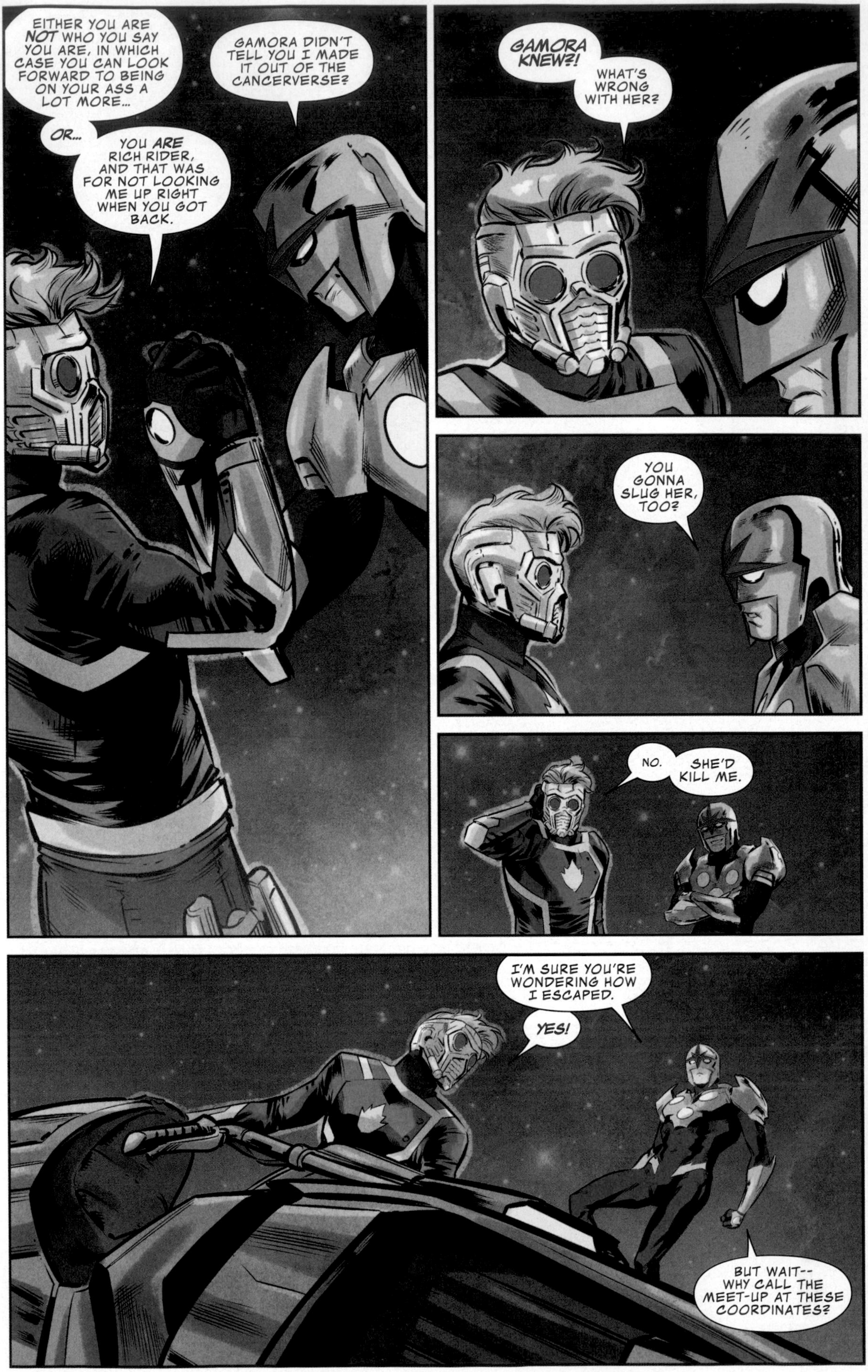
EITHER YOU ARE *NOT* WHO YOU SAY YOU ARE, IN WHICH CASE YOU CAN LOOK FORWARD TO BEING ON YOUR ASS A LOT MORE...
OR...
YOU *ARE* RICH RIDER, AND THAT WAS FOR NOT LOOKING ME UP RIGHT WHEN YOU GOT BACK.
GAMORA DIDN'T TELL YOU I MADE IT OUT OF THE CANCERVERSE?
GAMORA KNEW?!
WHAT'S WRONG WITH HER?
YOU GONNA SLUG HER, TOO?
NO.
SHE'D KILL ME.
I'M SURE YOU'RE WONDERING HOW I ESCAPED.
YES!
BUT WAIT-- WHY CALL THE MEET-UP AT THESE COORDINATES?

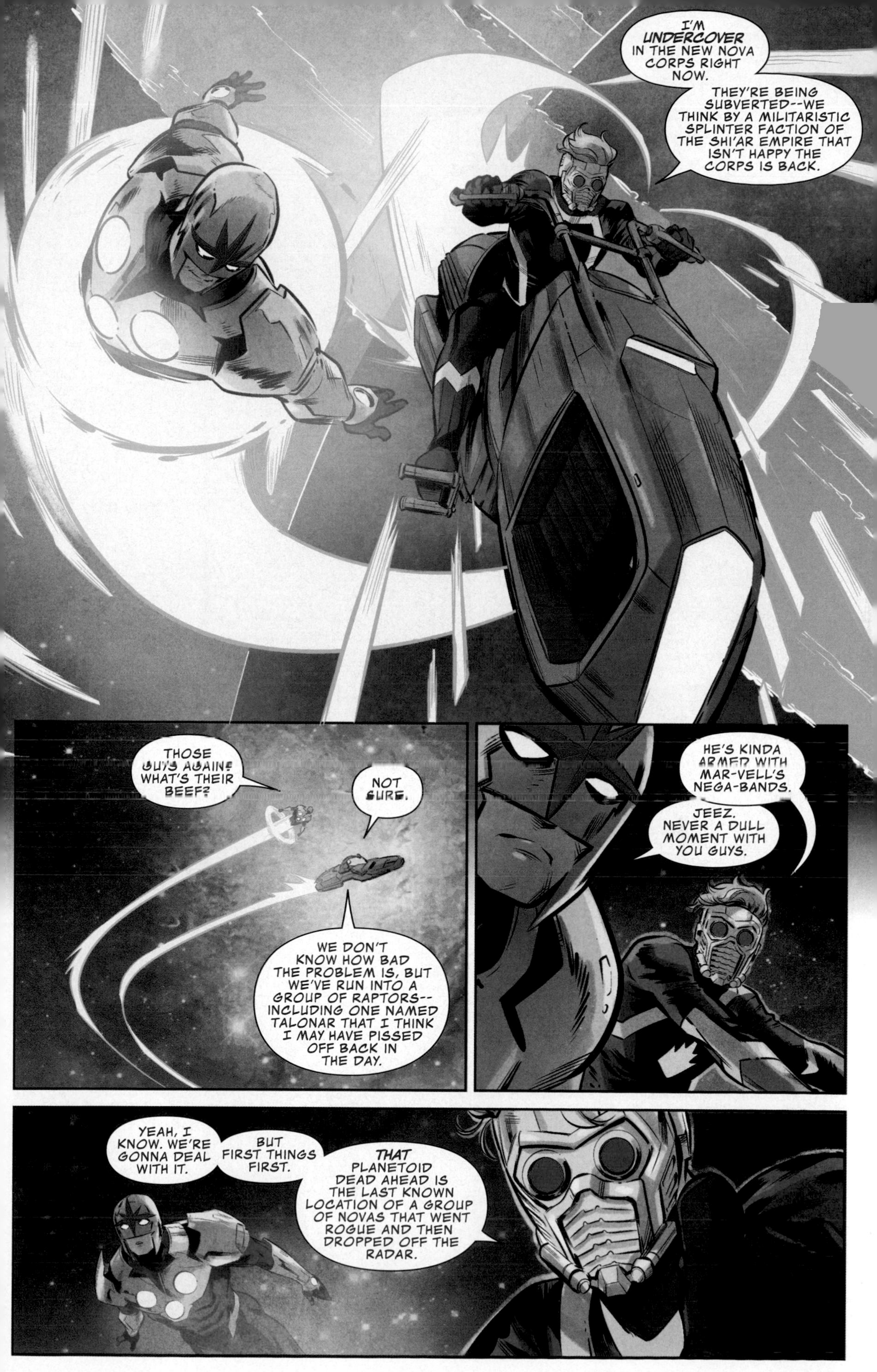
I'M *UNDERCOVER* IN THE NEW NOVA CORPS RIGHT NOW.
THEY'RE BEING SUBVERTED--WE THINK BY A MILITARISTIC SPLINTER FACTION OF THE SHI'AR EMPIRE THAT ISN'T HAPPY THE CORPS IS BACK.
THOSE GUYS AGAIN? WHAT'S THEIR BEEF?
NOT SURE.
WE DON'T KNOW HOW BAD THE PROBLEM IS, BUT WE'VE RUN INTO A GROUP OF RAPTORS--INCLUDING ONE NAMED TALONAR THAT I THINK I MAY HAVE PISSED OFF BACK IN THE DAY.
HE'S KINDA ARMED WITH MAR-VELL'S NEGA-BANDS.
JEEZ. NEVER A DULL MOMENT WITH YOU GUYS.
YEAH, I KNOW. WE'RE GONNA DEAL WITH IT.
BUT FIRST THINGS FIRST.
THAT PLANETOID DEAD AHEAD IS THE LAST KNOWN LOCATION OF A GROUP OF NOVAS THAT WENT ROGUE AND THEN DROPPED OFF THE RADAR.

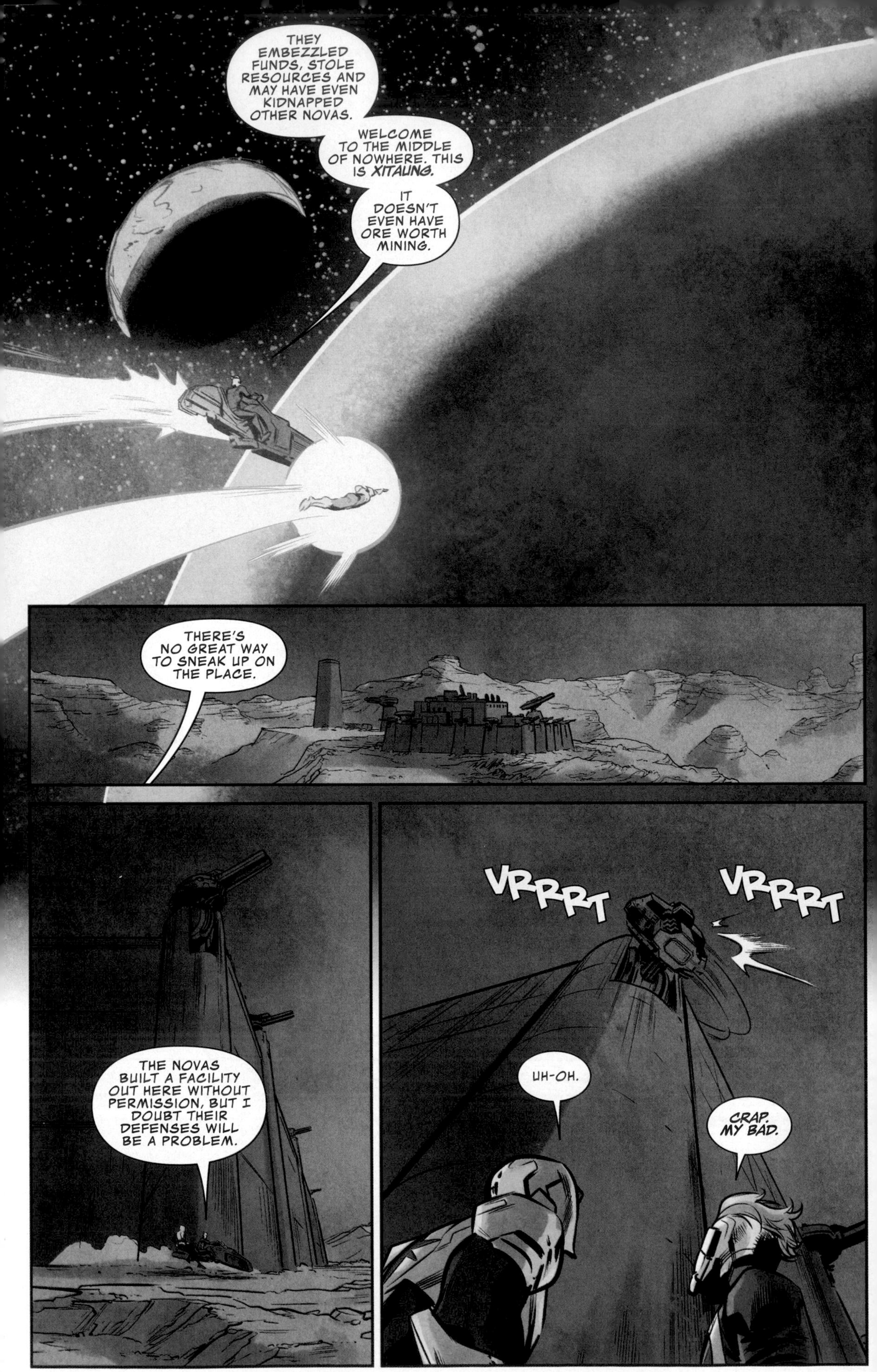
THEY EMBEZZLED FUNDS, STOLE RESOURCES AND MAY HAVE EVEN KIDNAPPED OTHER NOVAS.
WELCOME TO THE MIDDLE OF NOWHERE. THIS IS XITAUNG.
IT DOESN'T EVEN HAVE ORE WORTH MINING.
THERE'S NO GREAT WAY TO SNEAK UP ON THE PLACE.
THE NOVAS BUILT A FACILITY OUT HERE WITHOUT PERMISSION, BUT I DOUBT THEIR DEFENSES WILL BE A PROBLEM.
VRRRT
VRRRT
UH-OH.
CRAP. MY BAD.

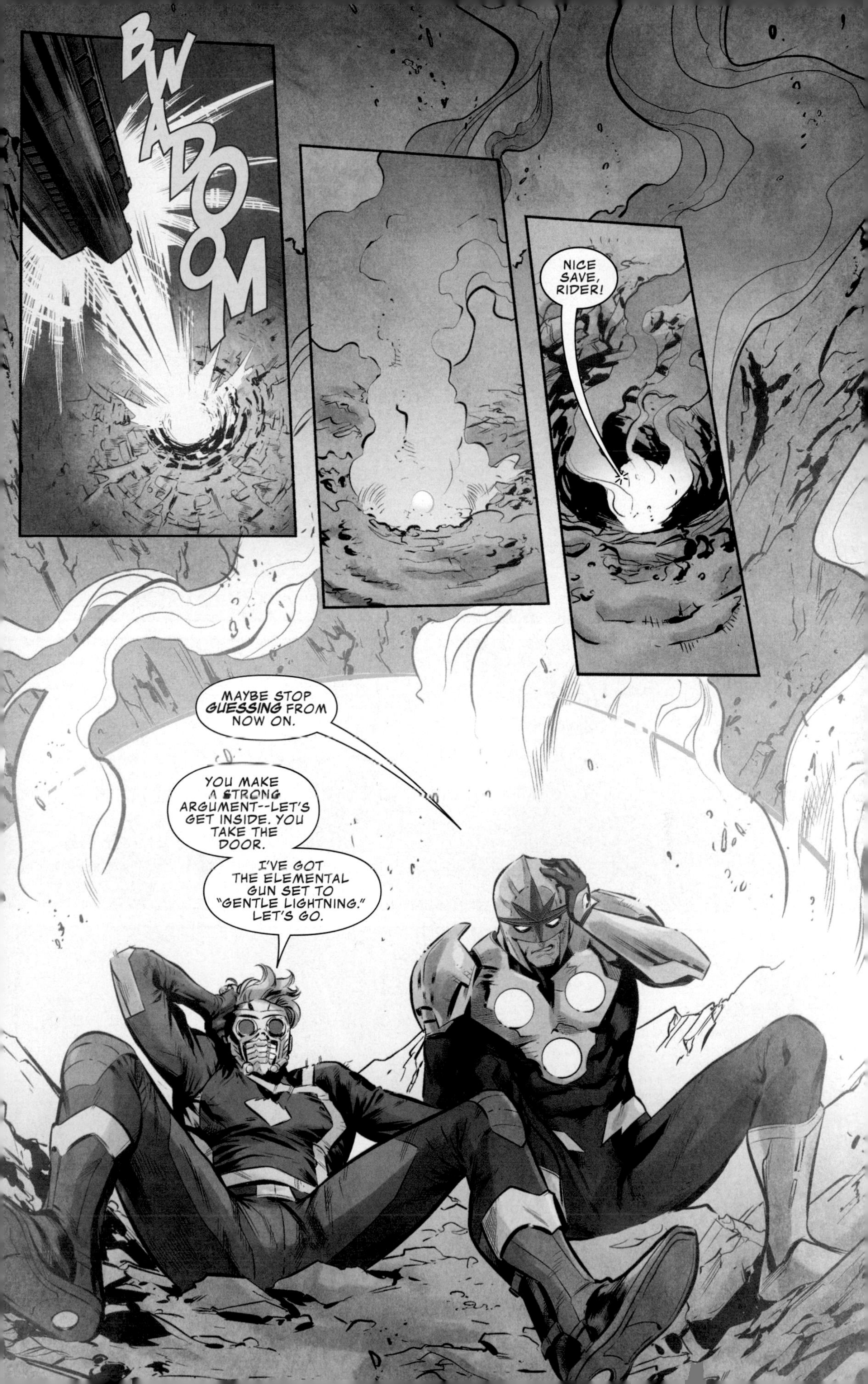
BWADOOM
NICE SAVE, RIDER!
MAYBE STOP GUESSING FROM NOW ON.
YOU MAKE A STRONG ARGUMENT--LET'S GET INSIDE. YOU TAKE THE DOOR.
I'VE GOT THE ELEMENTAL GUN SET TO "GENTLE LIGHTNING." LET'S GO.

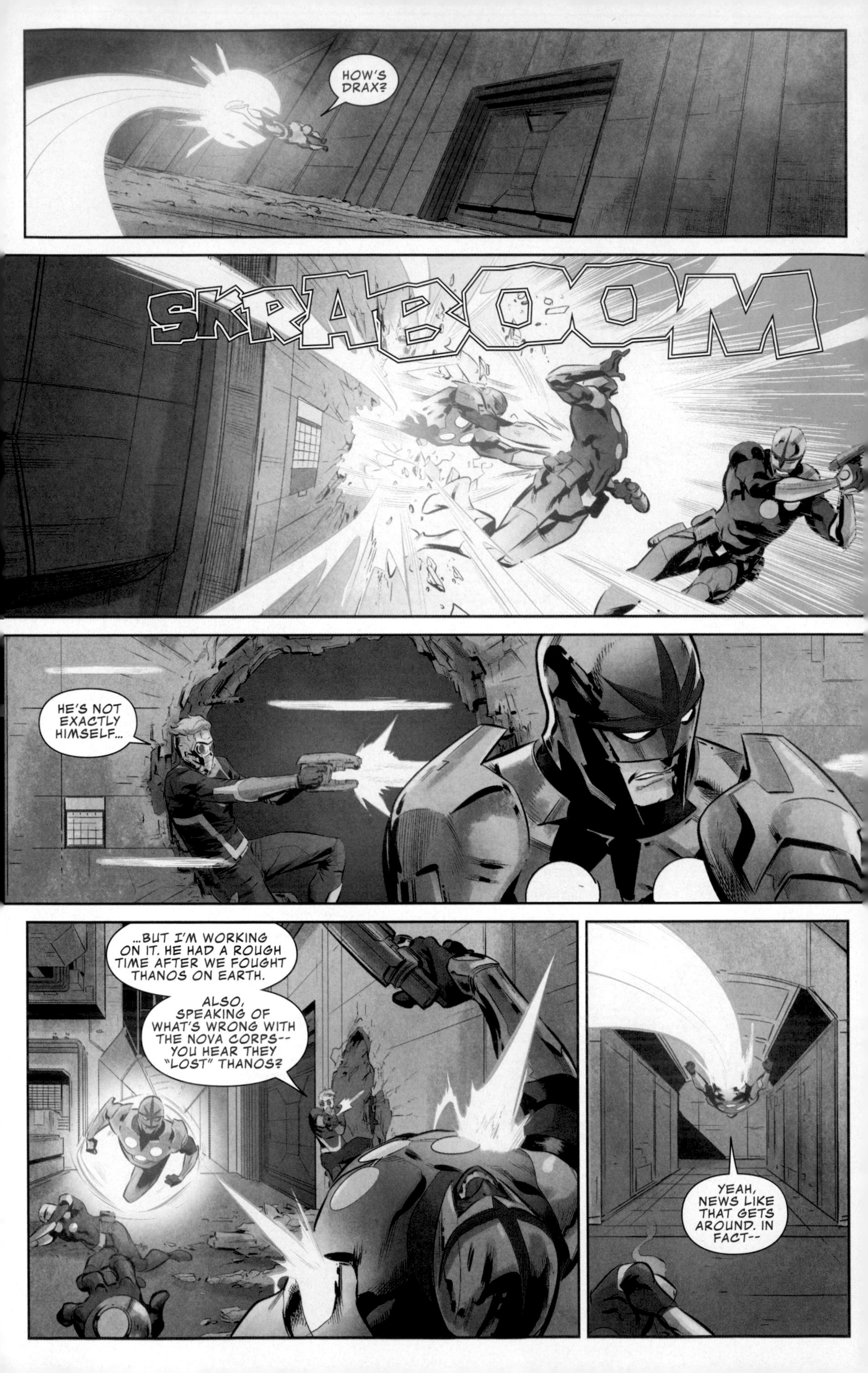
HOW'S DRAX?
SKRABOOM
HE'S NOT EXACTLY HIMSELF...
...BUT I'M WORKING ON IT. HE HAD A ROUGH TIME AFTER WE FOUGHT THANOS ON EARTH.
ALSO, SPEAKING OF WHAT'S WRONG WITH THE NOVA CORPS-- YOU HEAR THEY "LOST" THANOS?
YEAH, NEWS LIKE THAT GETS AROUND. IN FACT--

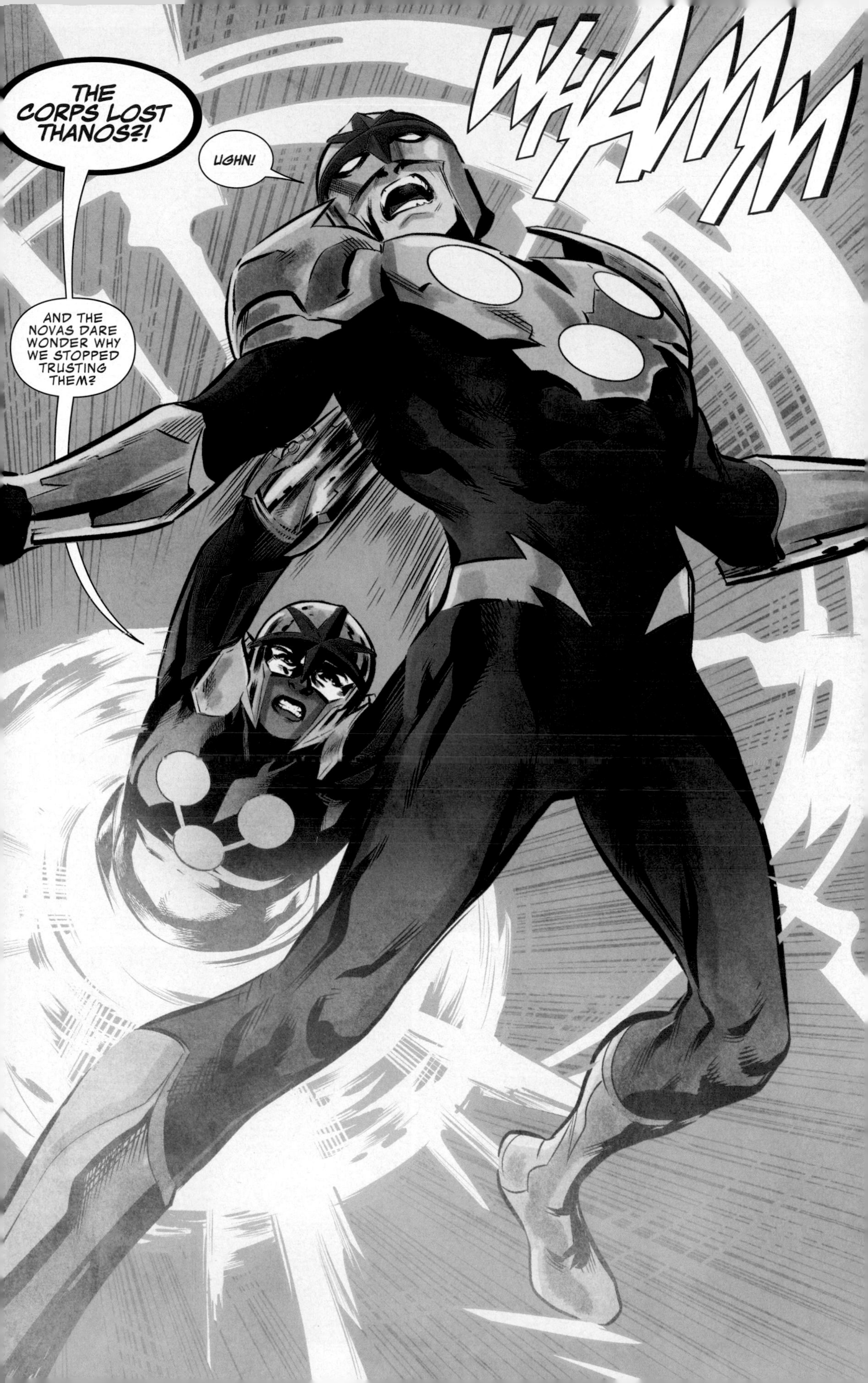
WHAMM
THE CORPS LOST THANOS?!
UGHN!
AND THE NOVAS DARE WONDER WHY WE STOPPED TRUSTING THEM?

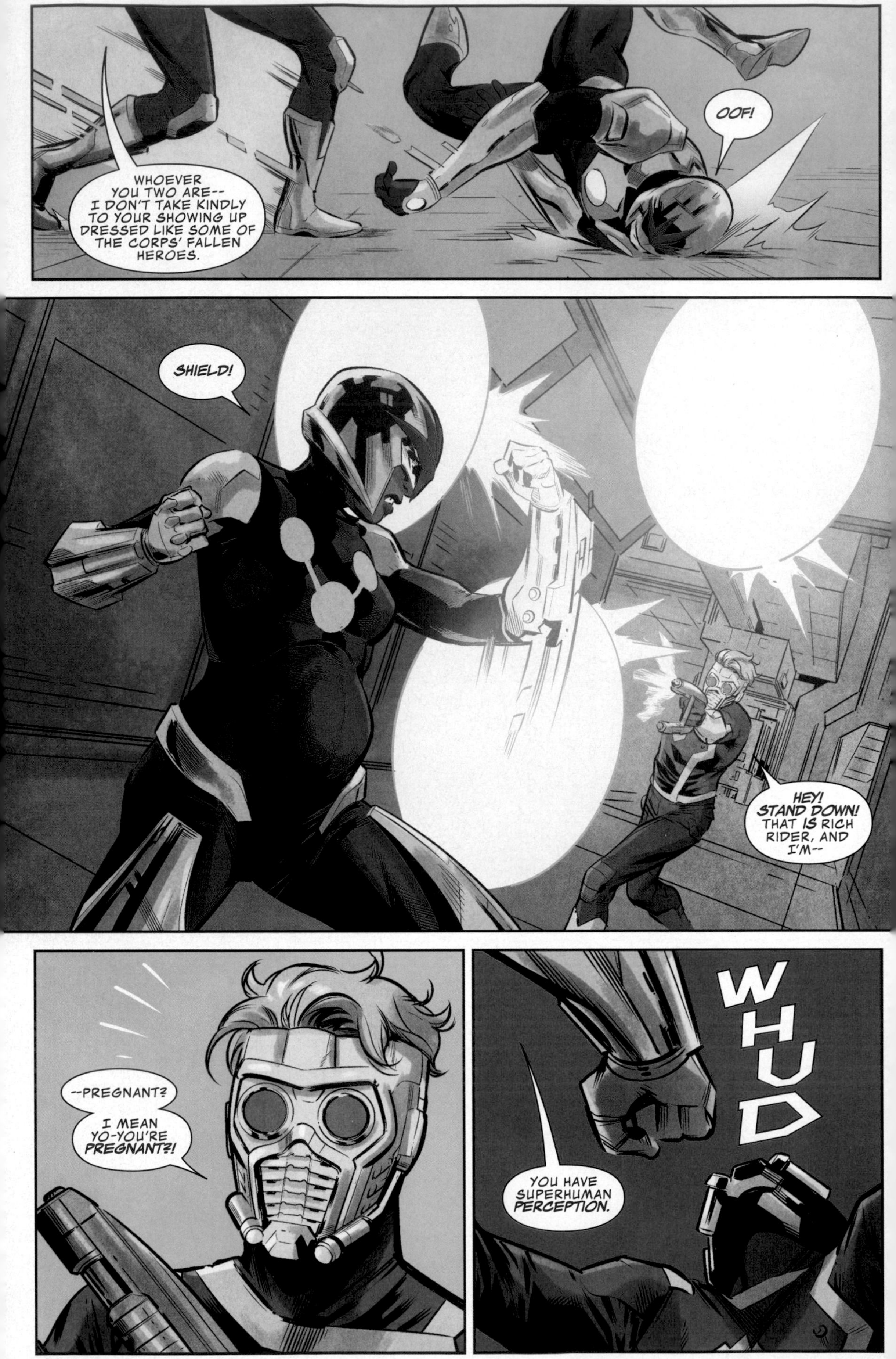
WHOEVER YOU TWO ARE-- I DON'T TAKE KINDLY TO YOUR SHOWING UP DRESSED LIKE SOME OF THE CORPS' FALLEN HEROES.
OOF!
SHIELD!
HEY! STAND DOWN! THAT IS RICH RIDER, AND I'M--
--PREGNANT?
I MEAN YO-YOU'RE PREGNANT?!
WHUD
YOU HAVE SUPERHUMAN PERCEPTION.

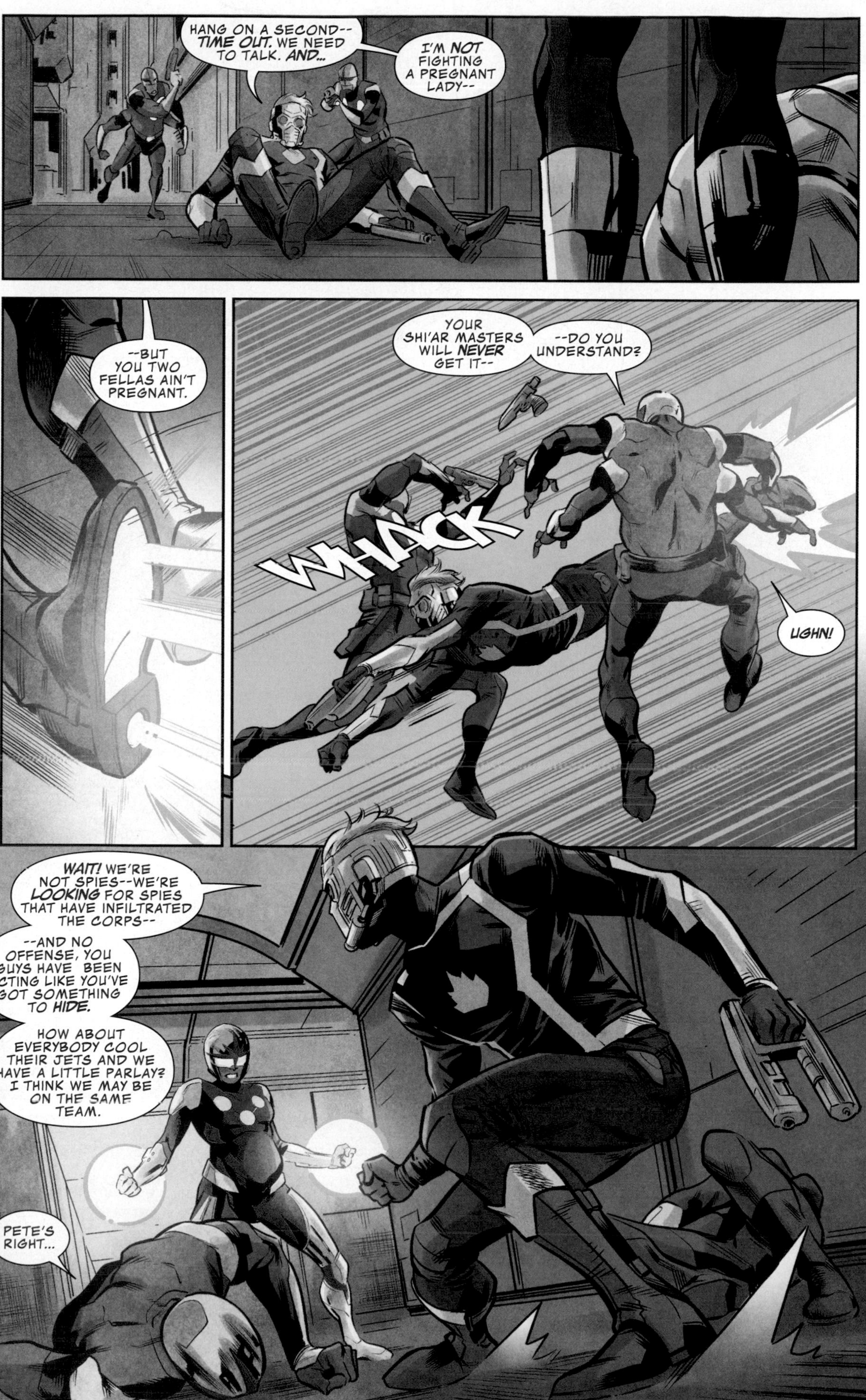
HANG ON A SECOND-- TIME OUT. WE NEED TO TALK. AND...
I'M NOT FIGHTING A PREGNANT LADY--
--BUT YOU TWO FELLAS AIN'T PREGNANT.
YOUR SHI'AR MASTERS WILL NEVER GET IT--
--DO YOU UNDERSTAND?
WHACK
UGHN!
WAIT! WE'RE NOT SPIES--WE'RE LOOKING FOR SPIES THAT HAVE INFILTRATED THE CORPS--
--AND NO OFFENSE, YOU GUYS HAVE BEEN ACTING LIKE YOU'VE GOT SOMETHING TO HIDE.
HOW ABOUT EVERYBODY COOL THEIR JETS AND WE HAVE A LITTLE PARLAY? I THINK WE MAY BE ON THE SAME TEAM.
PETE'S RIGHT...

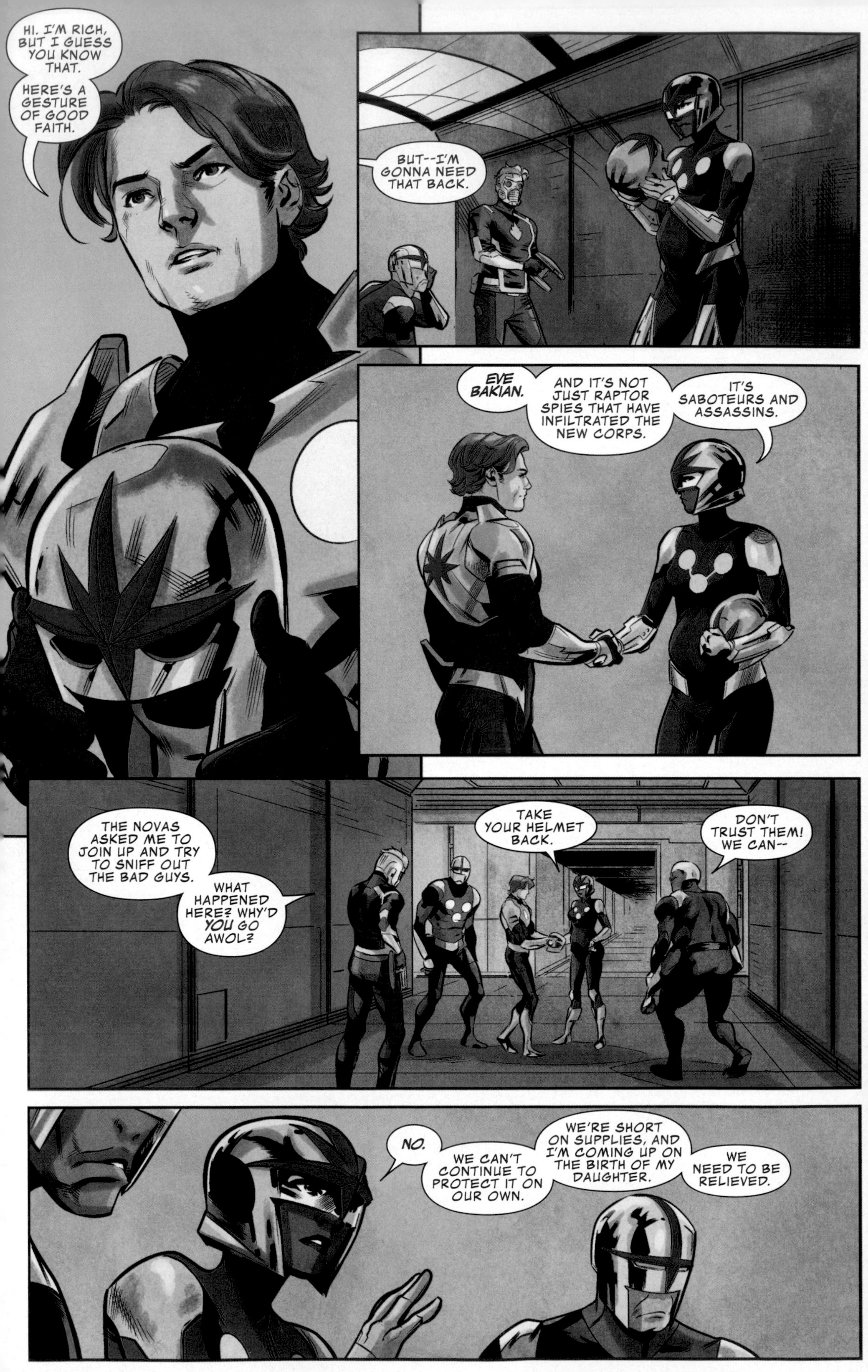
HI. I'M RICH, BUT I GUESS YOU KNOW THAT.
HERE'S A GESTURE OF GOOD FAITH.
BUT--I'M GONNA NEED THAT BACK.
EVE BAKIAN.
AND IT'S NOT JUST RAPTOR SPIES THAT HAVE INFILTRATED THE NEW CORPS.
IT'S SABOTEURS AND ASSASSINS.
THE NOVAS ASKED ME TO JOIN UP AND TRY TO SNIFF OUT THE BAD GUYS.
WHAT HAPPENED HERE? WHY'D YOU GO AWOL?
TAKE YOUR HELMET BACK.
DON'T TRUST THEM! WE CAN--
NO.
WE CAN'T CONTINUE TO PROTECT IT ON OUR OWN.
WE'RE SHORT ON SUPPLIES, AND I'M COMING UP ON THE BIRTH OF MY DAUGHTER.
WE NEED TO BE RELIEVED.

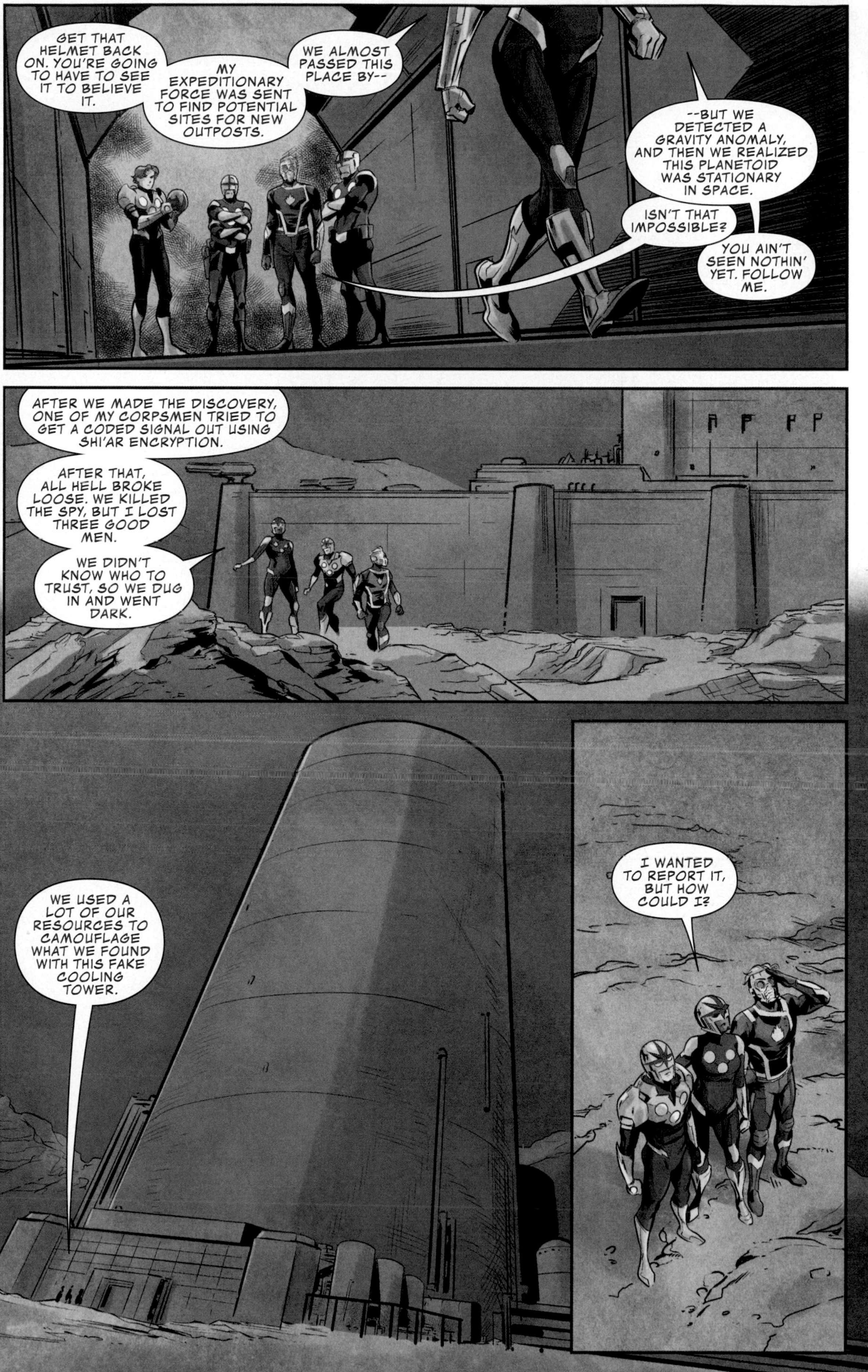
GET THAT HELMET BACK ON. YOU'RE GOING TO HAVE TO SEE IT TO BELIEVE IT.
MY EXPEDITIONARY FORCE WAS SENT TO FIND POTENTIAL SITES FOR NEW OUTPOSTS.
WE ALMOST PASSED THIS PLACE BY--
--BUT WE DETECTED A GRAVITY ANOMALY, AND THEN WE REALIZED THIS PLANETOID WAS STATIONARY IN SPACE.
ISN'T THAT IMPOSSIBLE?
YOU AIN'T SEEN NOTHIN' YET. FOLLOW ME.
AFTER WE MADE THE DISCOVERY, ONE OF MY CORPSMEN TRIED TO GET A CODED SIGNAL OUT USING SHI'AR ENCRYPTION.
AFTER THAT, ALL HELL BROKE LOOSE. WE KILLED THE SPY, BUT I LOST THREE GOOD MEN.
WE DIDN'T KNOW WHO TO TRUST, SO WE DUG IN AND WENT DARK.
WE USED A LOT OF OUR RESOURCES TO CAMOUFLAGE WHAT WE FOUND WITH THIS FAKE COOLING TOWER.
I WANTED TO REPORT IT, BUT HOW COULD I?

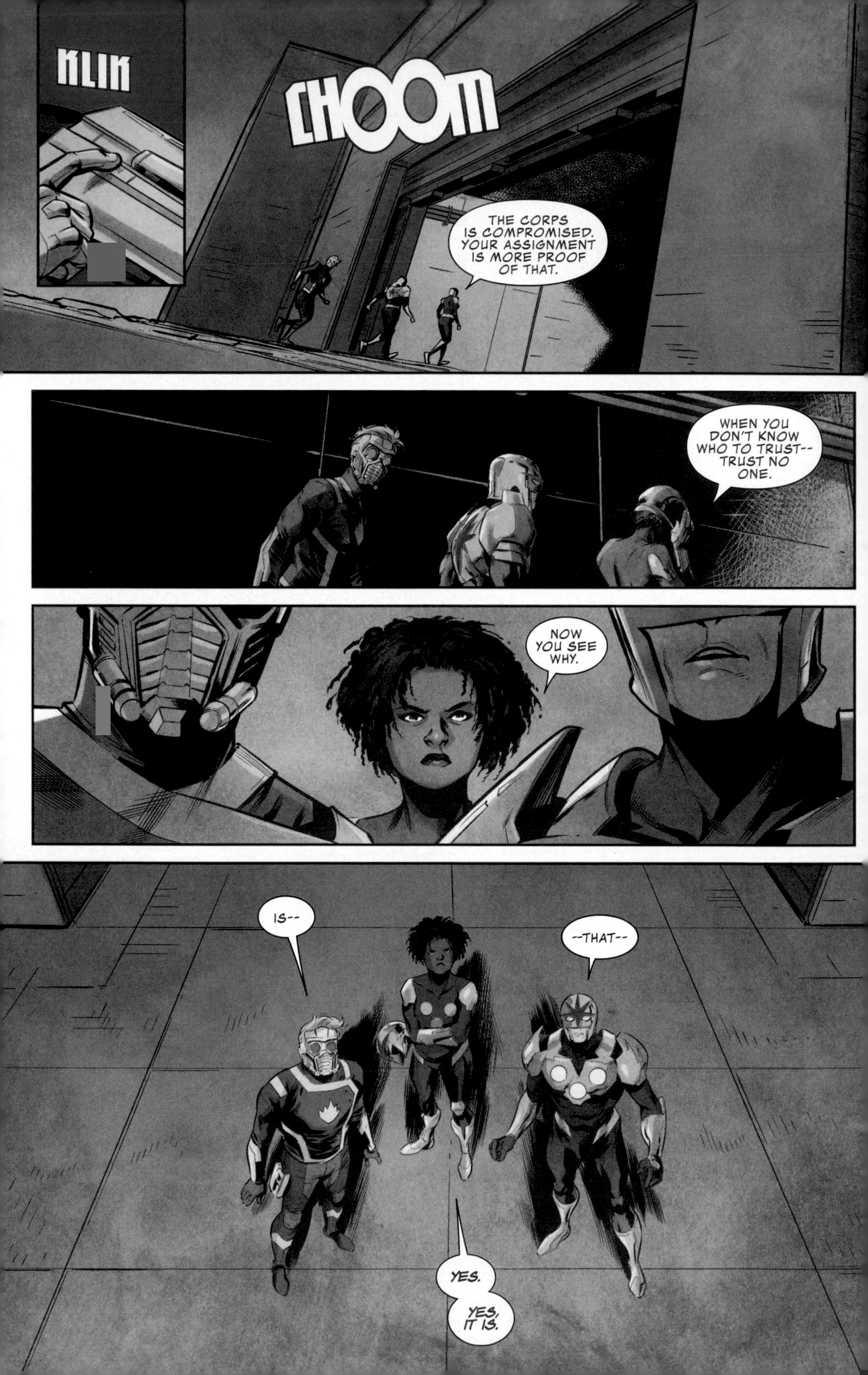
KLIK
CHOOM
THE CORPS IS COMPROMISED. YOUR ASSIGNMENT IS MORE PROOF OF THAT.
WHEN YOU DON'T KNOW WHO TO TRUST-- TRUST NO ONE.
NOW YOU SEE WHY.
IS--
--THAT--
YES.
YES, IT IS.

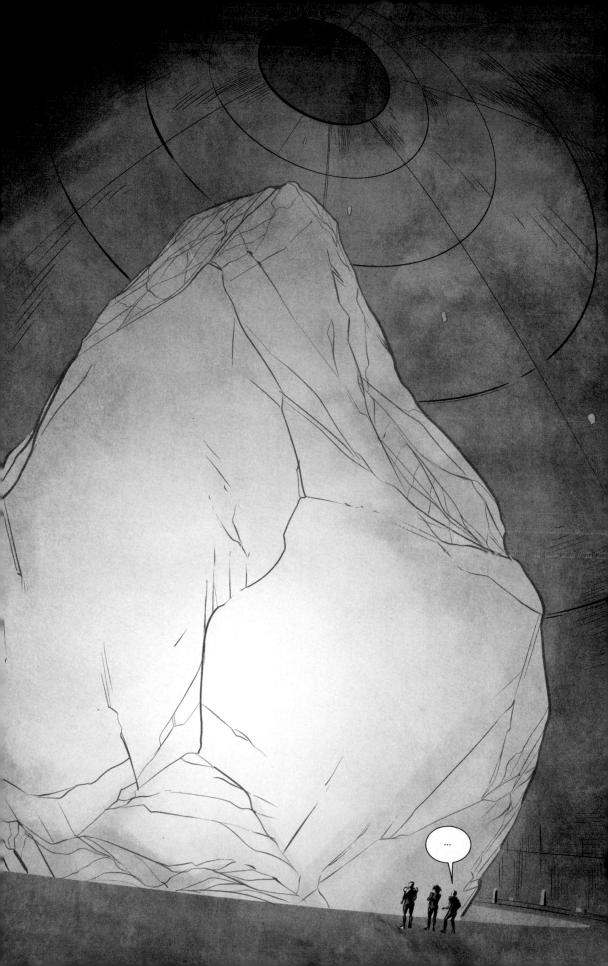

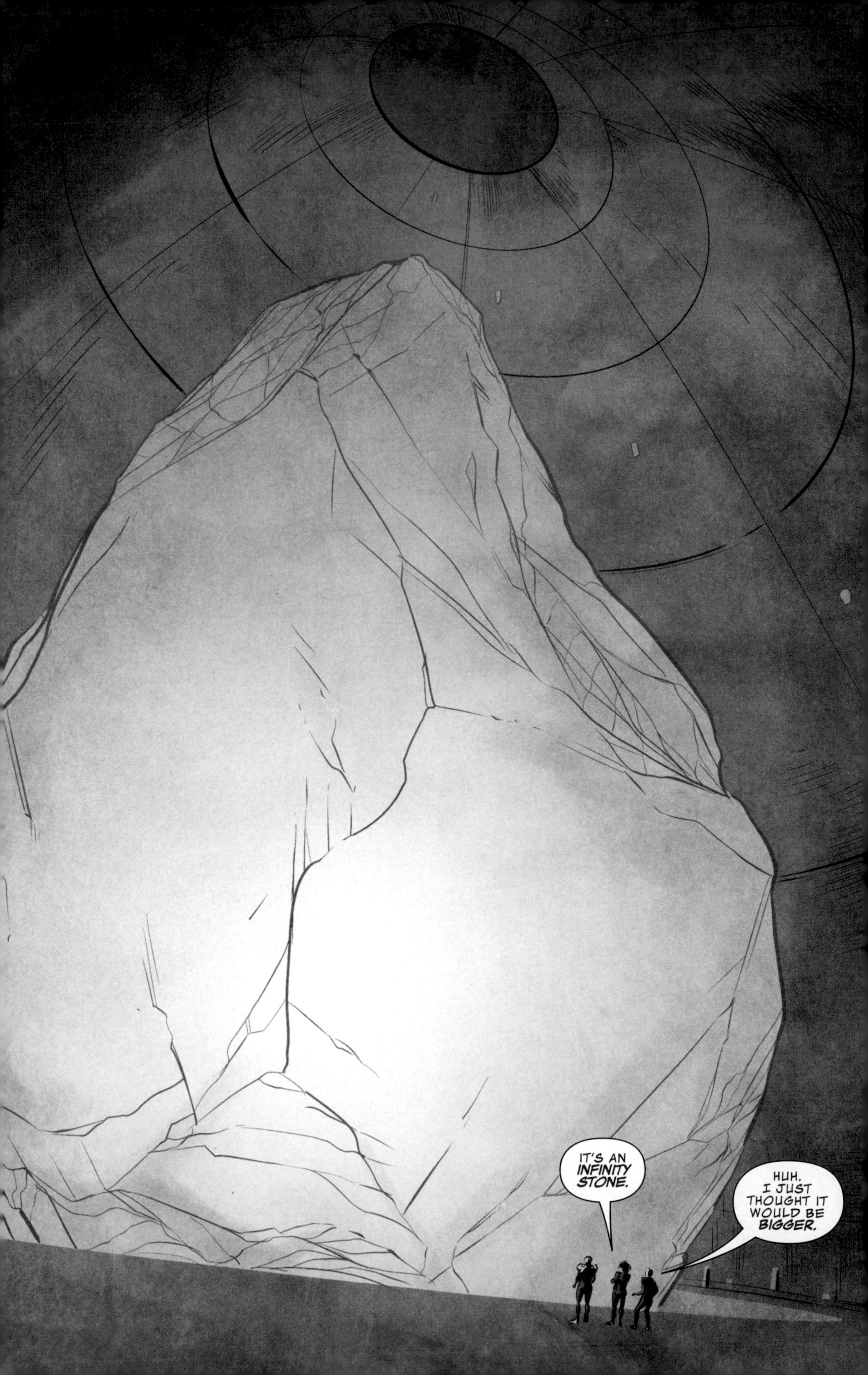
IT'S AN INFINITY STONE.
HUH. I JUST THOUGHT IT WOULD BE BIGGER.

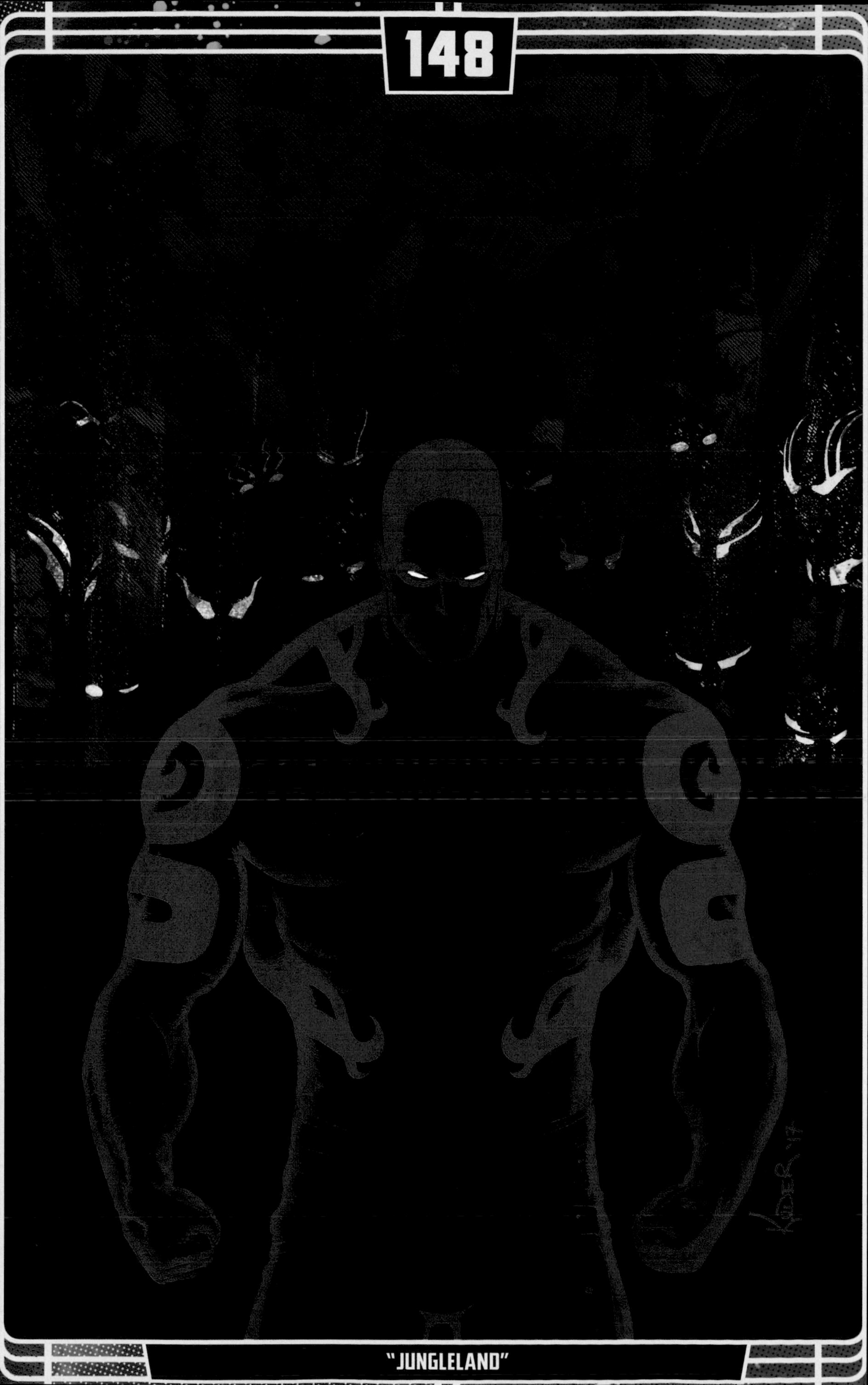
148
"JUNGLELAND"

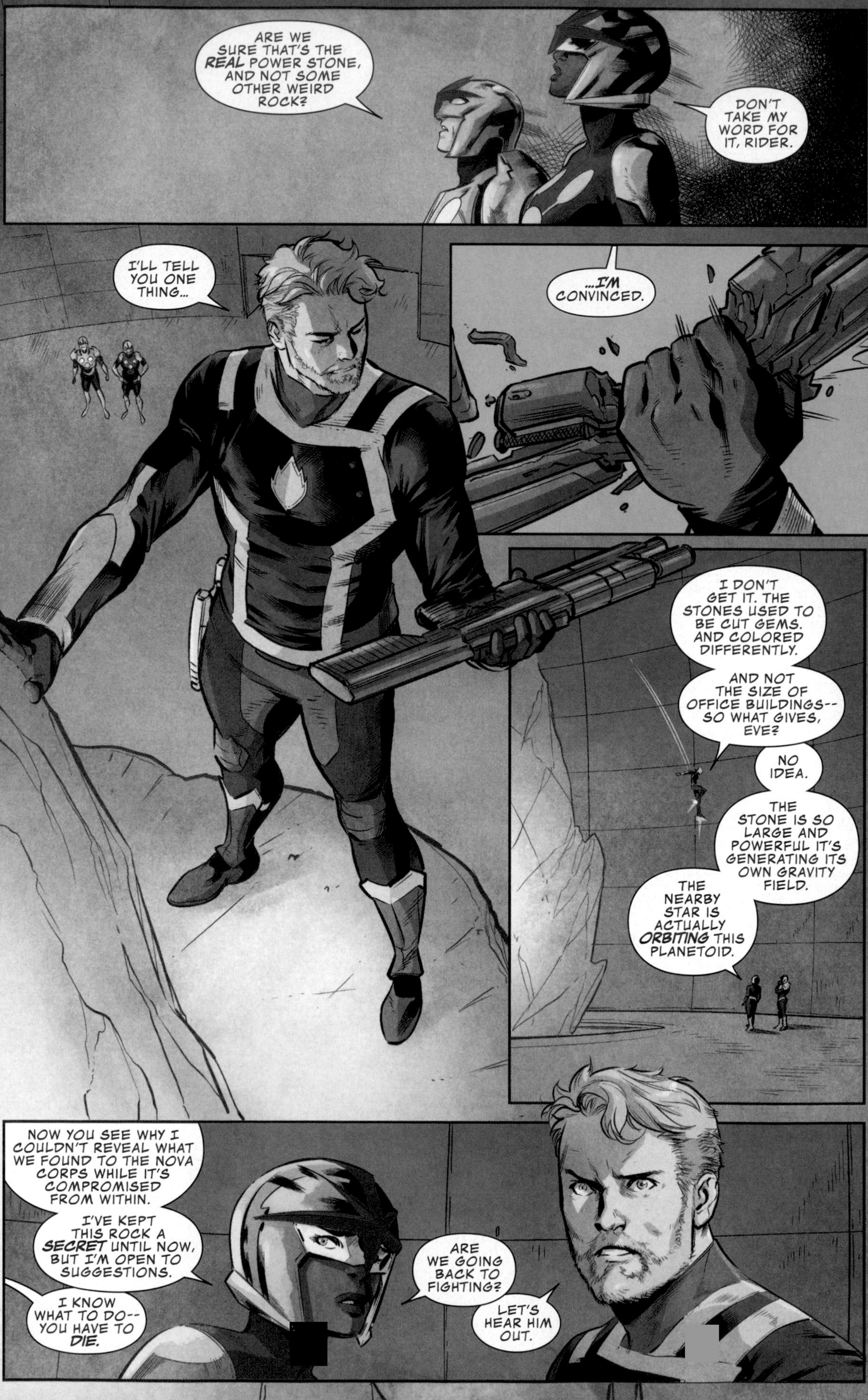
ARE WE SURE THAT'S THE REAL POWER STONE, AND NOT SOME OTHER WEIRD ROCK?
DON'T TAKE MY WORD FOR IT, RIDER.
I'LL TELL YOU ONE THING...
...I'M CONVINCED.
I DON'T GET IT. THE STONES USED TO BE CUT GEMS. AND COLORED DIFFERENTLY.
AND NOT THE SIZE OF OFFICE BUILDINGS-- SO WHAT GIVES, EVE?
NO IDEA.
THE STONE IS SO LARGE AND POWERFUL IT'S GENERATING ITS OWN GRAVITY FIELD.
THE NEARBY STAR IS ACTUALLY ORBITING THIS PLANETOID.
NOW YOU SEE WHY I COULDN'T REVEAL WHAT WE FOUND TO THE NOVA CORPS WHILE IT'S COMPROMISED FROM WITHIN.
I'VE KEPT THIS ROCK A SECRET UNTIL NOW, BUT I'M OPEN TO SUGGESTIONS.
I KNOW WHAT TO DO-- YOU HAVE TO DIE.
ARE WE GOING BACK TO FIGHTING?
LET'S HEAR HIM OUT.

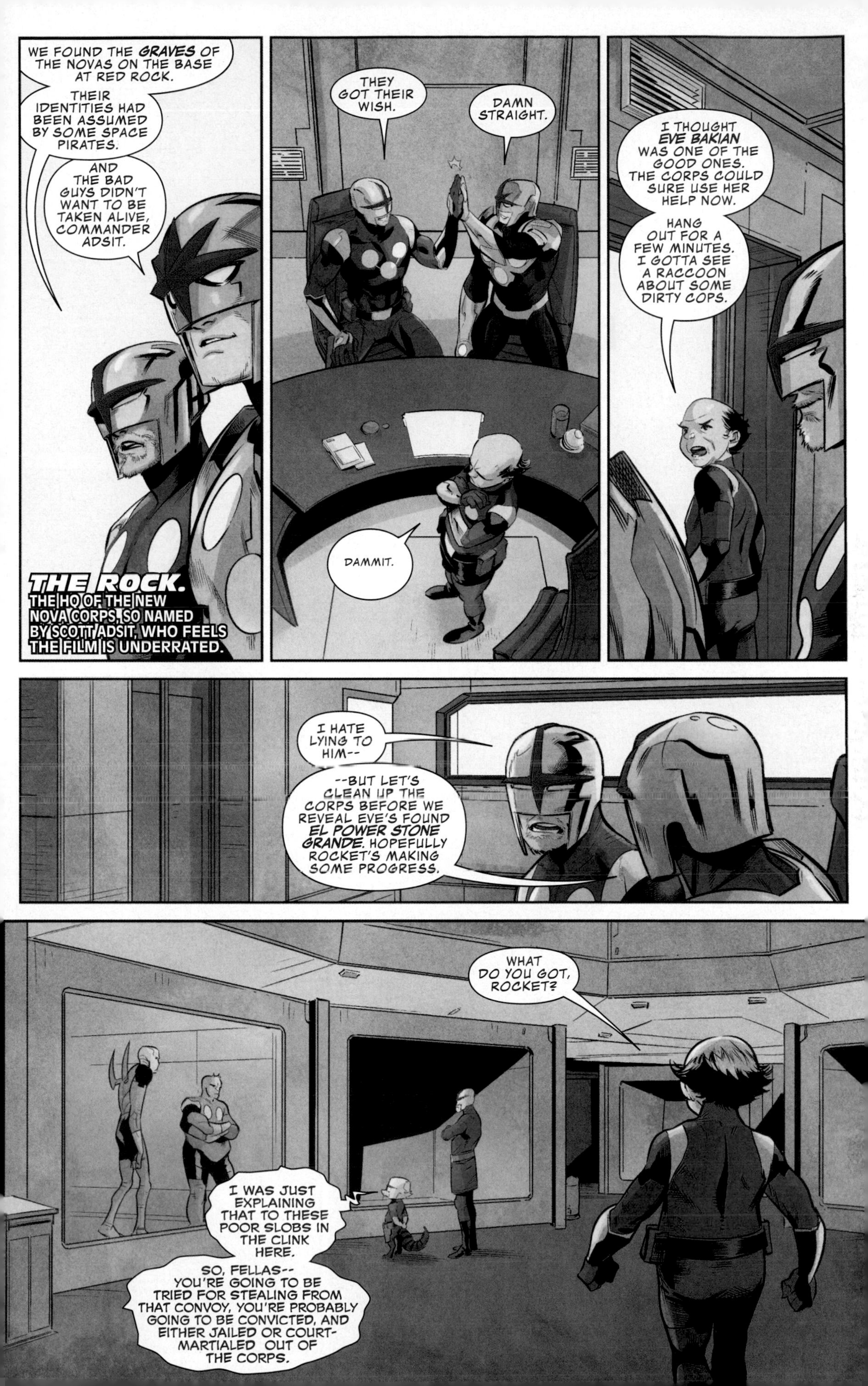
WE FOUND THE GRAVES OF THE NOVAS ON THE BASE AT RED ROCK.
THEIR IDENTITIES HAD BEEN ASSUMED BY SOME SPACE PIRATES.
AND THE BAD GUYS DIDN'T WANT TO BE TAKEN ALIVE, COMMANDER ADSIT.
THE ROCK. THE HQ OF THE NEW NOVA CORPS, SO NAMED BY SCOTT ADSIT, WHO FEELS THE FILM IS UNDERRATED.
THEY GOT THEIR WISH.
DAMN STRAIGHT.
DAMMIT.
I THOUGHT EVE BAKIAN WAS ONE OF THE GOOD ONES. THE CORPS COULD SURE USE HER HELP NOW.
HANG OUT FOR A FEW MINUTES. I GOTTA SEE A RACCOON ABOUT SOME DIRTY COPS.
I HATE LYING TO HIM--
--BUT LET'S CLEAN UP THE CORPS BEFORE WE REVEAL EVE'S FOUND EL POWER STONE GRANDE. HOPEFULLY ROCKET'S MAKING SOME PROGRESS.
WHAT DO YOU GOT, ROCKET?
I WAS JUST EXPLAINING THAT TO THESE POOR SLOBS IN THE CLINK HERE.
SO, FELLAS-- YOU'RE GOING TO BE TRIED FOR STEALING FROM THAT CONVOY, YOU'RE PROBABLY GOING TO BE CONVICTED, AND EITHER JAILED OR COURT-MARTIALED OUT OF THE CORPS.

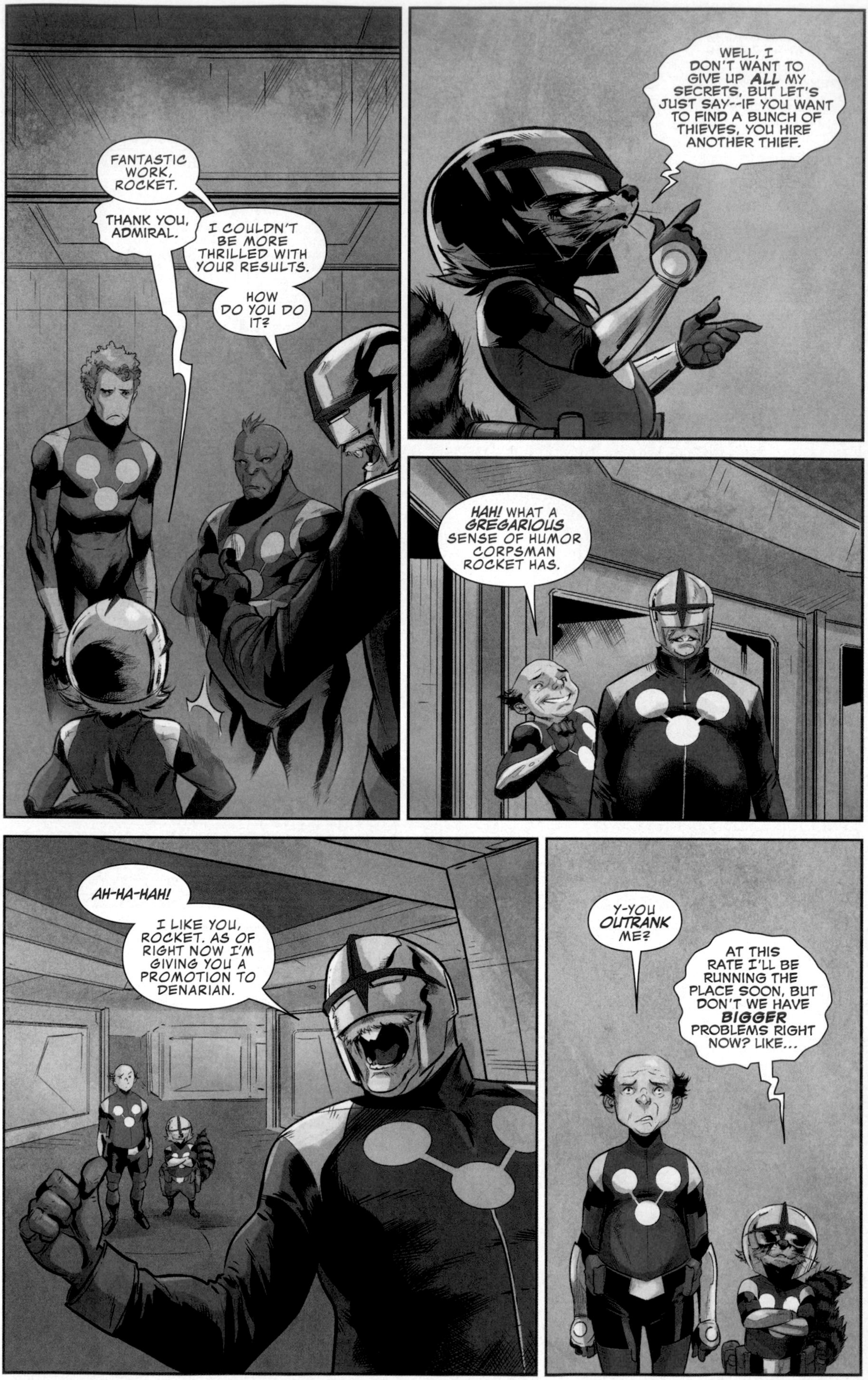
FANTASTIC WORK, ROCKET.
THANK YOU, ADMIRAL.
I COULDN'T BE MORE THRILLED WITH YOUR RESULTS.
HOW DO YOU DO IT?
WELL, I DON'T WANT TO GIVE UP ALL MY SECRETS, BUT LET'S JUST SAY--IF YOU WANT TO FIND A BUNCH OF THIEVES, YOU HIRE ANOTHER THIEF.
HAH! WHAT A GREGARIOUS SENSE OF HUMOR CORPSMAN ROCKET HAS.
AH-HA-HAH!
I LIKE YOU, ROCKET. AS OF RIGHT NOW I'M GIVING YOU A PROMOTION TO DENARIAN.
Y-YOU OUTRANK ME?
AT THIS RATE I'LL BE RUNNING THE PLACE SOON, BUT DON'T WE HAVE BIGGER PROBLEMS RIGHT NOW? LIKE...

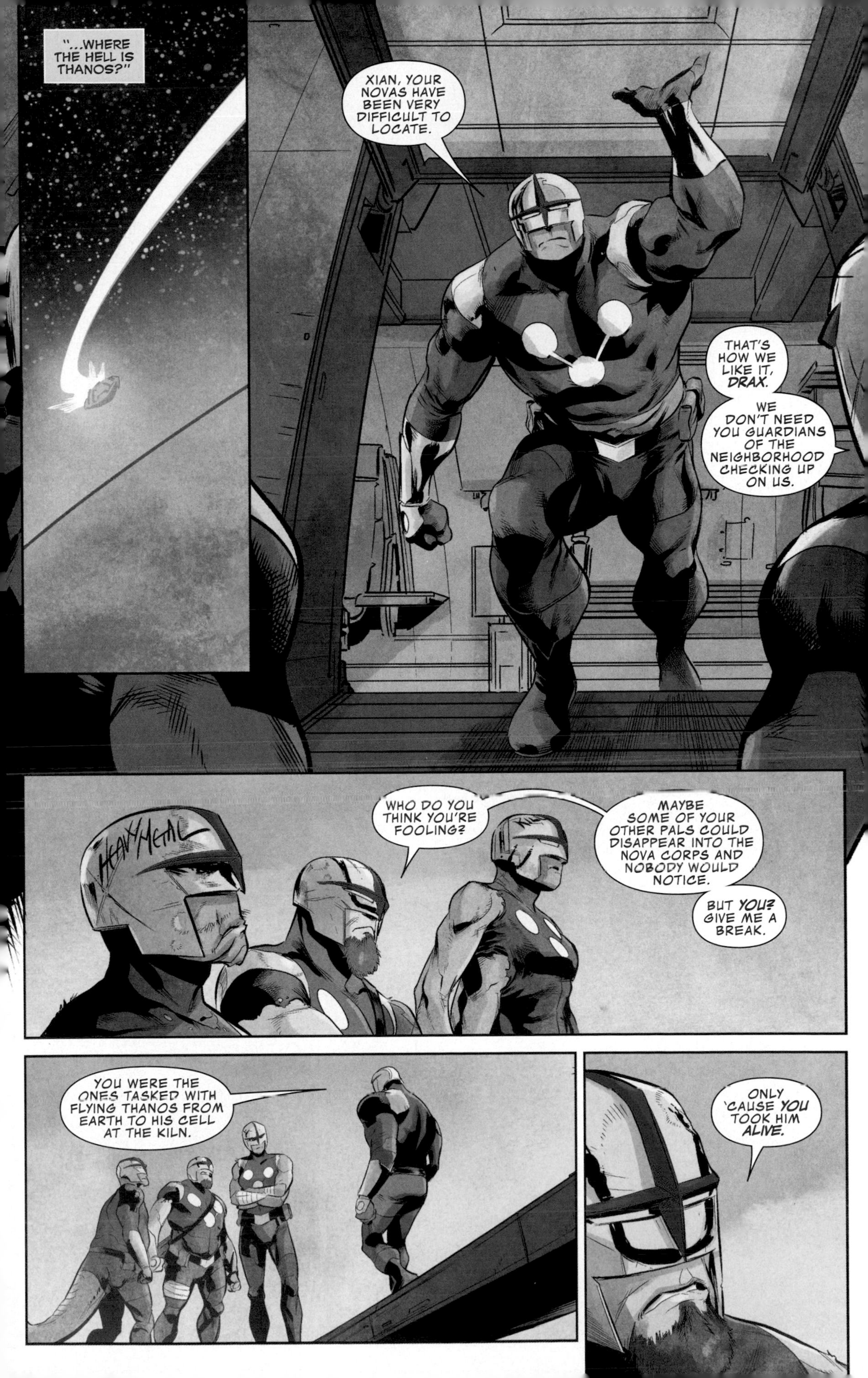
"...WHERE THE HELL IS THANOS?"
XIAN, YOUR NOVAS HAVE BEEN VERY DIFFICULT TO LOCATE.
THAT'S HOW WE LIKE IT, DRAX.
WE DON'T NEED YOU GUARDIANS OF THE NEIGHBORHOOD CHECKING UP ON US.
HEAVY METAL
WHO DO YOU THINK YOU'RE FOOLING?
MAYBE SOME OF YOUR OTHER PALS COULD DISAPPEAR INTO THE NOVA CORPS AND NOBODY WOULD NOTICE.
BUT YOU? GIVE ME A BREAK.
YOU WERE THE ONES TASKED WITH FLYING THANOS FROM EARTH TO HIS CELL AT THE KILN.
ONLY 'CAUSE YOU TOOK HIM ALIVE.

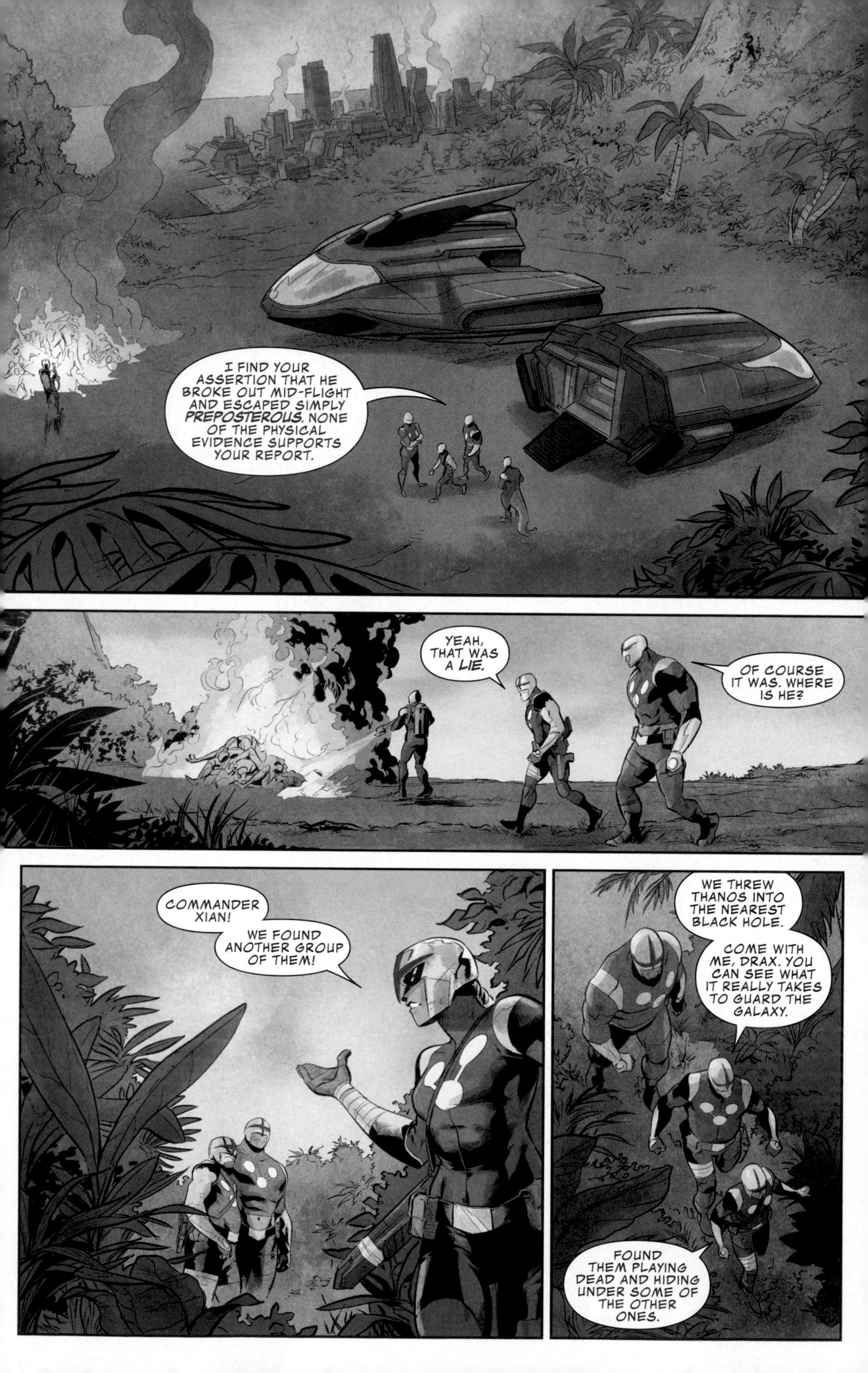
I FIND YOUR ASSERTION THAT HE BROKE OUT MID-FLIGHT AND ESCAPED SIMPLY PREPOSTEROUS. NONE OF THE PHYSICAL EVIDENCE SUPPORTS YOUR REPORT.
YEAH, THAT WAS A LIE.
OF COURSE IT WAS. WHERE IS HE?
COMMANDER XIAN!
WE FOUND ANOTHER GROUP OF THEM!
WE THREW THANOS INTO THE NEAREST BLACK HOLE.
COME WITH ME, DRAX. YOU CAN SEE WHAT IT REALLY TAKES TO GUARD THE GALAXY.
FOUND THEM PLAYING DEAD AND HIDING UNDER SOME OF THE OTHER ONES.

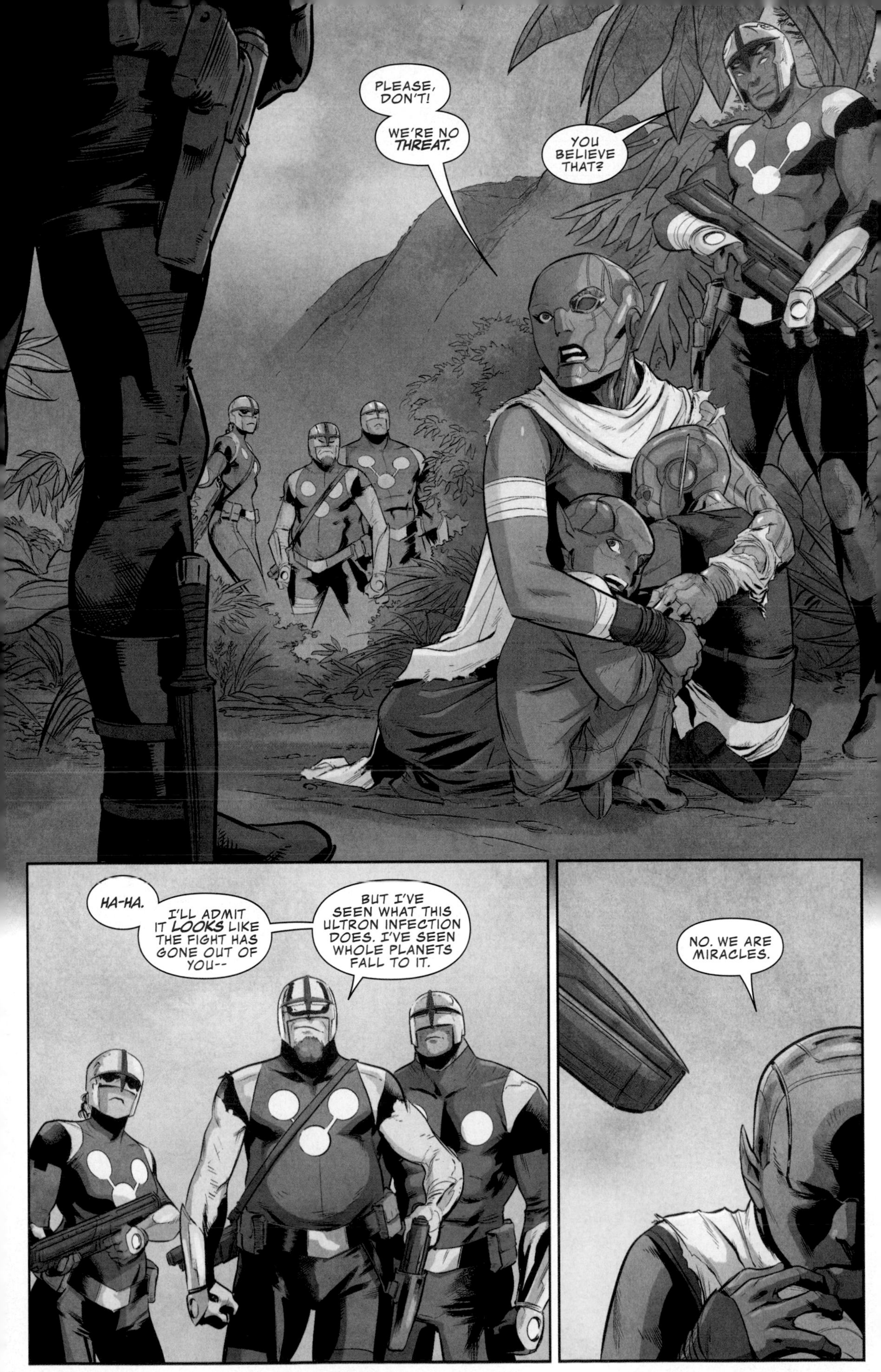
PLEASE, DON'T!
WE'RE NO THREAT.
YOU BELIEVE THAT?
HA-HA.
I'LL ADMIT IT LOOKS LIKE THE FIGHT HAS GONE OUT OF YOU--
BUT I'VE SEEN WHAT THIS ULTRON INFECTION DOES. I'VE SEEN WHOLE PLANETS FALL TO IT.
NO. WE ARE MIRACLES.

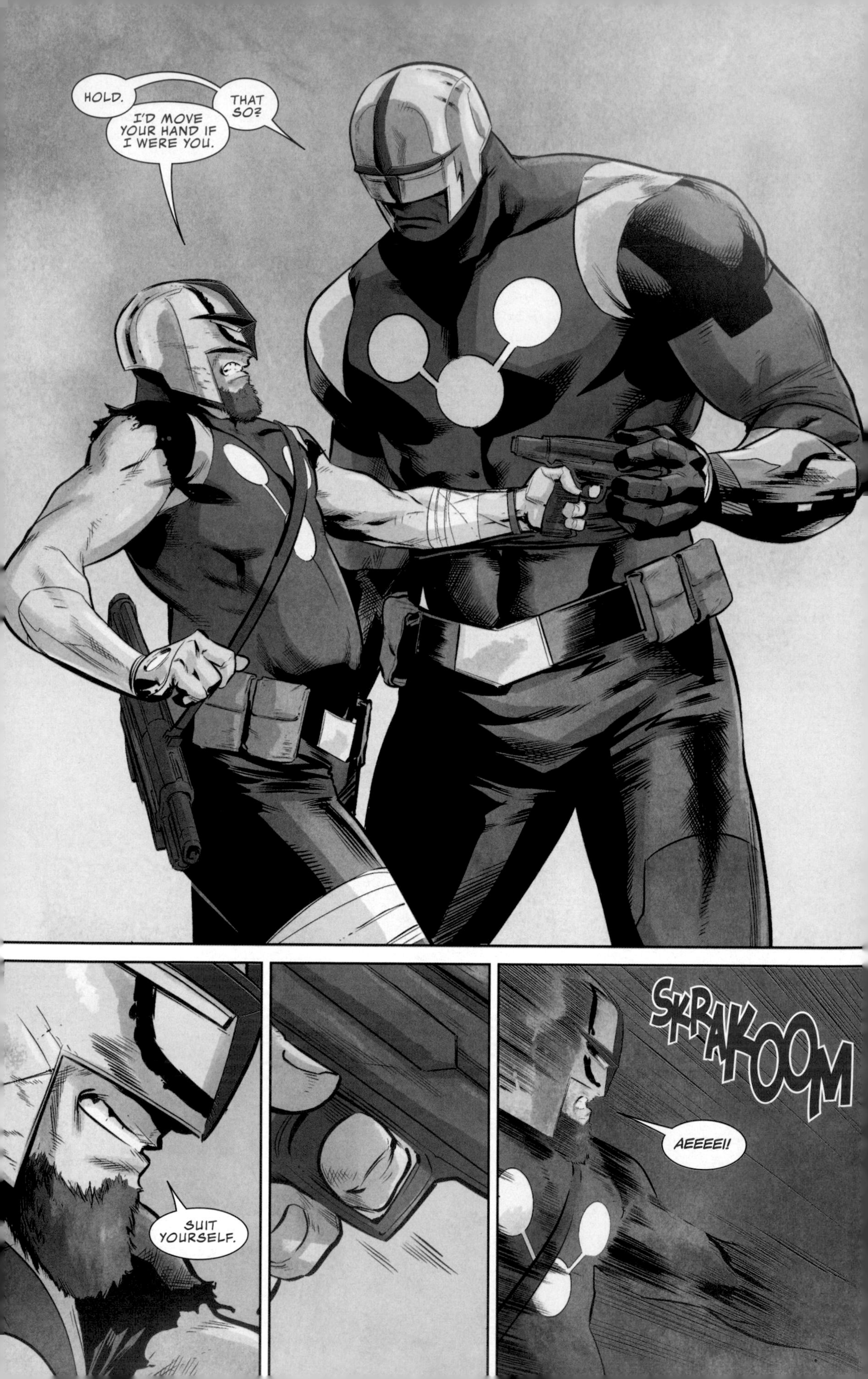
HOLD.
I'D MOVE YOUR HAND IF I WERE YOU.
THAT SO?
SUIT YOURSELF.
SKRAKOOM
AEEEEI!

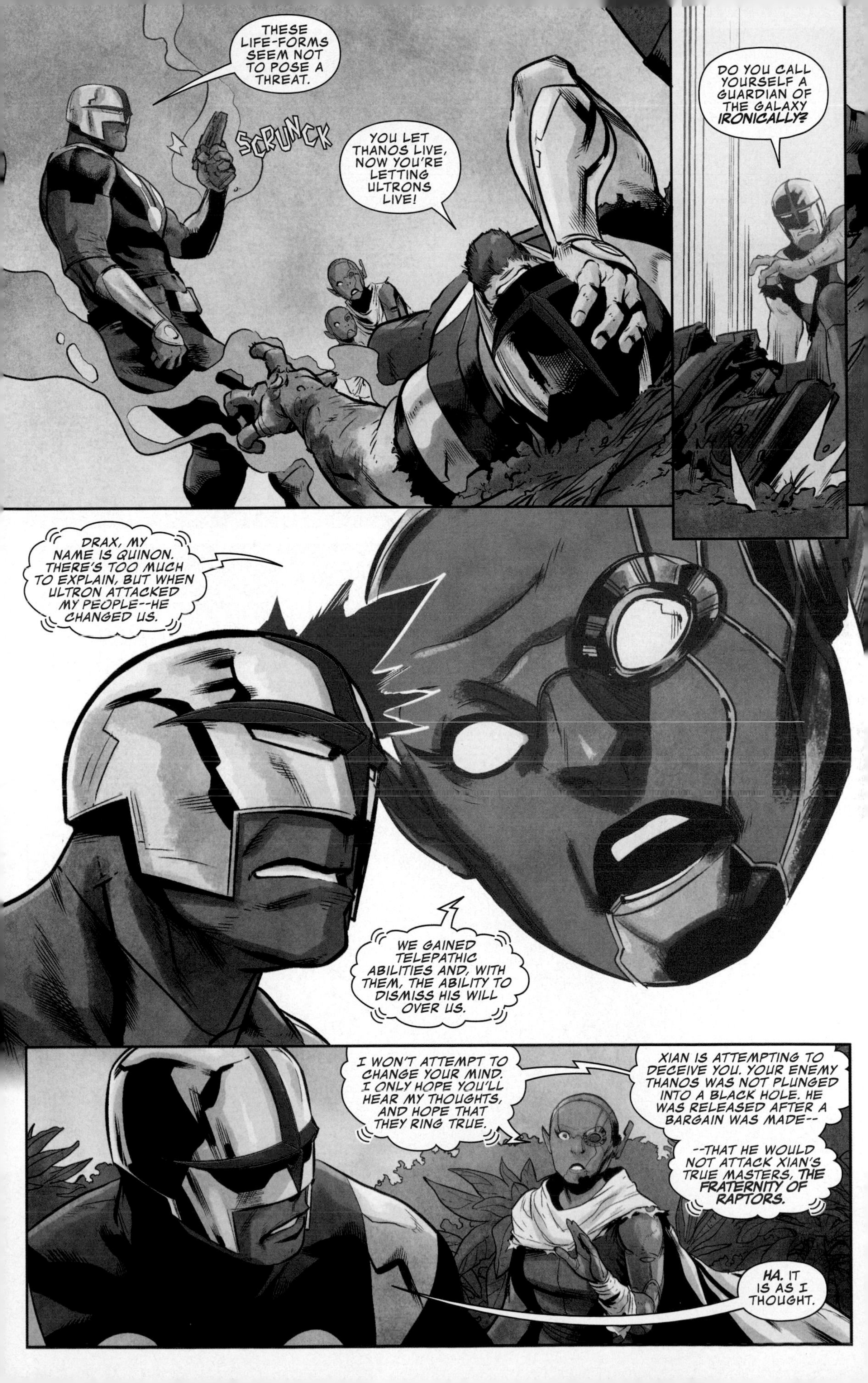
THESE LIFE-FORMS SEEM NOT TO POSE A THREAT.
SCRUNCK
YOU LET THANOS LIVE, NOW YOU'RE LETTING ULTRONS LIVE!
DO YOU CALL YOURSELF A GUARDIAN OF THE GALAXY IRONICALLY?
DRAX, MY NAME IS QUINON. THERE'S TOO MUCH TO EXPLAIN, BUT WHEN ULTRON ATTACKED MY PEOPLE--HE CHANGED US.
WE GAINED TELEPATHIC ABILITIES AND, WITH THEM, THE ABILITY TO DISMISS HIS WILL OVER US.
I WON'T ATTEMPT TO CHANGE YOUR MIND. I ONLY HOPE YOU'LL HEAR MY THOUGHTS, AND HOPE THAT THEY RING TRUE.
XIAN IS ATTEMPTING TO DECEIVE YOU. YOUR ENEMY THANOS WAS NOT PLUNGED INTO A BLACK HOLE. HE WAS RELEASED AFTER A BARGAIN WAS MADE--
--THAT HE WOULD NOT ATTACK XIAN'S TRUE MASTERS, THE FRATERNITY OF RAPTORS.
HA. IT IS AS I THOUGHT.

YOU ARE THE SHI'AR SPIES THAT SEEK TO SUBVERT THE NOVA CORPS.

YOU WILL *NOT* RESIST ARREST.

WHAT THE HELL? HOW DID HE--

HOLY FLARK, THIS THING IS A TELEPATHIC.

KILL IT!

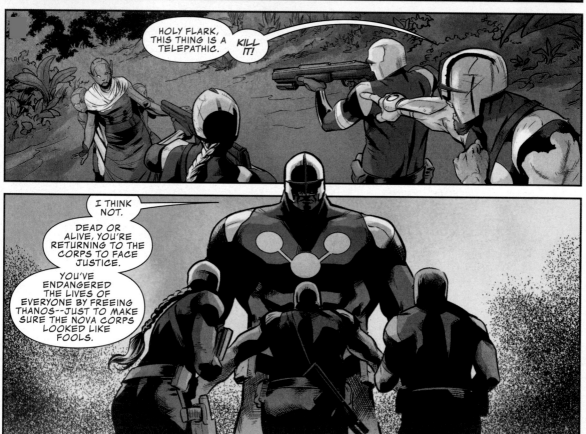

I THINK NOT.

DEAD OR ALIVE, YOU'RE RETURNING TO THE CORPS TO FACE JUSTICE.

YOU'VE ENDANGERED THE LIVES OF EVERYONE BY FREEING THANOS--JUST TO MAKE SURE THE NOVA CORPS LOOKED LIKE FOOLS.

JUST ONE PROBLEM, DRAX. EVERYBODY KNOWS YOU'VE LOST YOUR TASTE FOR KILLING, AND WE--

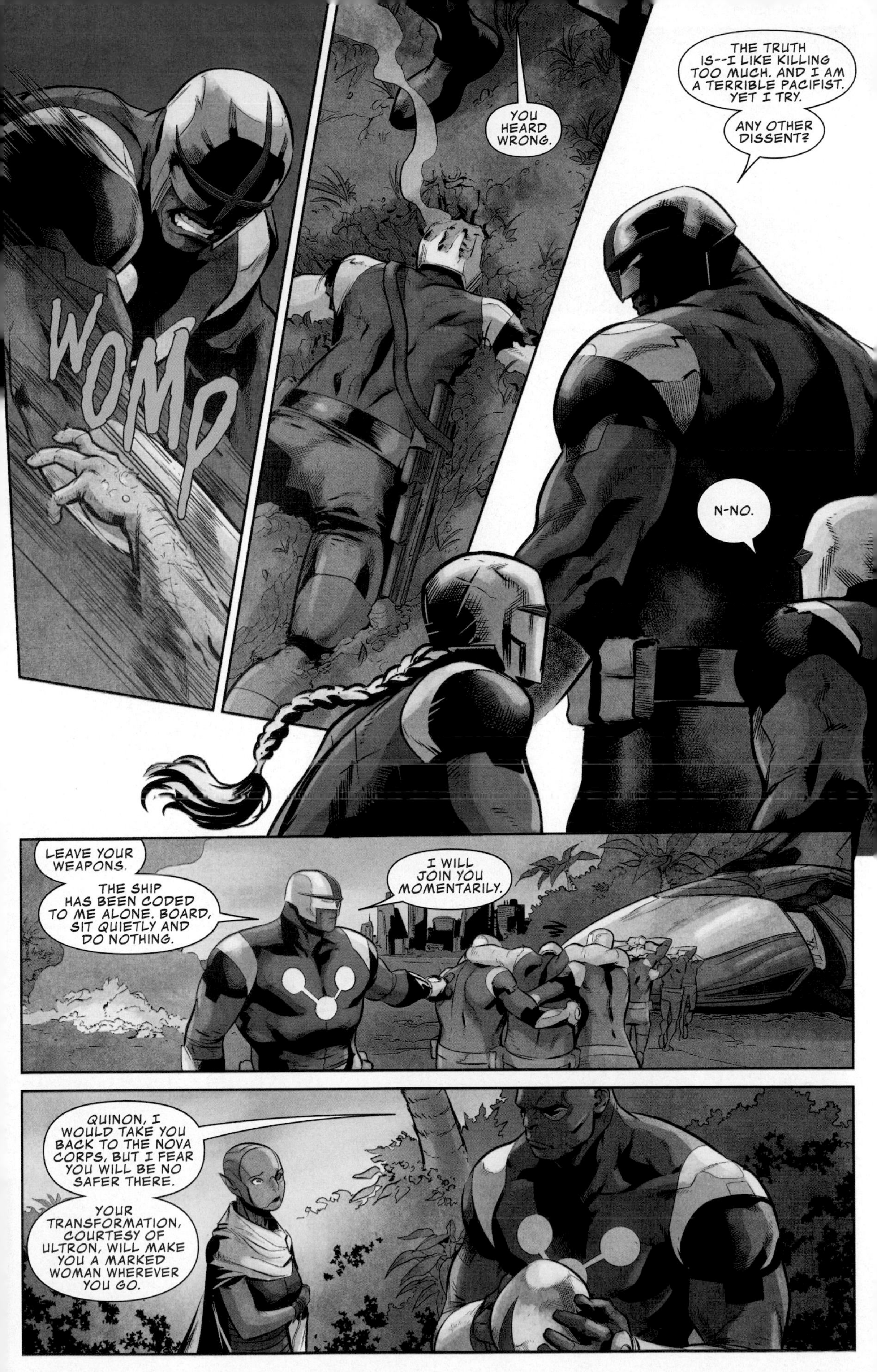
WOMP
YOU HEARD WRONG.
THE TRUTH IS--I LIKE KILLING TOO MUCH. AND I AM A TERRIBLE PACIFIST. YET I TRY.
ANY OTHER DISSENT?
N-NO.
LEAVE YOUR WEAPONS.
THE SHIP HAS BEEN CODED TO ME ALONE. BOARD, SIT QUIETLY AND DO NOTHING.
I WILL JOIN YOU MOMENTARILY.
QUINON, I WOULD TAKE YOU BACK TO THE NOVA CORPS, BUT I FEAR YOU WILL BE NO SAFER THERE.
YOUR TRANSFORMATION, COURTESY OF ULTRON, WILL MAKE YOU A MARKED WOMAN WHEREVER YOU GO.

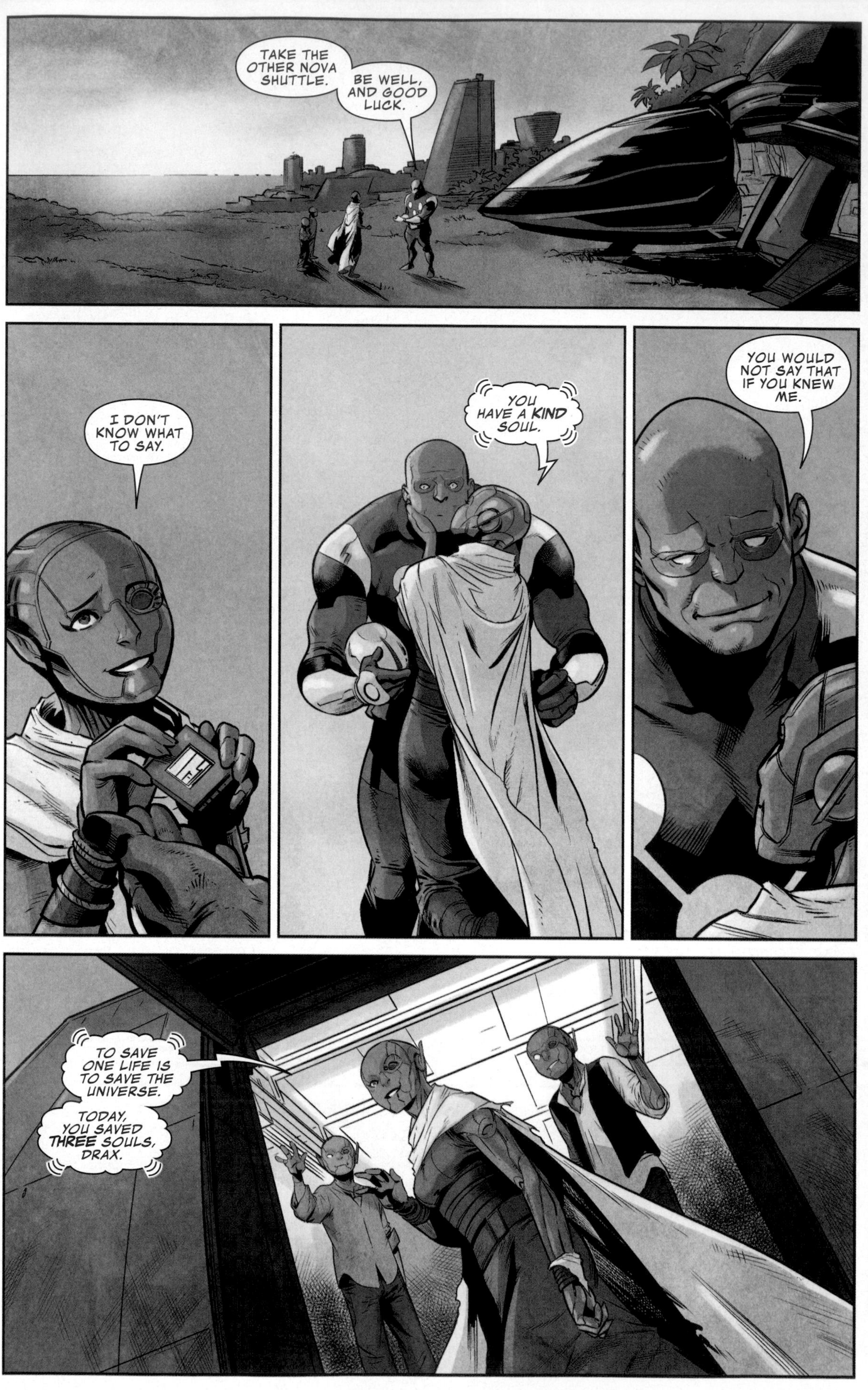
TAKE THE OTHER NOVA SHUTTLE.
BE WELL, AND GOOD LUCK.
I DON'T KNOW WHAT TO SAY.
YOU HAVE A KIND SOUL.
YOU WOULD NOT SAY THAT IF YOU KNEW ME.
TO SAVE ONE LIFE IS TO SAVE THE UNIVERSE.
TODAY, YOU SAVED THREE SOULS, DRAX.

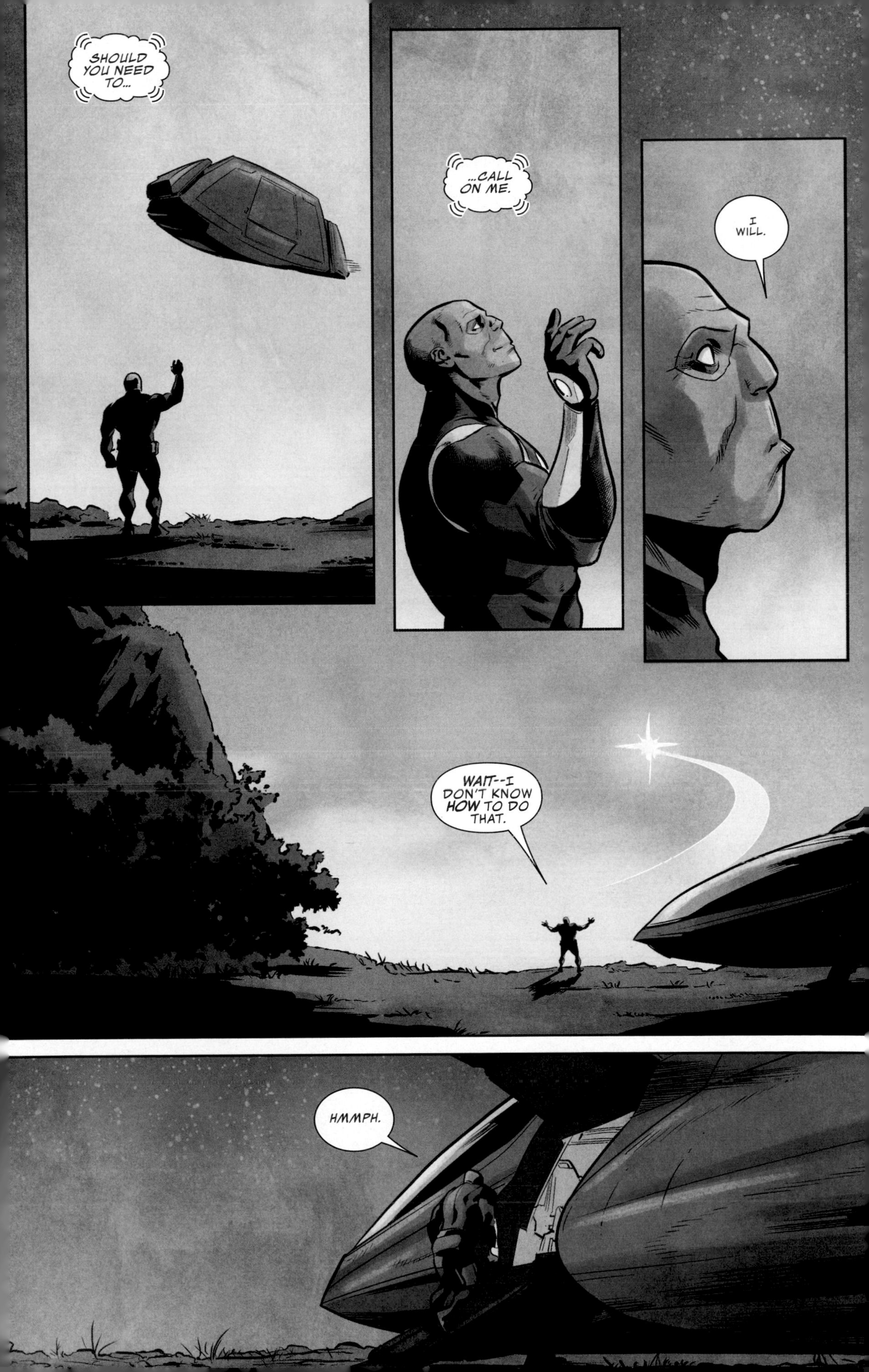
SHOULD YOU NEED TO...
...CALL ON ME.
I WILL.
WAIT--I DON'T KNOW HOW TO DO THAT.
HMMPH.

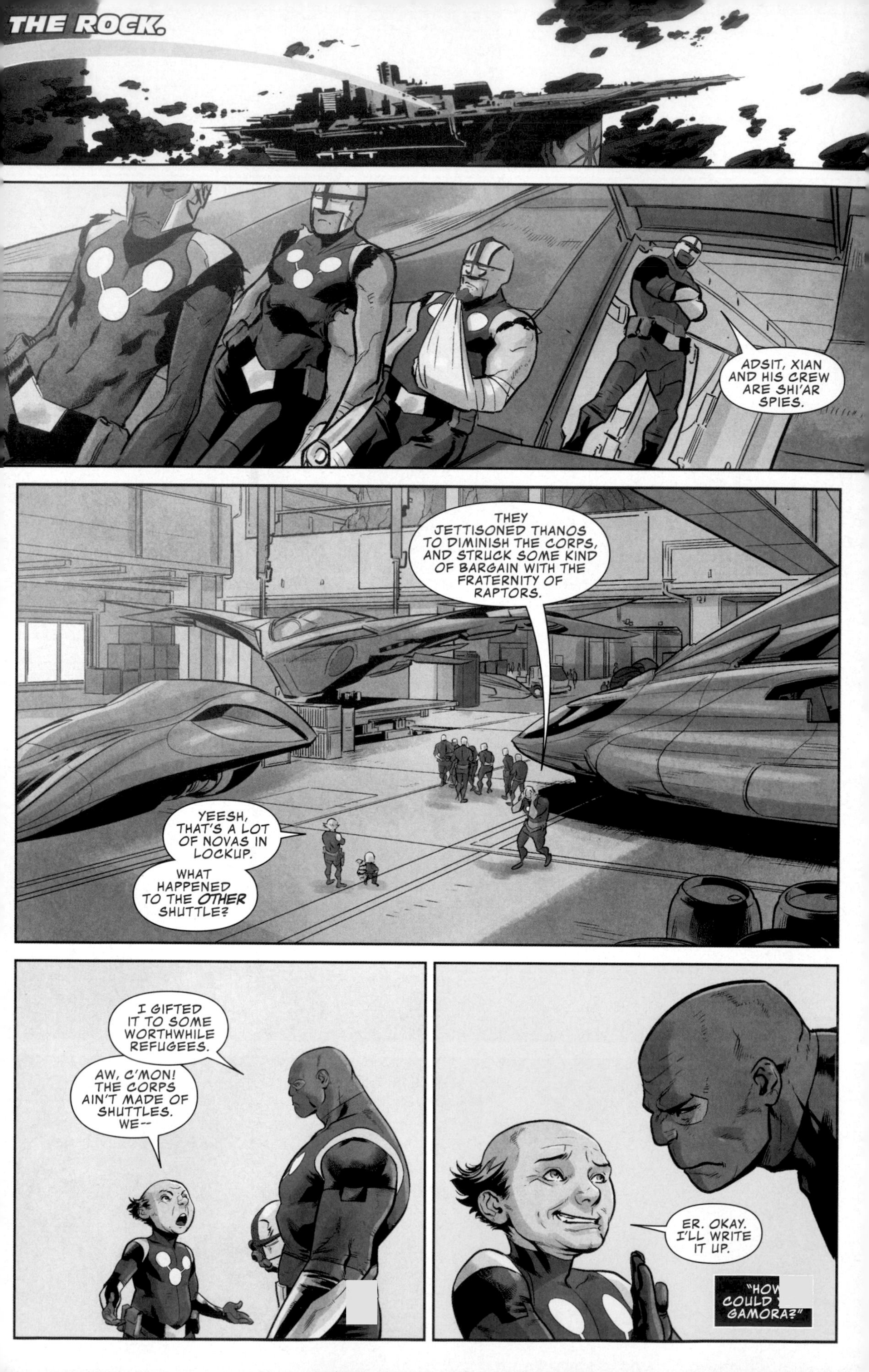
THE ROCK.
ADSIT, XIAN AND HIS CREW ARE SHI'AR SPIES.
THEY JETTISONED THANOS TO DIMINISH THE CORPS, AND STRUCK SOME KIND OF BARGAIN WITH THE FRATERNITY OF RAPTORS.
YEESH, THAT'S A LOT OF NOVAS IN LOCKUP.
WHAT HAPPENED TO THE *OTHER* SHUTTLE?
I GIFTED IT TO SOME WORTHWHILE REFUGEES.
AW, C'MON! THE CORPS AIN'T MADE OF SHUTTLES. WE--
ER. OKAY. I'LL WRITE IT UP.
"HOW COULD
GAMORA?"

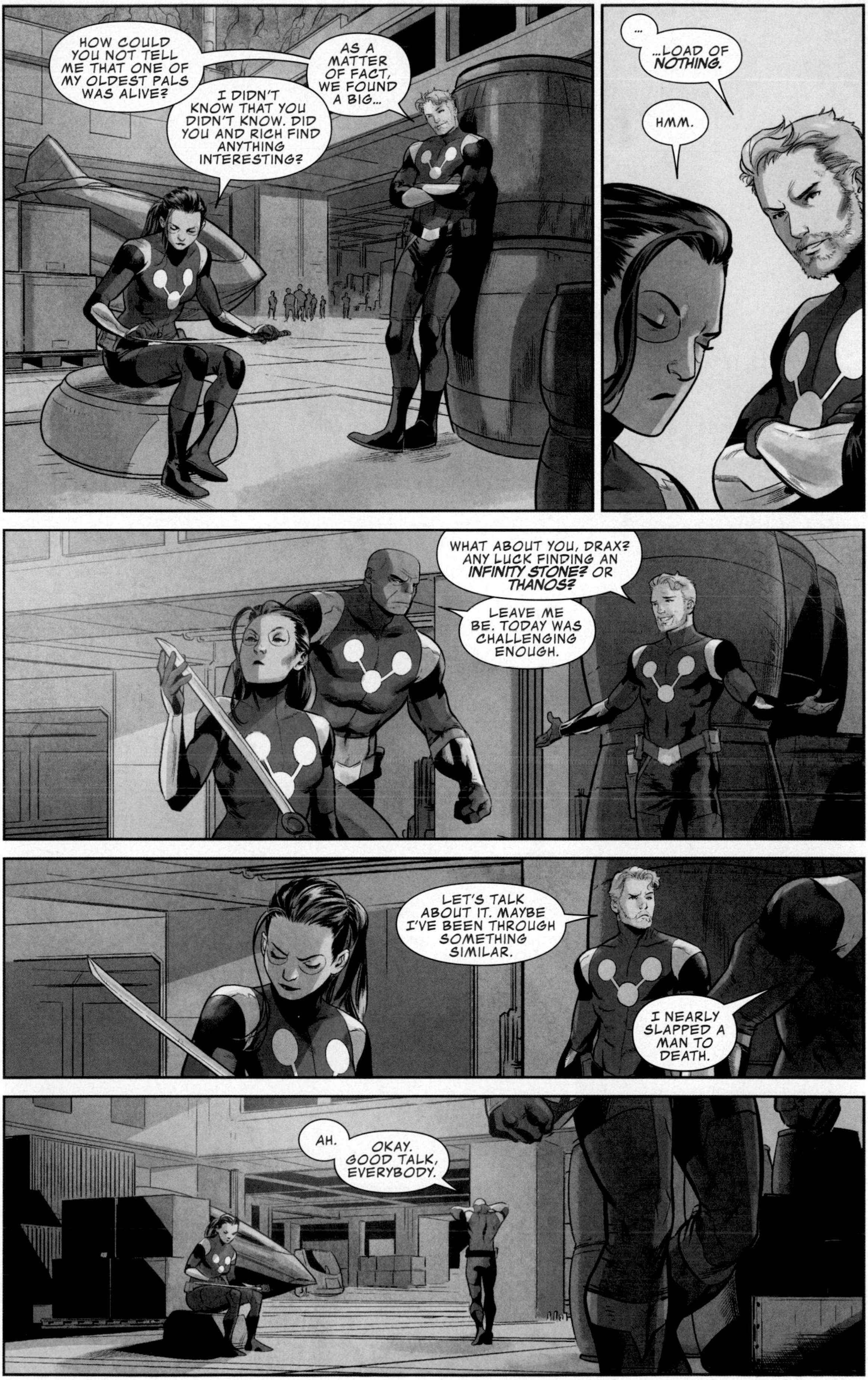
HOW COULD YOU NOT TELL ME THAT ONE OF MY OLDEST PALS WAS ALIVE?
I DIDN'T KNOW THAT YOU DIDN'T KNOW. DID YOU AND RICH FIND ANYTHING INTERESTING?
AS A MATTER OF FACT, WE FOUND A BIG...
...
...LOAD OF *NOTHING.*
HMM.
WHAT ABOUT YOU, DRAX? ANY LUCK FINDING AN *INFINITY STONE?* OR *THANOS?*
LEAVE ME BE. TODAY WAS CHALLENGING ENOUGH.
LET'S TALK ABOUT IT. MAYBE I'VE BEEN THROUGH SOMETHING SIMILAR.
I NEARLY SLAPPED A MAN TO DEATH.
AH.
OKAY. GOOD TALK, EVERYBODY.

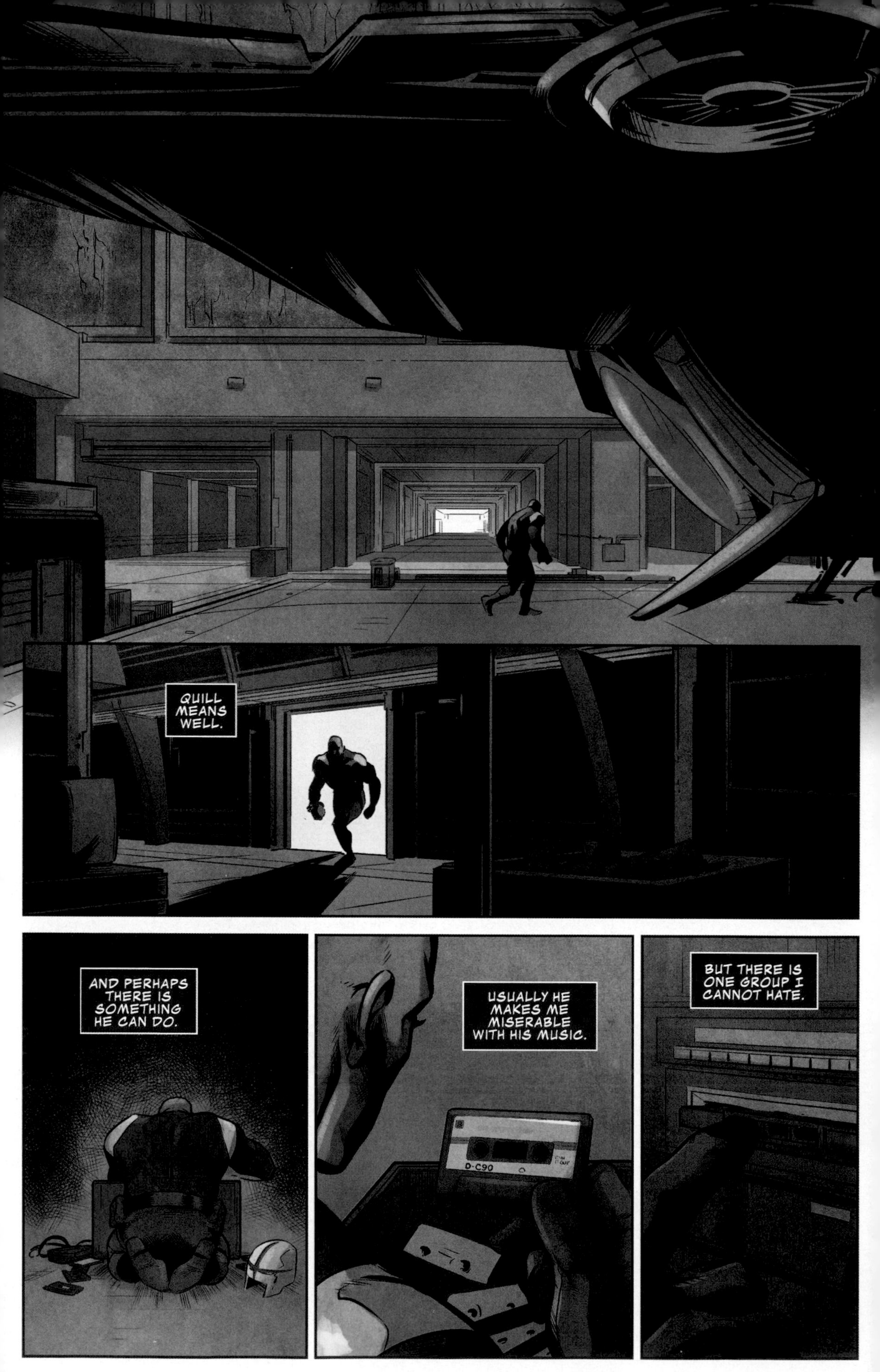
QUILL MEANS WELL.
AND PERHAPS THERE IS SOMETHING HE CAN DO.
USUALLY HE MAKES ME MISERABLE WITH HIS MUSIC.
BUT THERE IS ONE GROUP I CANNOT HATE.

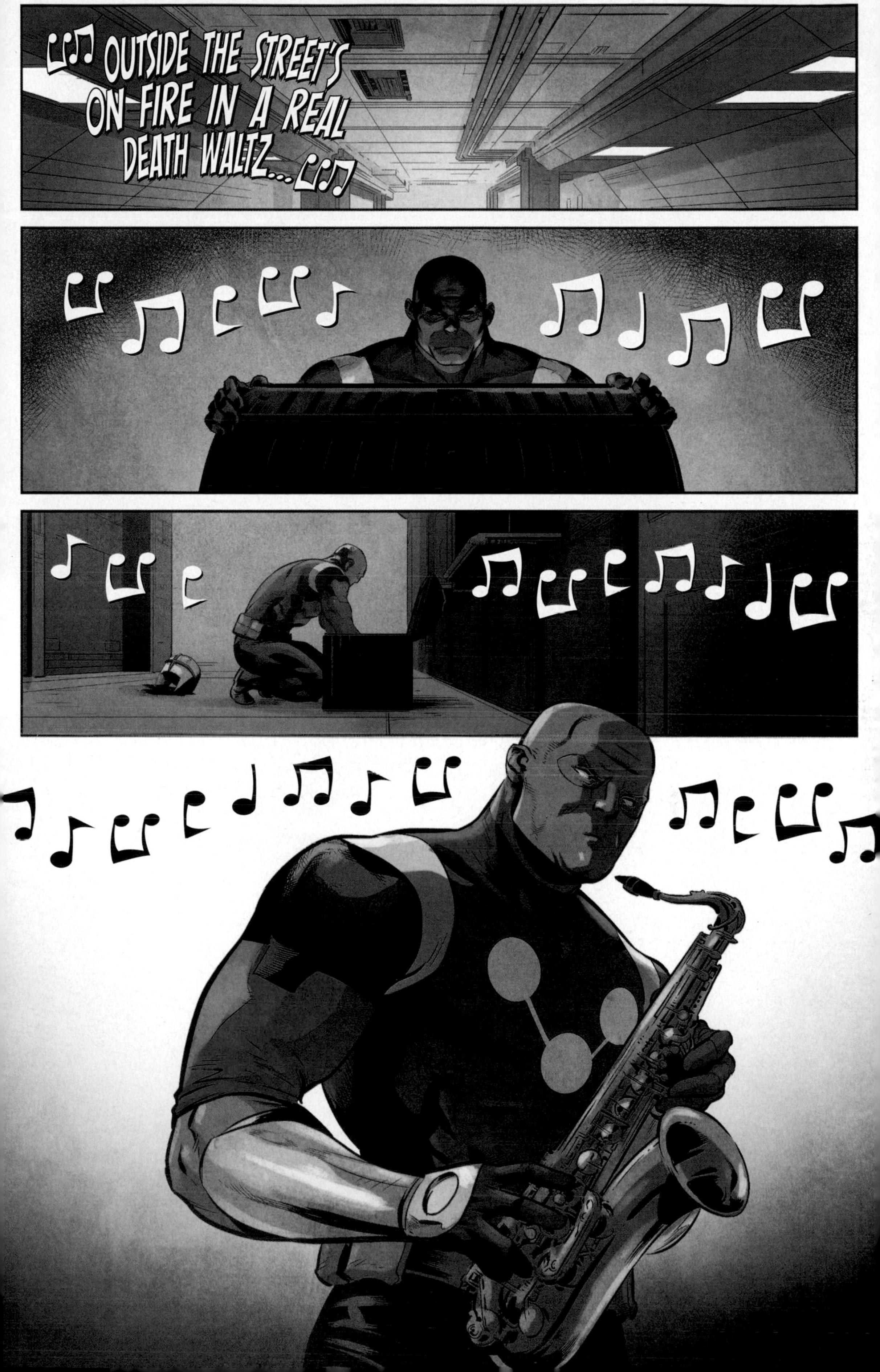
OUTSIDE THE STREET'S ON FIRE IN A REAL DEATH WALTZ...

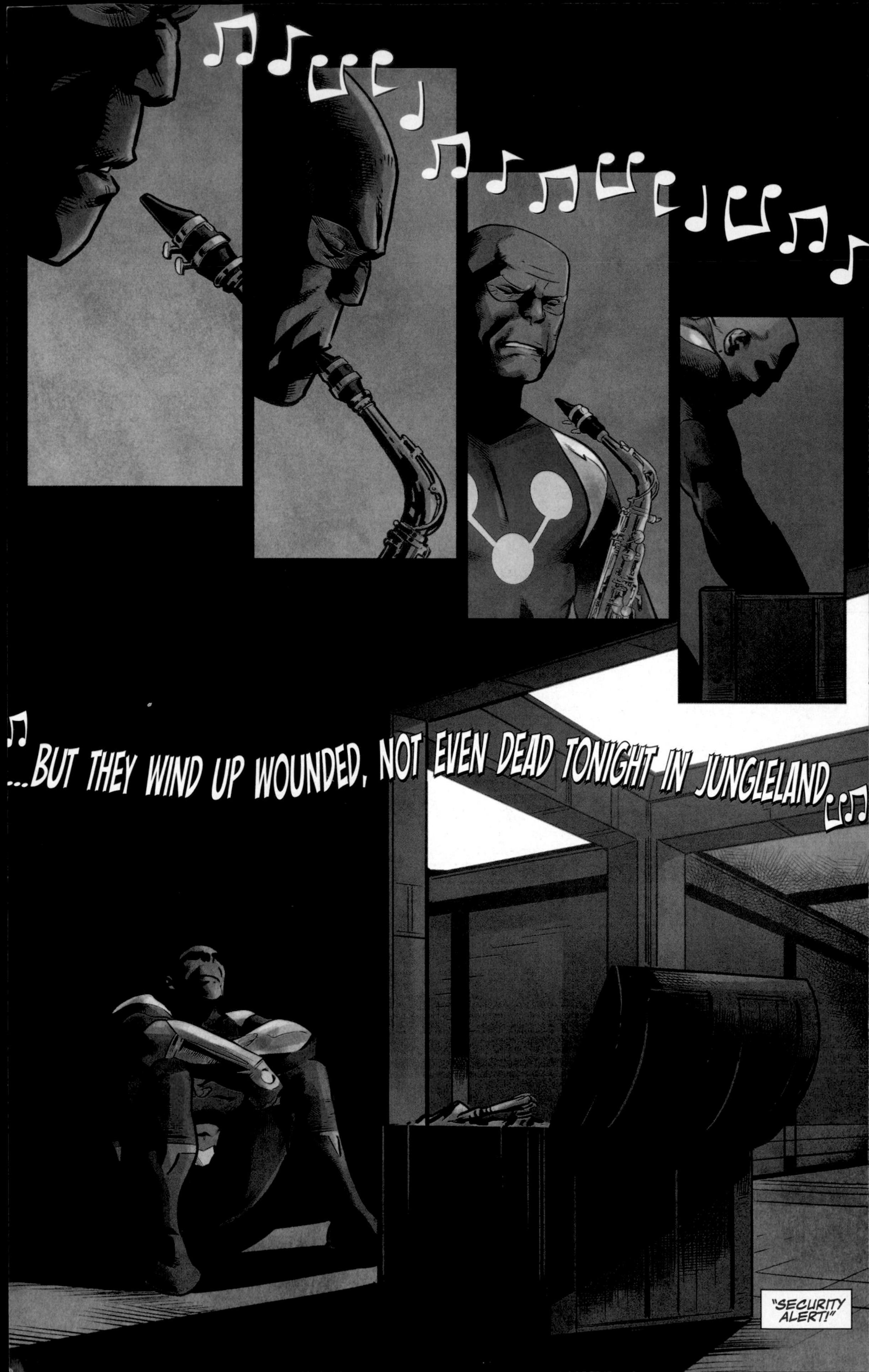
...BUT THEY WIND UP WOUNDED, NOT EVEN DEAD TONIGHT IN JUNGLELAND.
"SECURITY ALERT!"

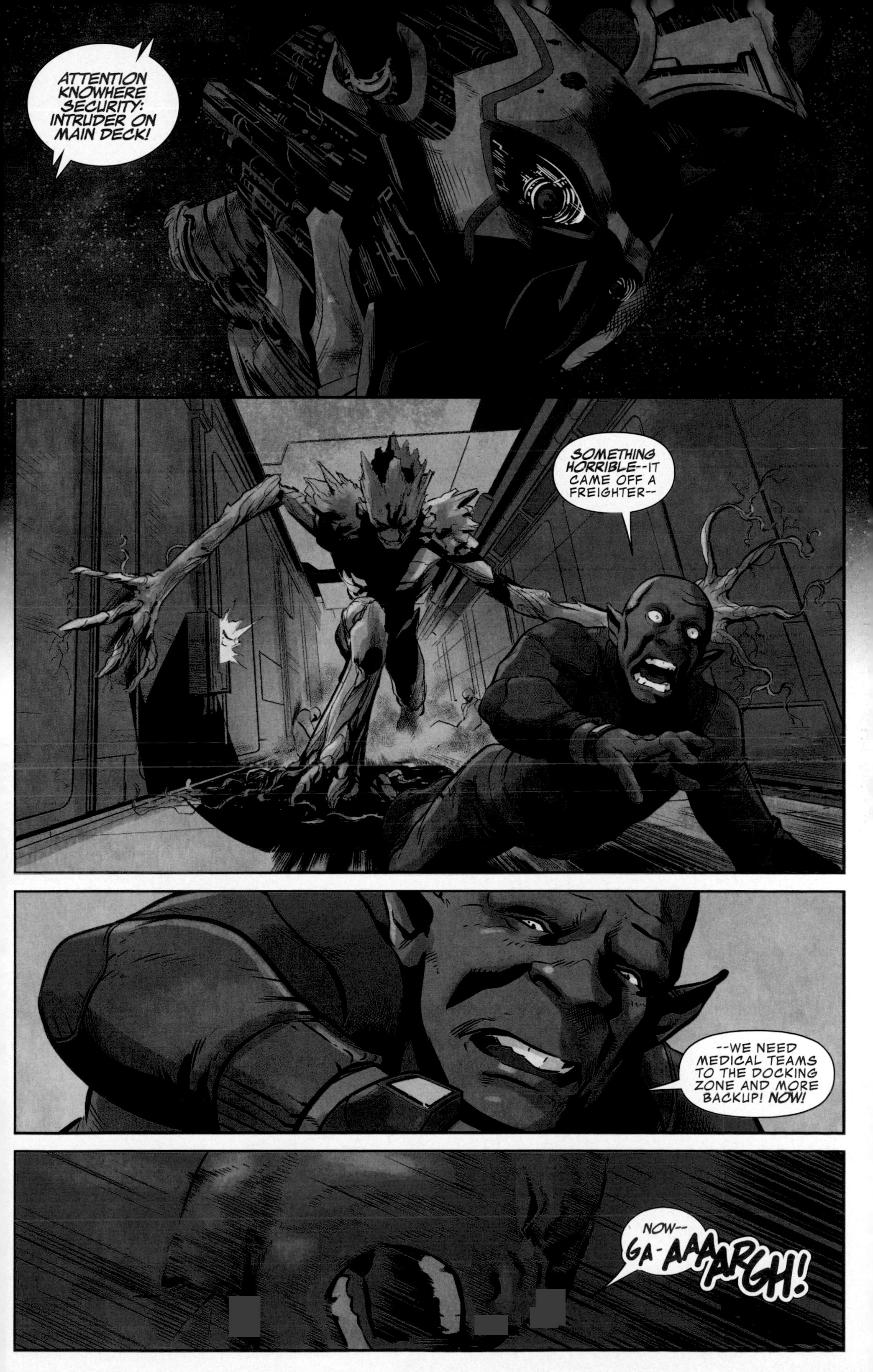
ATTENTION KNOWHERE SECURITY: INTRUDER ON MAIN DECK!
SOMETHING HORRIBLE--IT CAME OFF A FREIGHTER--
--WE NEED MEDICAL TEAMS TO THE DOCKING ZONE AND MORE BACKUP! NOW!
NOW-- GA-AAAARGH!

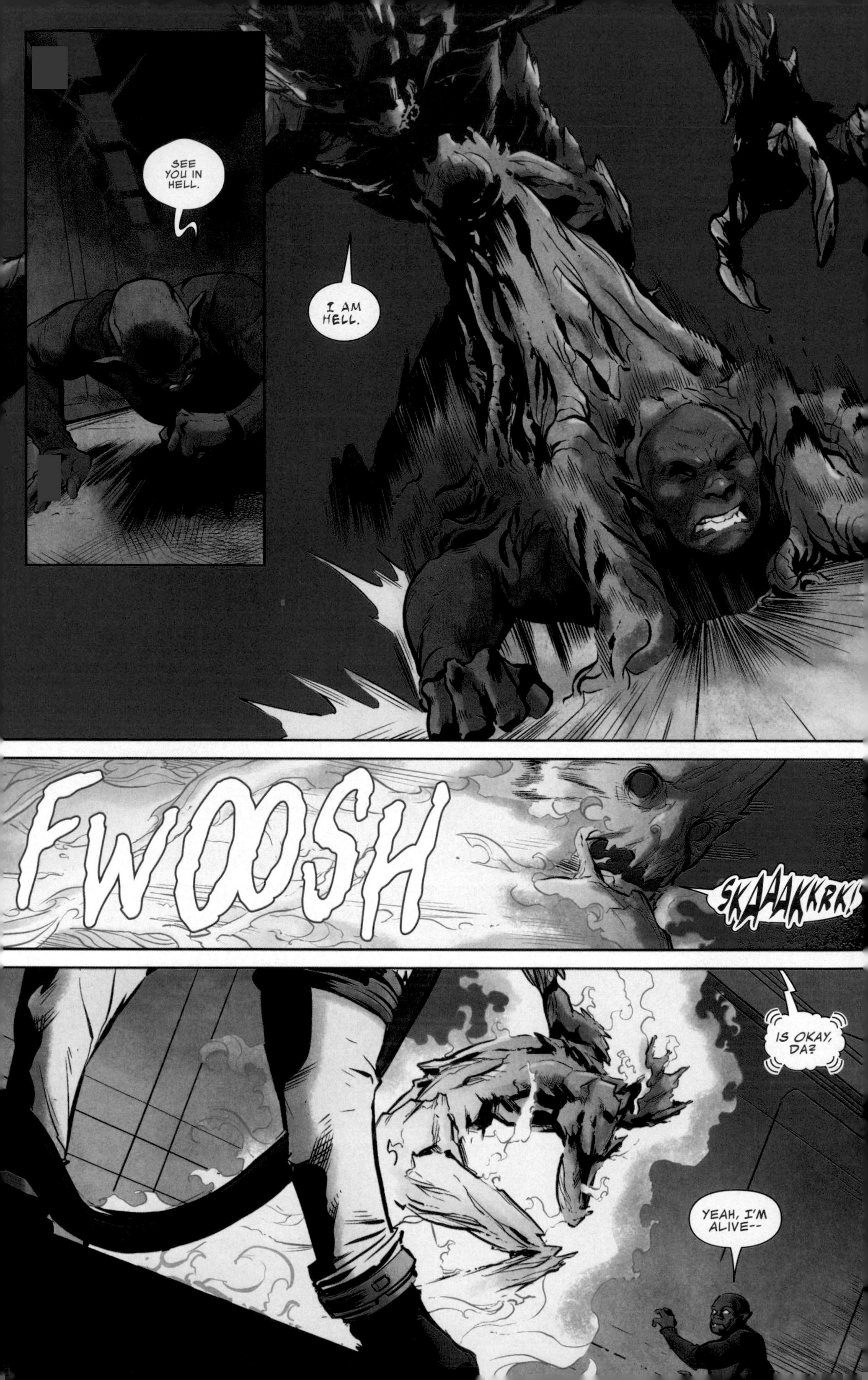
SEE YOU IN HELL.
I AM HELL.
FWOOSH
SKAAAKKRK!
IS OKAY, DA?
YEAH, I'M ALIVE--

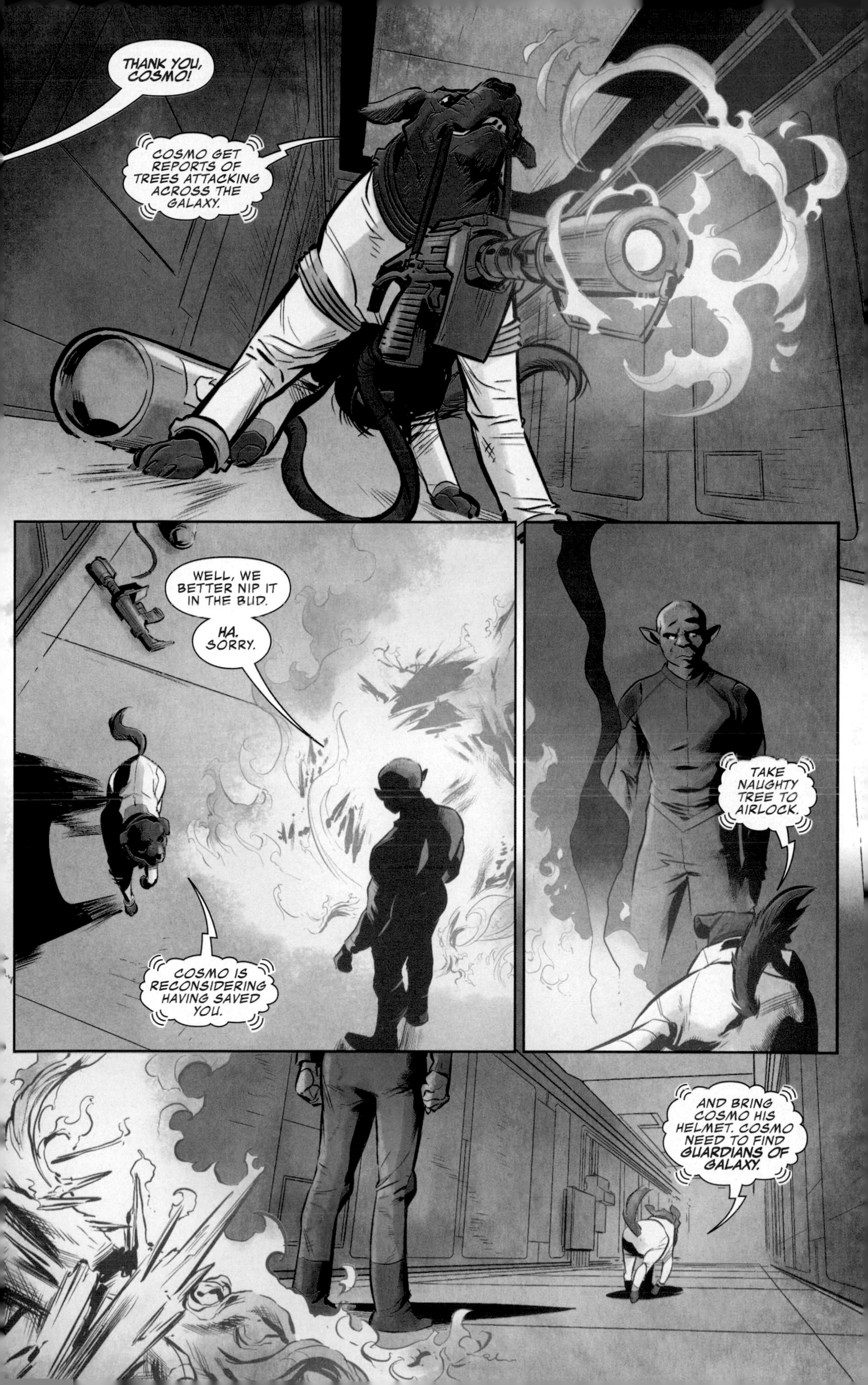
THANK YOU, COSMO!
COSMO GET REPORTS OF TREES ATTACKING ACROSS THE GALAXY.
WELL, WE BETTER NIP IT IN THE BUD.
HA. SORRY.
COSMO IS RECONSIDERING HAVING SAVED YOU.
TAKE NAUGHTY TREE TO AIRLOCK.
AND BRING COSMO HIS HELMET. COSMO NEED TO FIND GUARDIANS OF GALAXY.

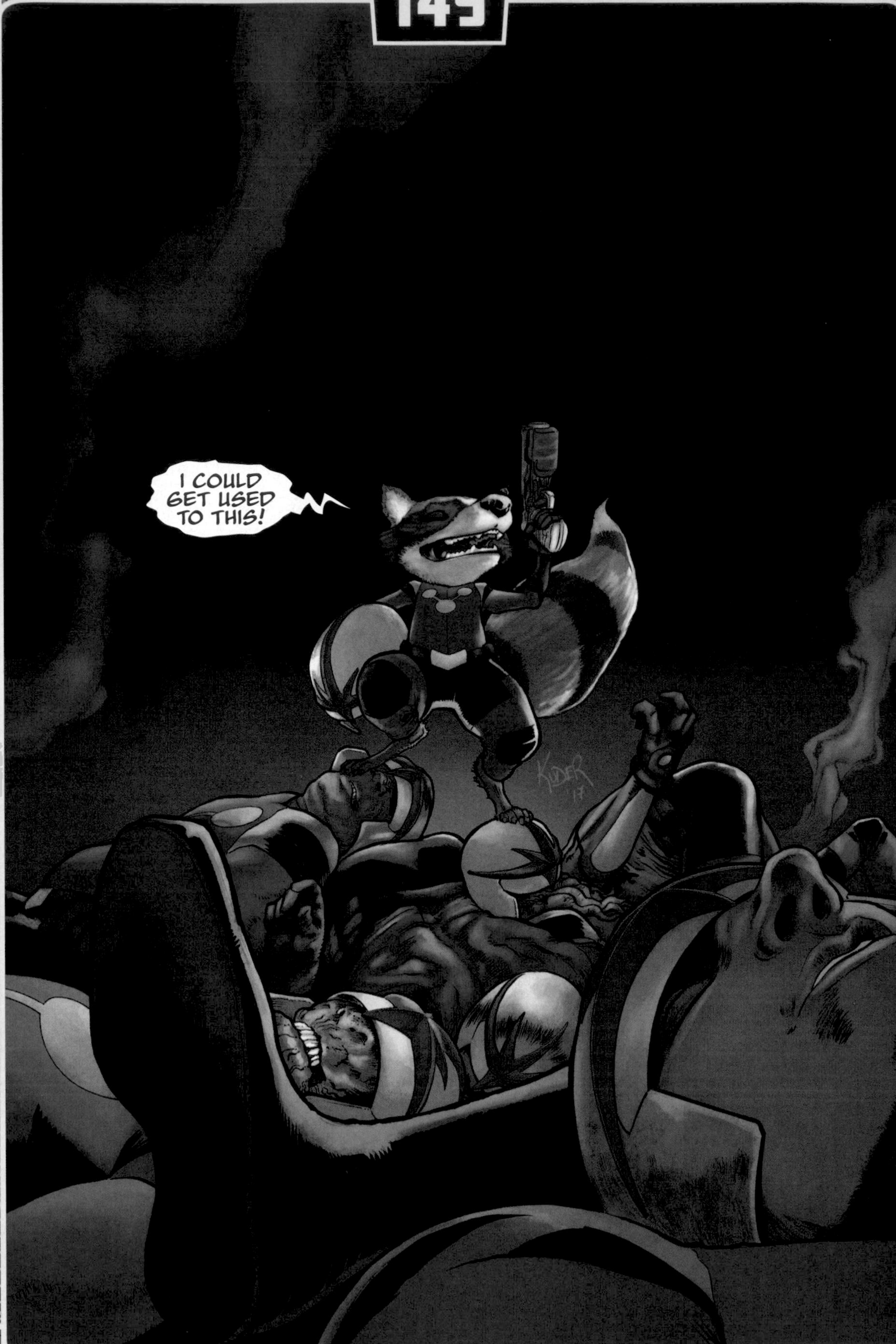
I COULD GET USED TO THIS!
KUDER '17

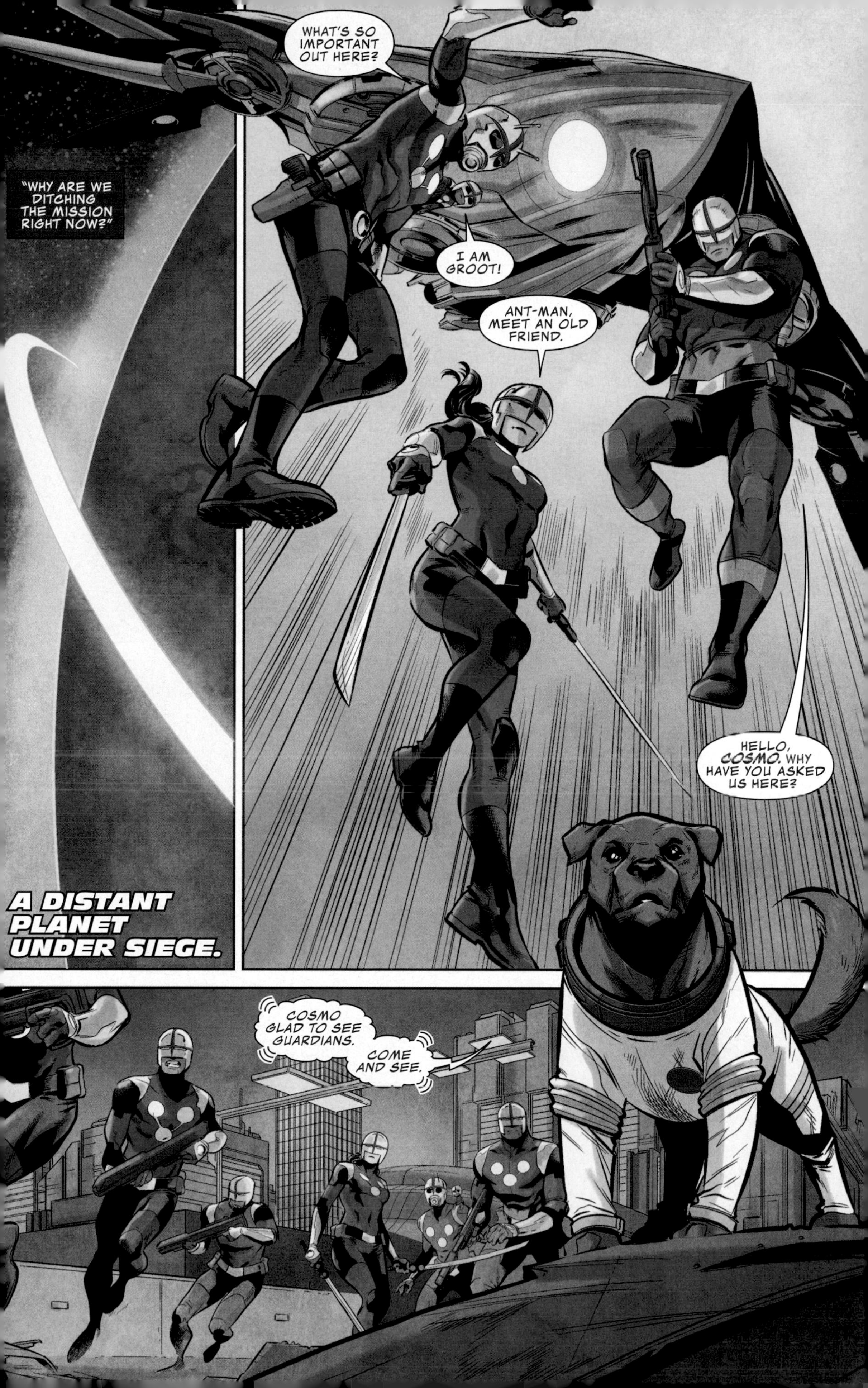
"WHY ARE WE DITCHING THE MISSION RIGHT NOW?"
WHAT'S SO IMPORTANT OUT HERE?
I AM GROOT!
ANT-MAN, MEET AN OLD FRIEND.
HELLO, COSMO. WHY HAVE YOU ASKED US HERE?
A DISTANT PLANET UNDER SIEGE.
COSMO GLAD TO SEE GUARDIANS.
COME AND SEE.

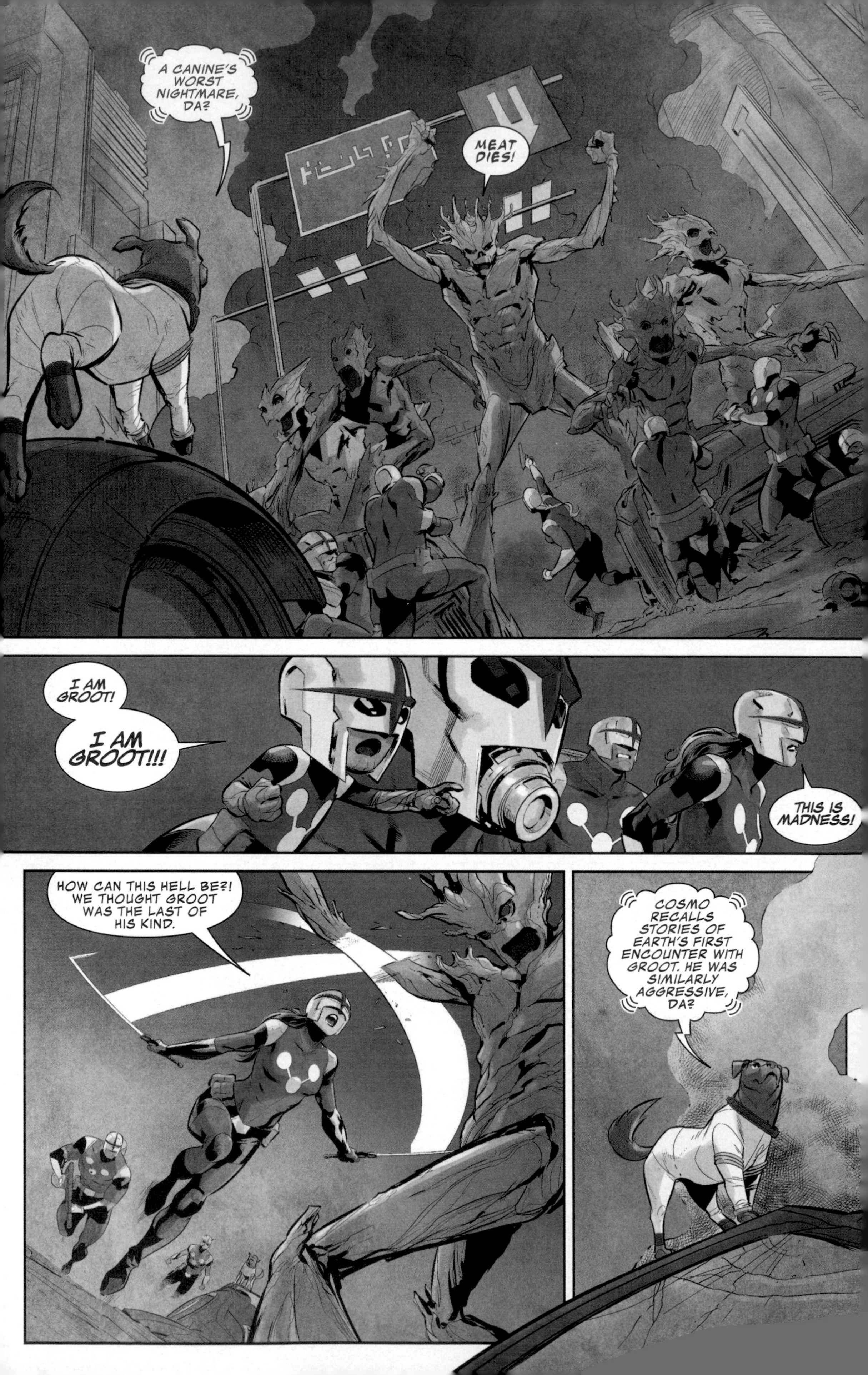

A CANINE'S WORST NIGHTMARE, DA?
MEAT DIES!
I AM GROOT!
I AM GROOT!!!
THIS IS MADNESS!
HOW CAN THIS HELL BE?! WE THOUGHT GROOT WAS THE LAST OF HIS KIND.
COSMO RECALLS STORIES OF EARTH'S FIRST ENCOUNTER WITH GROOT. HE WAS SIMILARLY AGGRESSIVE, DA?

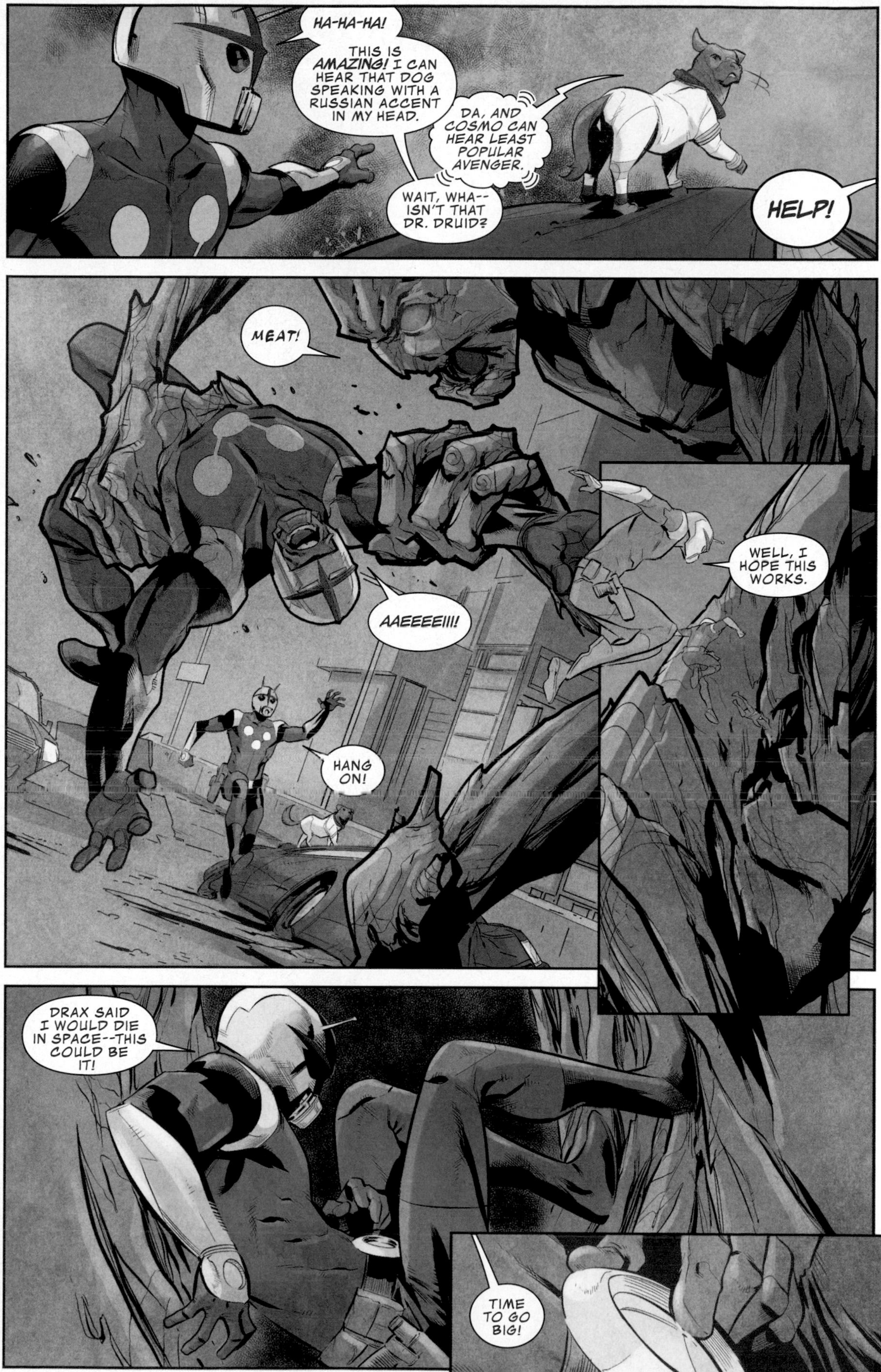
HA-HA-HA!
THIS IS AMAZING! I CAN HEAR THAT DOG SPEAKING WITH A RUSSIAN ACCENT IN MY HEAD.
DA, AND COSMO CAN HEAR LEAST POPULAR AVENGER.
WAIT, WHA-- ISN'T THAT DR. DRUID?
HELP!
MEAT!
AAEEEEIII!
WELL, I HOPE THIS WORKS.
HANG ON!
DRAX SAID I WOULD DIE IN SPACE--THIS COULD BE IT!
TIME TO GO BIG!

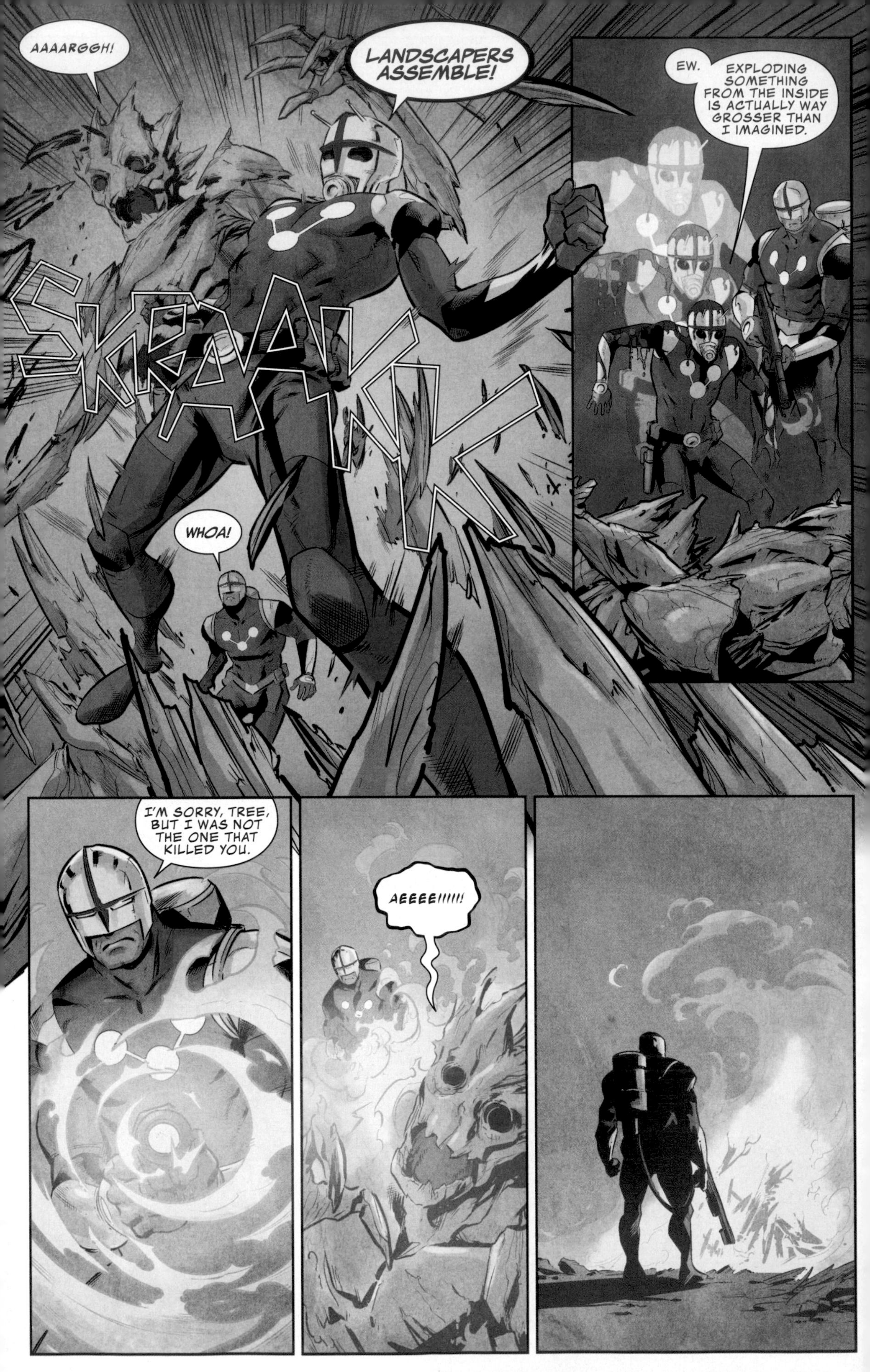
AAAARGGH!
LANDSCAPERS ASSEMBLE!
SKRAAAWK
WHOA!
EW.
EXPLODING SOMETHING FROM THE INSIDE IS ACTUALLY WAY GROSSER THAN I IMAGINED.
I'M SORRY, TREE, BUT I WAS NOT THE ONE THAT KILLED YOU.
AEEEE!!!!!!

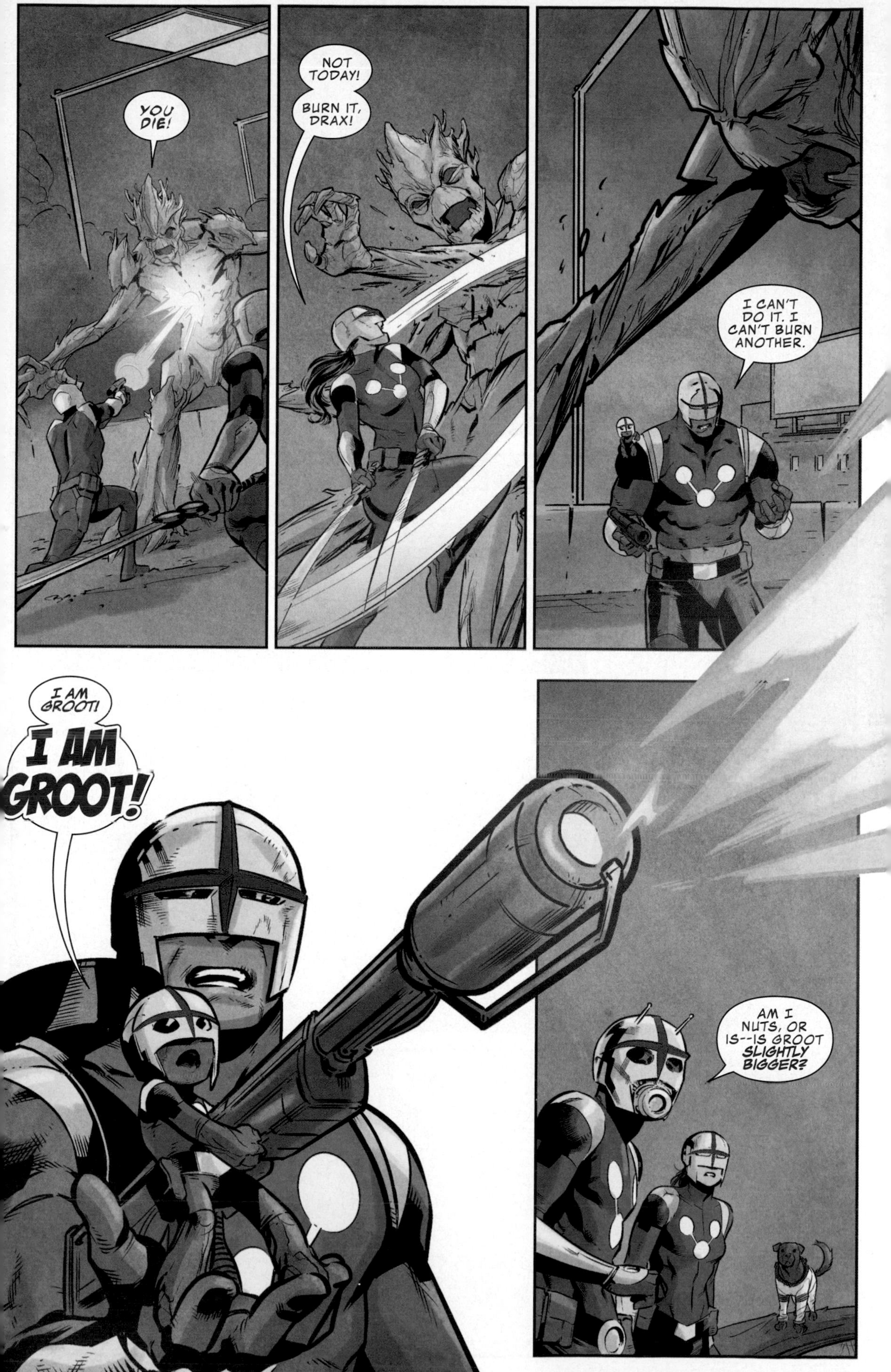
YOU DIE!
NOT TODAY!
BURN IT, DRAX!
I CAN'T DO IT. I CAN'T BURN ANOTHER.
I AM GROOT!
I AM GROOT!
AM I NUTS, OR IS--IS GROOT SLIGHTLY BIGGER?

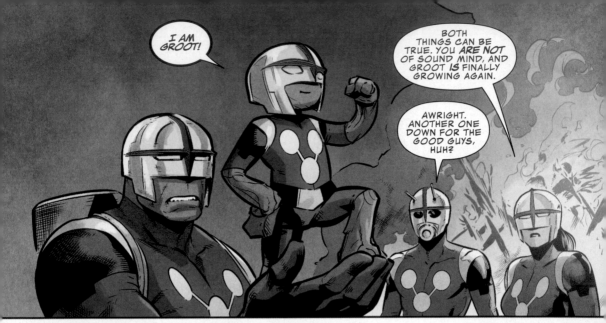

I AM GROOT!

BOTH THINGS CAN BE TRUE. YOU *ARE NOT* OF SOUND MIND, AND GROOT *IS* FINALLY GROWING AGAIN.

AWRIGHT. ANOTHER ONE DOWN FOR THE GOOD GUYS, HUH?

C'MERE BUDDY. WHO'S A GOOD BOY? MY DAUGHTER WILL NEVER BELIEVE THIS.

ANT-MAN HAVE BRAIN SIZE OF ANT?

COSMO HAVE BAD NEWS. GUARDIANS STOPPED FLORA COLOSSI *HERE*--BUT THEY ARE SPREADING *EVERYWHERE.*

SEVERAL PLANETS IN THIS SYSTEM REPORTING ANGRY TREES DROPPING FROM SPACE.

HOW IS THAT POSSIBLE?

COSMO CAN FEEL AN INTELLIGENCE IN THE TREES. A DISCIPLINE OF STONE DRIVES THEM.

MORE OF THEM THREATENING A VILLAGE THIS WAY!

LET US WIN THIS WAR WITH HASTE AND RETURN TO NOVA HEADQUARTERS. BY NOW, ROCKET'S PLAN WILL BE REACHING FRUITION.

QUILL SHOULD HAVE DONE MORE TO RECOVER THOSE *NEGA-BANDS...*

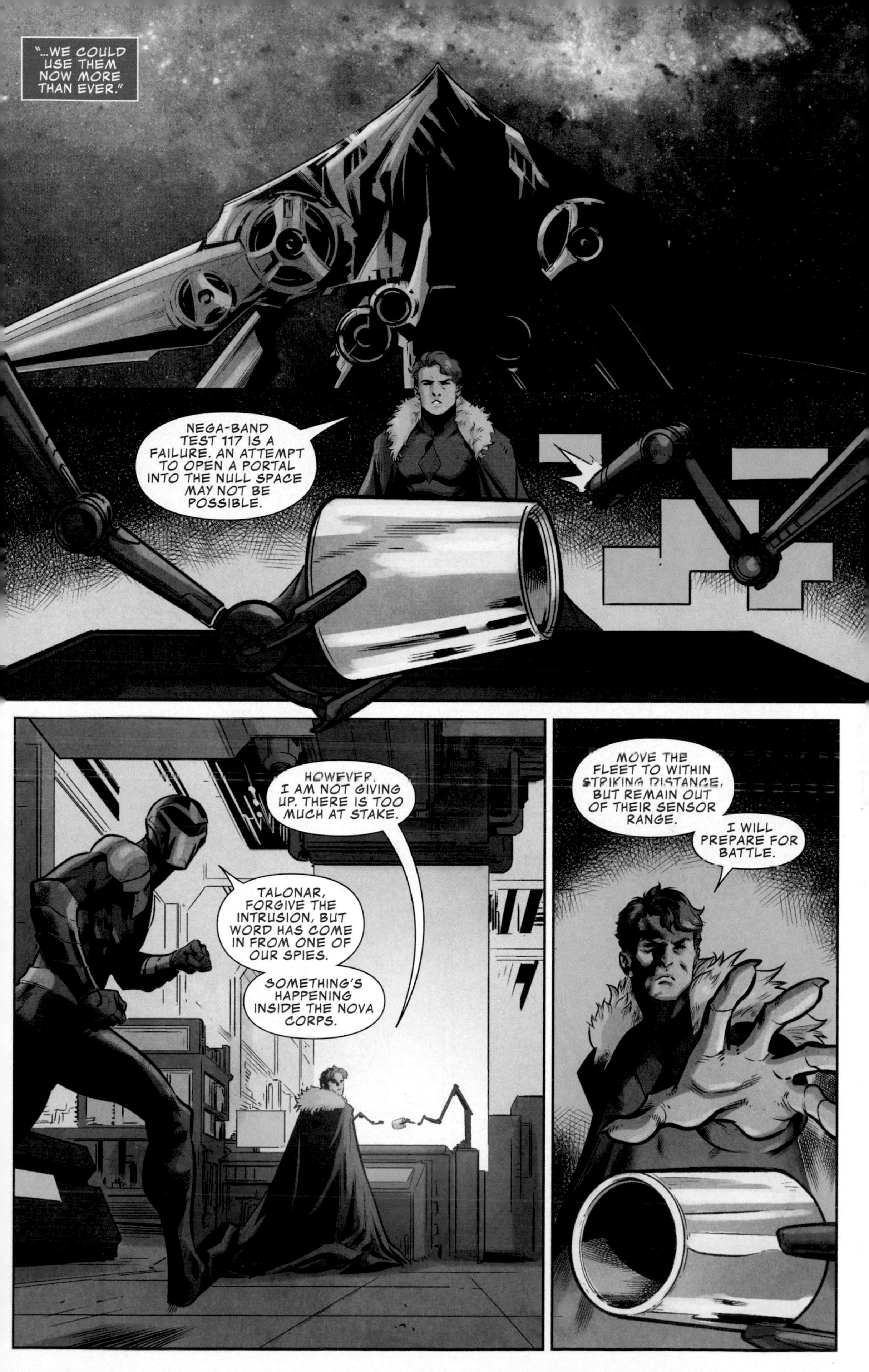
"...WE COULD USE THEM NOW MORE THAN EVER."
NEGA-BAND TEST 117 IS A FAILURE. AN ATTEMPT TO OPEN A PORTAL INTO THE NULL SPACE MAY NOT BE POSSIBLE.
HOWEVER, I AM NOT GIVING UP. THERE IS TOO MUCH AT STAKE.
TALONAR, FORGIVE THE INTRUSION, BUT WORD HAS COME IN FROM ONE OF OUR SPIES.
SOMETHING'S HAPPENING INSIDE THE NOVA CORPS.
MOVE THE FLEET TO WITHIN STRIKING DISTANCE, BUT REMAIN OUT OF THEIR SENSOR RANGE.
I WILL PREPARE FOR BATTLE.

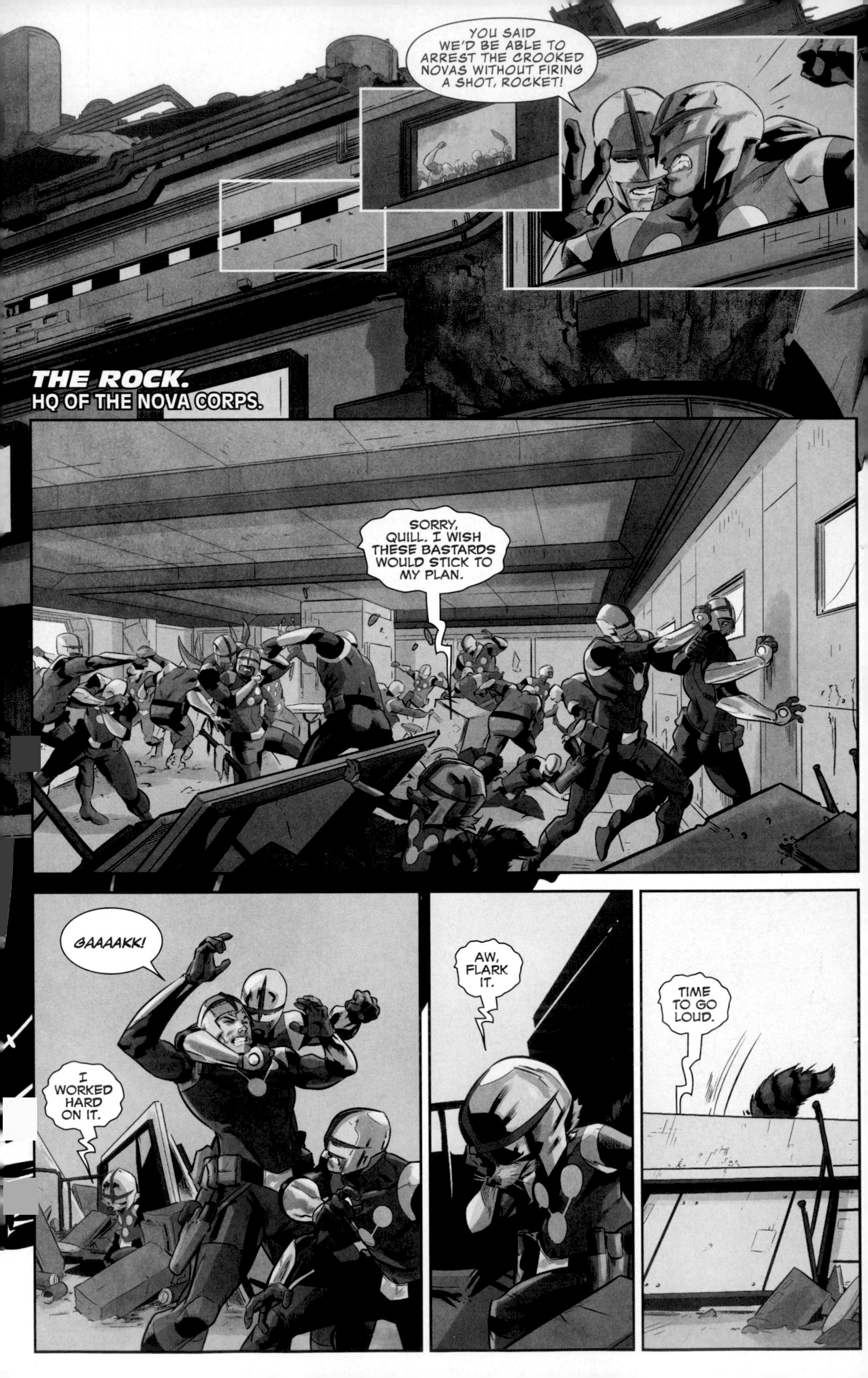
YOU SAID WE'D BE ABLE TO ARREST THE CROOKED NOVAS WITHOUT FIRING A SHOT, ROCKET!
THE ROCK.
HQ OF THE NOVA CORPS.
SORRY, QUILL. I WISH THESE BASTARDS WOULD STICK TO MY PLAN.
GAAAAKK!
I WORKED HARD ON IT.
AW, FLARK IT.
TIME TO GO LOUD.

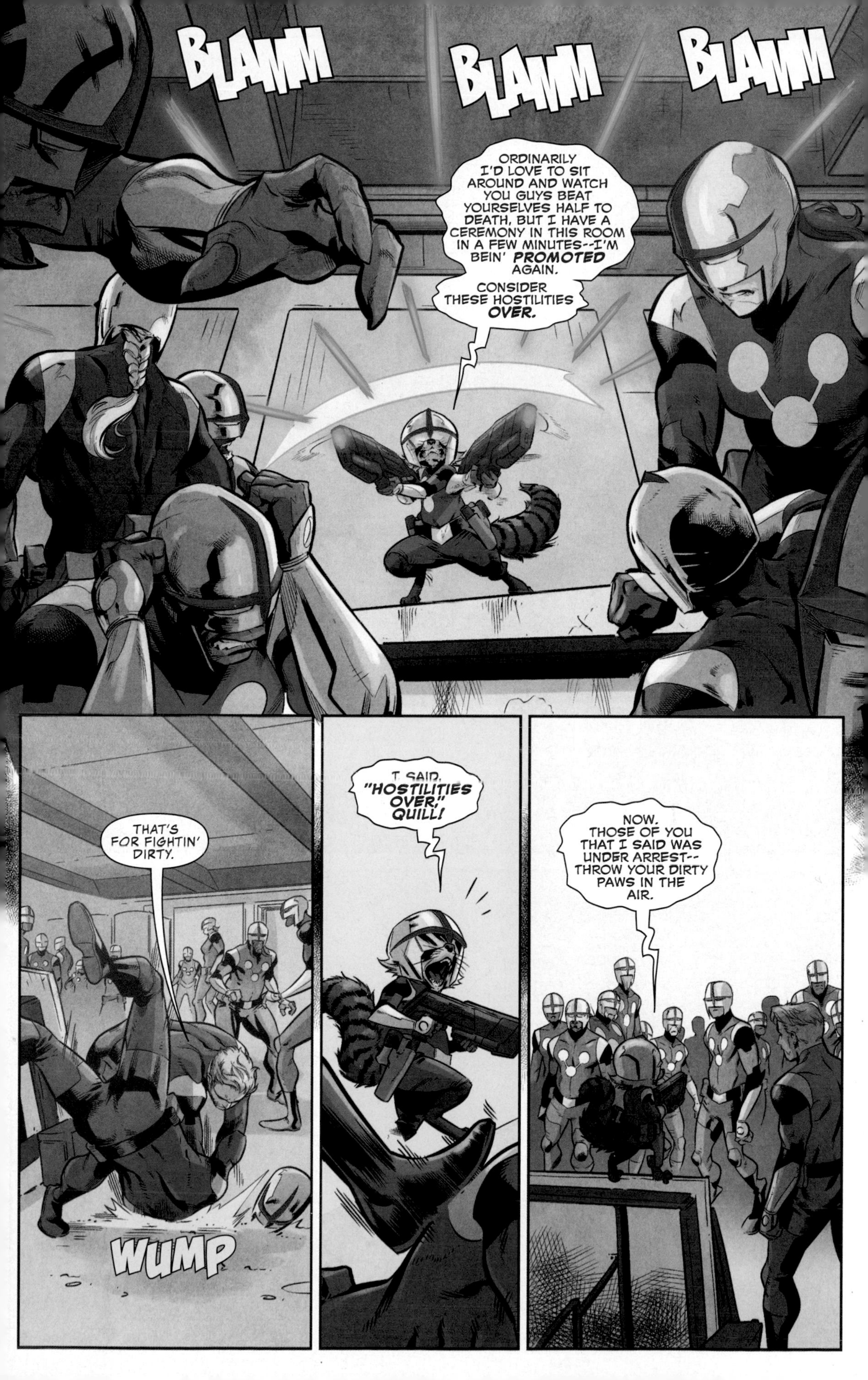
BLAMM
BLAMM
BLAMM
ORDINARILY I'D LOVE TO SIT AROUND AND WATCH YOU GUYS BEAT YOURSELVES HALF TO DEATH, BUT I HAVE A CEREMONY IN THIS ROOM IN A FEW MINUTES--I'M BEIN' PROMOTED AGAIN.
CONSIDER THESE HOSTILITIES OVER.
THAT'S FOR FIGHTIN' DIRTY.
WUMP
I SAID, "HOSTILITIES OVER," QUILL!
NOW. THOSE OF YOU THAT I SAID WAS UNDER ARREST-- THROW YOUR DIRTY PAWS IN THE AIR.

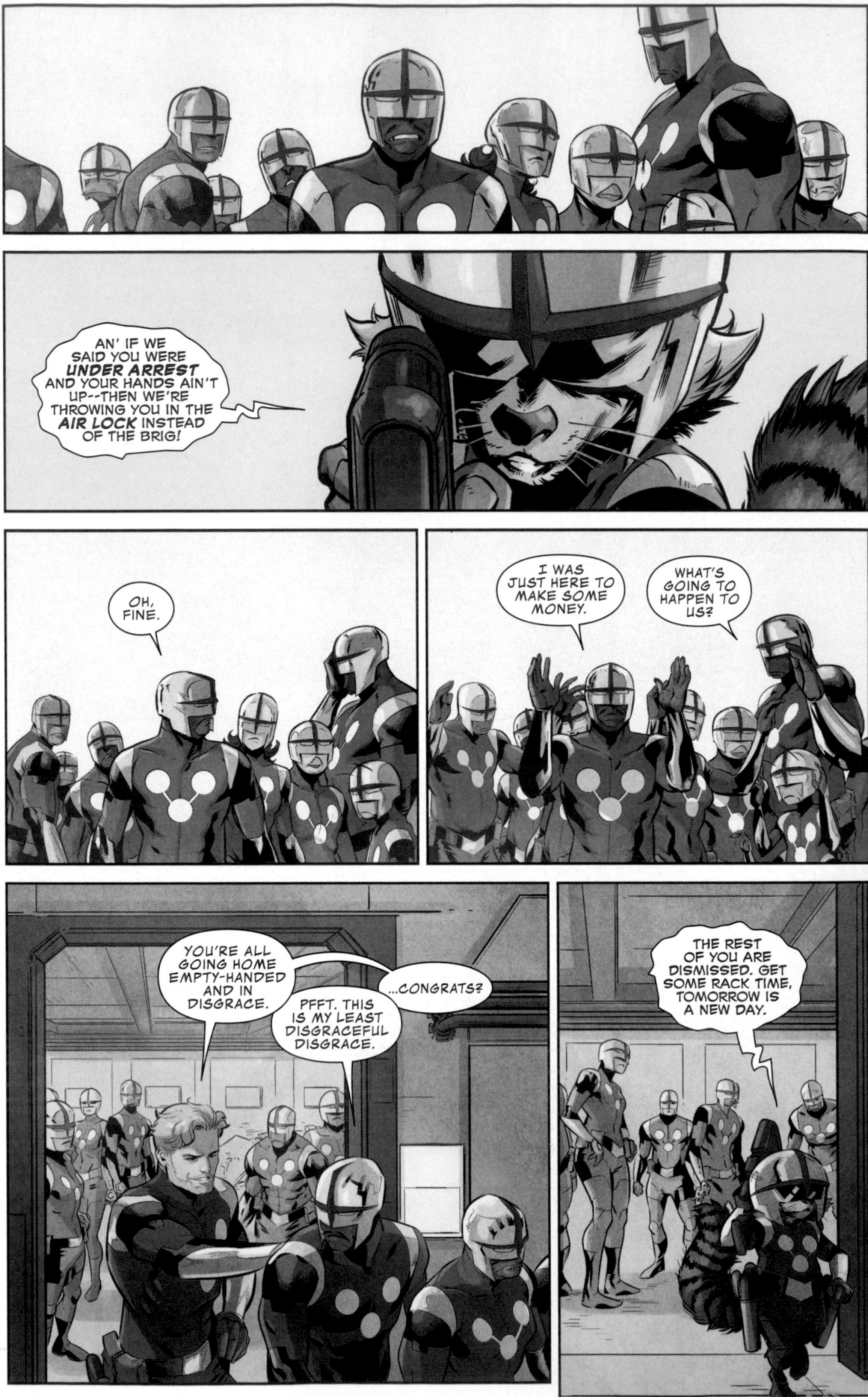
AN' IF WE SAID YOU WERE UNDER ARREST AND YOUR HANDS AIN'T UP--THEN WE'RE THROWING YOU IN THE AIR LOCK INSTEAD OF THE BRIG!
OH, FINE.
I WAS JUST HERE TO MAKE SOME MONEY.
WHAT'S GOING TO HAPPEN TO US?
YOU'RE ALL GOING HOME EMPTY-HANDED AND IN DISGRACE.
...CONGRATS?
PFFT. THIS IS MY LEAST DISGRACEFUL DISGRACE.
THE REST OF YOU ARE DISMISSED. GET SOME RACK TIME, TOMORROW IS A NEW DAY.

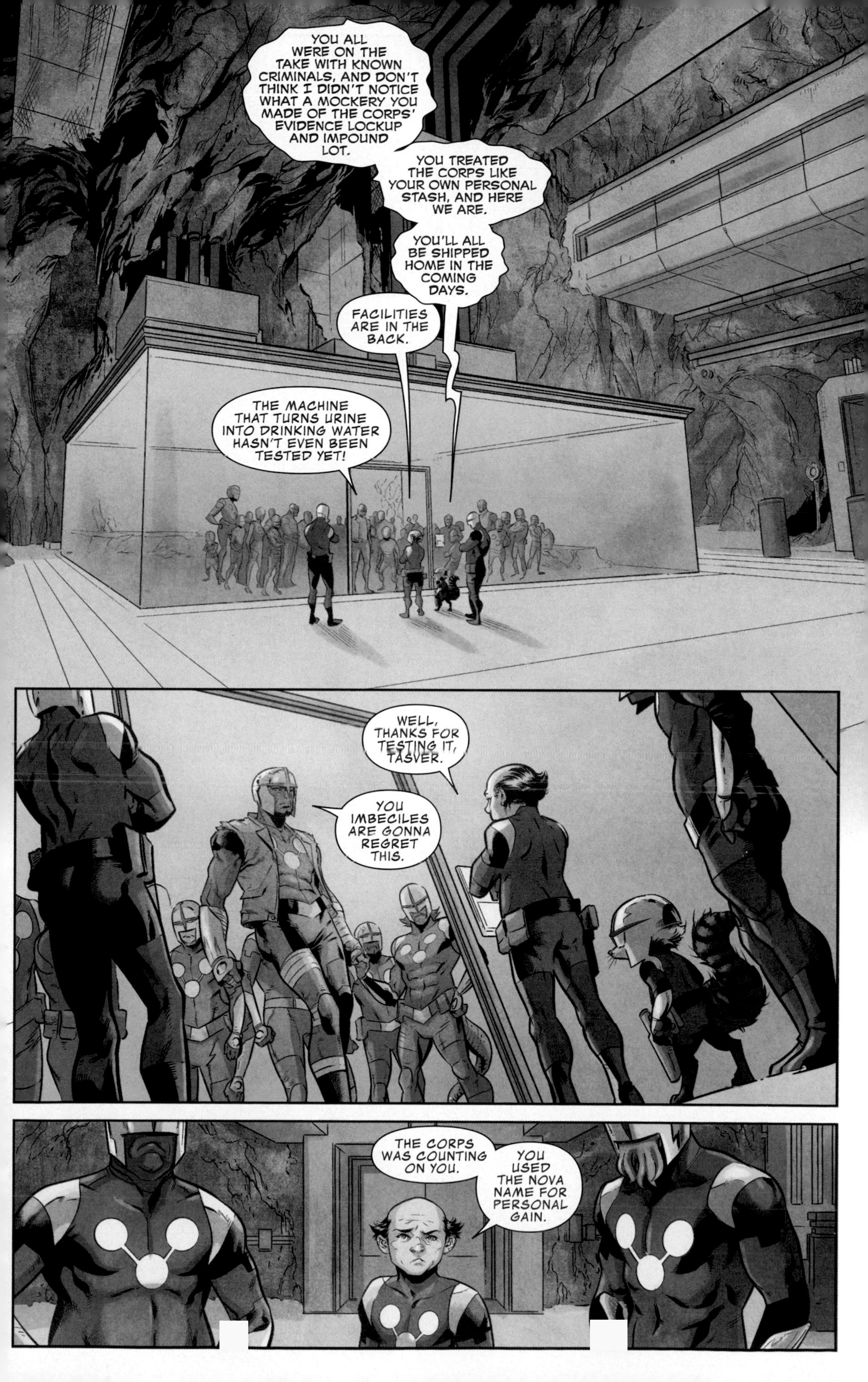
YOU ALL WERE ON THE TAKE WITH KNOWN CRIMINALS, AND DON'T THINK I DIDN'T NOTICE WHAT A MOCKERY YOU MADE OF THE CORPS' EVIDENCE LOCKUP AND IMPOUND LOT.
YOU TREATED THE CORPS LIKE YOUR OWN PERSONAL STASH, AND HERE WE ARE.
YOU'LL ALL BE SHIPPED HOME IN THE COMING DAYS.
FACILITIES ARE IN THE BACK.
THE MACHINE THAT TURNS URINE INTO DRINKING WATER HASN'T EVEN BEEN TESTED YET!
WELL, THANKS FOR TESTING IT, TASVER.
YOU IMBECILES ARE GONNA REGRET THIS.
THE CORPS WAS COUNTING ON YOU.
YOU USED THE NOVA NAME FOR PERSONAL GAIN.

EVERY SINGLE LAST ONE OF YOU IS A REAL DISGRACE-- BUT ESPECIALLY YOU, TASVER...
...I HAD SUCH HIGH HOPES FOR YOU.
MORROW, DID YOU EVEN KNOW THEY WERE CARVING A BRIG?
YEAH, BUT I DIDN'T KNOW I WAS GONNA END UP IN IT.
GUARD THESE CLOWNS. MAKE SURE NOBODY ESCAPES.
YES, SIR.

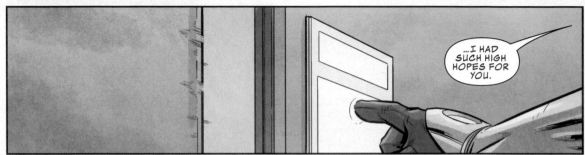

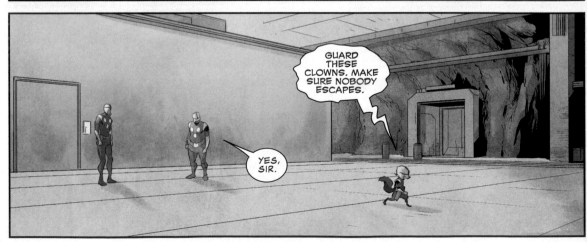

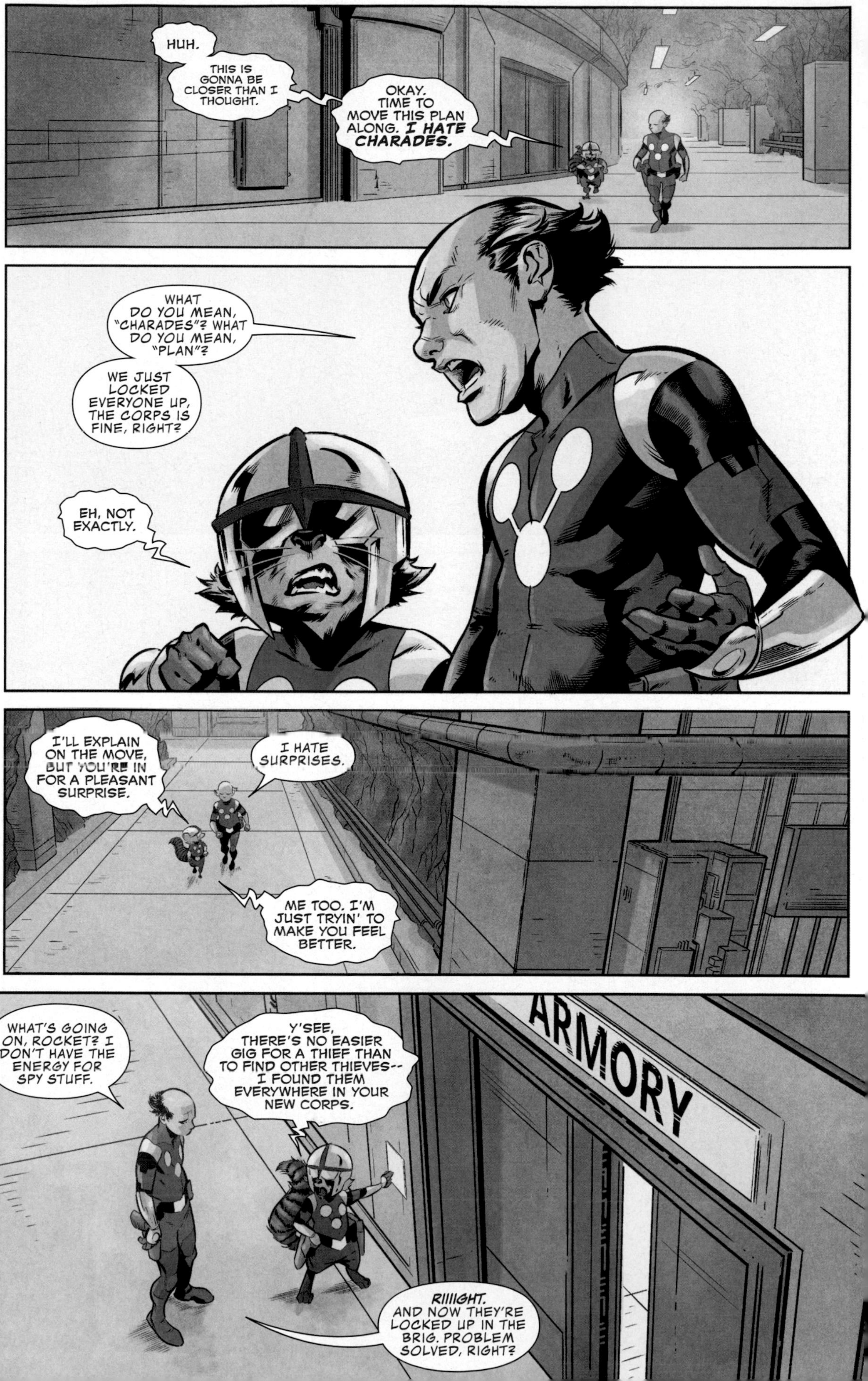
HUH.
THIS IS GONNA BE CLOSER THAN I THOUGHT.
OKAY. TIME TO MOVE THIS PLAN ALONG. I HATE CHARADES.
WHAT DO YOU MEAN, "CHARADES"? WHAT DO YOU MEAN, "PLAN"?
WE JUST LOCKED EVERYONE UP, THE CORPS IS FINE, RIGHT?
EH, NOT EXACTLY.
I'LL EXPLAIN ON THE MOVE, BUT YOU'RE IN FOR A PLEASANT SURPRISE.
I HATE SURPRISES.
ME TOO. I'M JUST TRYIN' TO MAKE YOU FEEL BETTER.
ARMORY
WHAT'S GOING ON, ROCKET? I DON'T HAVE THE ENERGY FOR SPY STUFF.
Y'SEE, THERE'S NO EASIER GIG FOR A THIEF THAN TO FIND OTHER THIEVES-- I FOUND THEM EVERYWHERE IN YOUR NEW CORPS.
RIIIIGHT. AND NOW THEY'RE LOCKED UP IN THE BRIG. PROBLEM SOLVED, RIGHT?

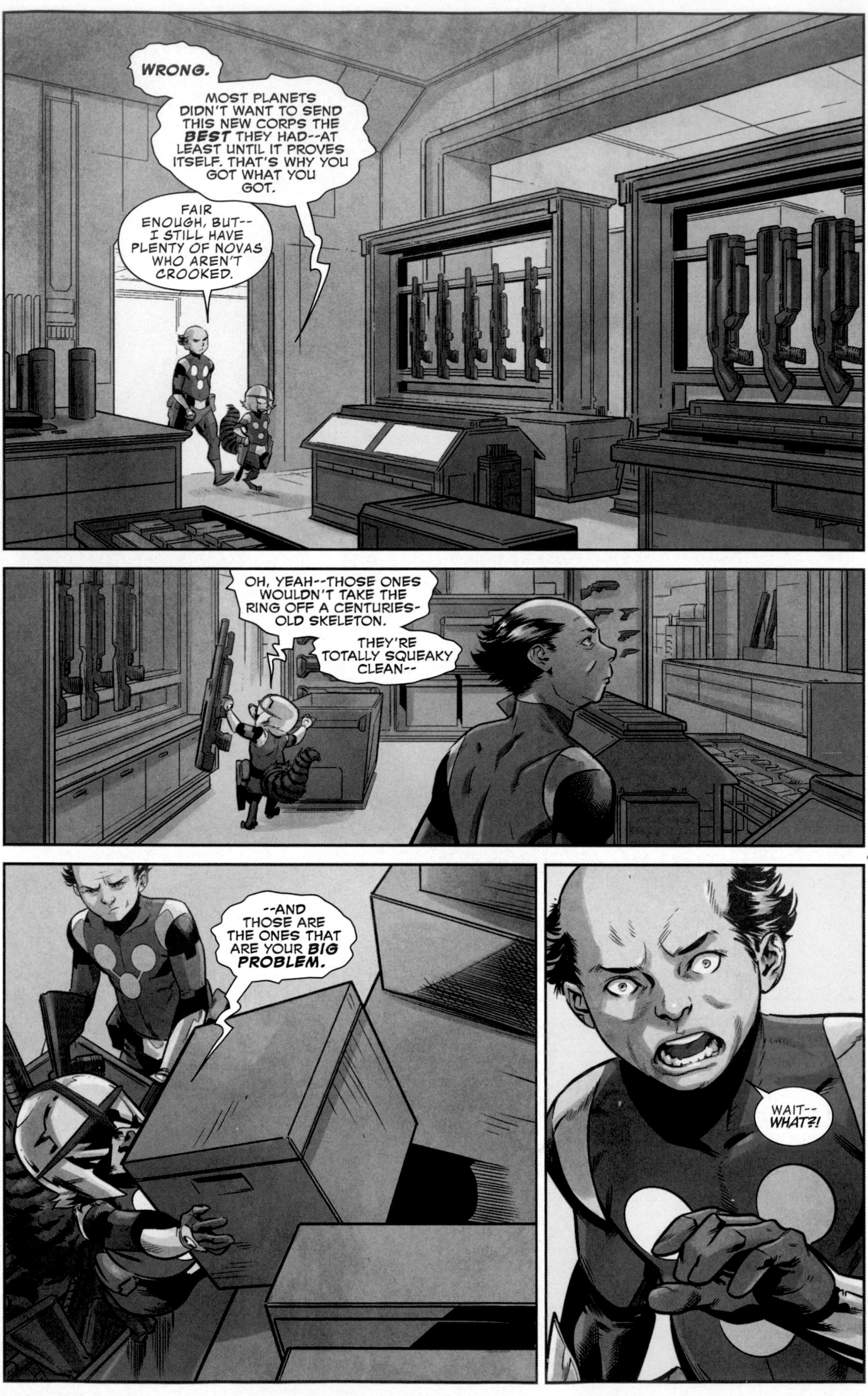
WRONG.
MOST PLANETS DIDN'T WANT TO SEND THIS NEW CORPS THE BEST THEY HAD--AT LEAST UNTIL IT PROVES ITSELF. THAT'S WHY YOU GOT WHAT YOU GOT.
FAIR ENOUGH, BUT-- I STILL HAVE PLENTY OF NOVAS WHO AREN'T CROOKED.
OH, YEAH--THOSE ONES WOULDN'T TAKE THE RING OFF A CENTURIES-OLD SKELETON.
THEY'RE TOTALLY SQUEAKY CLEAN--
--AND THOSE ARE THE ONES THAT ARE YOUR BIG PROBLEM.
WAIT-- WHAT?!

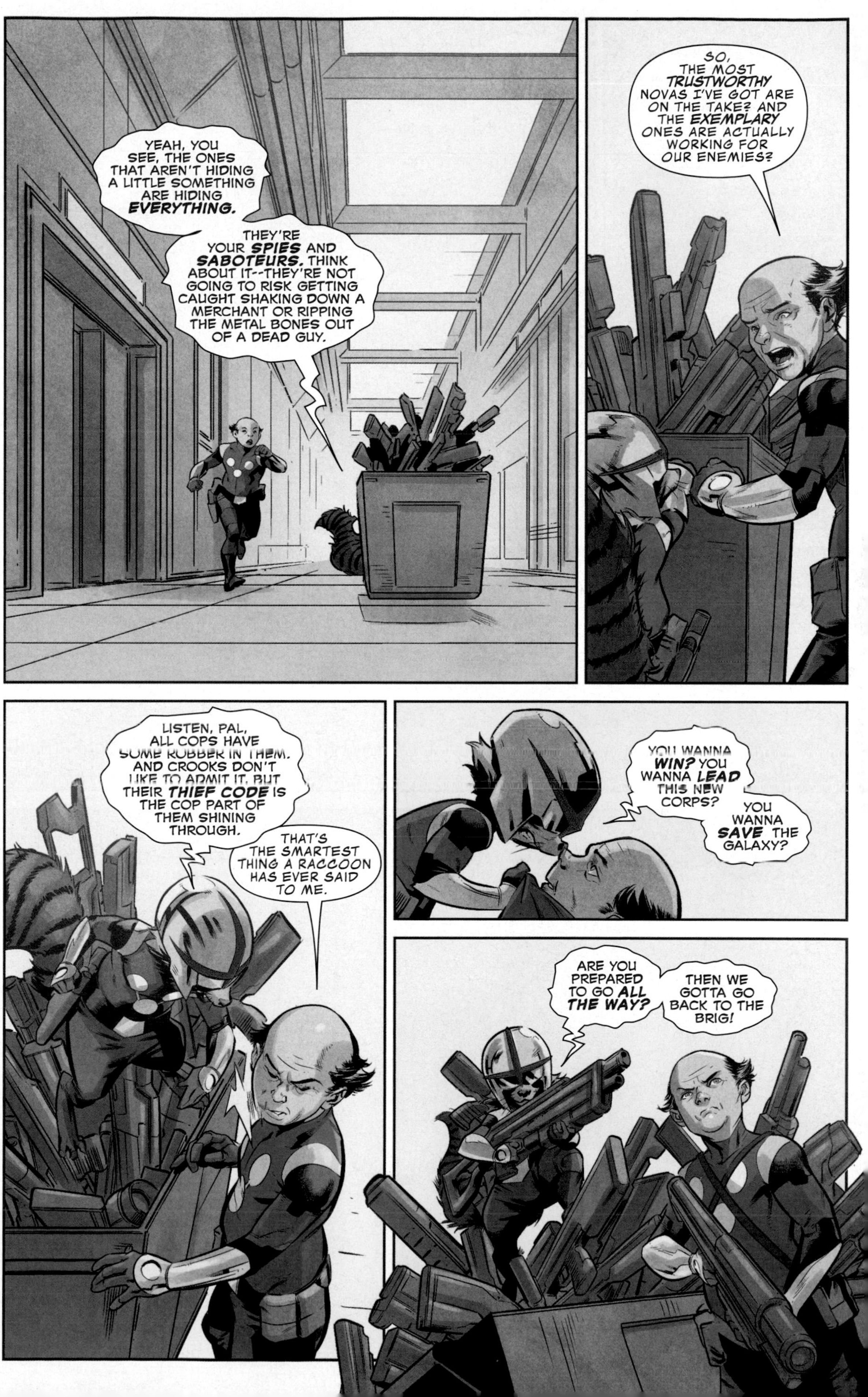
YEAH, YOU SEE, THE ONES THAT AREN'T HIDING A LITTLE SOMETHING ARE HIDING EVERYTHING.
THEY'RE YOUR SPIES AND SABOTEURS. THINK ABOUT IT--THEY'RE NOT GOING TO RISK GETTING CAUGHT SHAKING DOWN A MERCHANT OR RIPPING THE METAL BONES OUT OF A DEAD GUY.
SO, THE MOST TRUSTWORTHY NOVAS I'VE GOT ARE ON THE TAKE? AND THE EXEMPLARY ONES ARE ACTUALLY WORKING FOR OUR ENEMIES?
LISTEN, PAL, ALL COPS HAVE SOME ROBBER IN THEM. AND CROOKS DON'T LIKE TO ADMIT IT, BUT THEIR THIEF CODE IS THE COP PART OF THEM SHINING THROUGH.
THAT'S THE SMARTEST THING A RACCOON HAS EVER SAID TO ME.
YOU WANNA WIN? YOU WANNA LEAD THIS NEW CORPS?
YOU WANNA SAVE THE GALAXY?
ARE YOU PREPARED TO GO ALL THE WAY?
THEN WE GOTTA GO BACK TO THE BRIG!

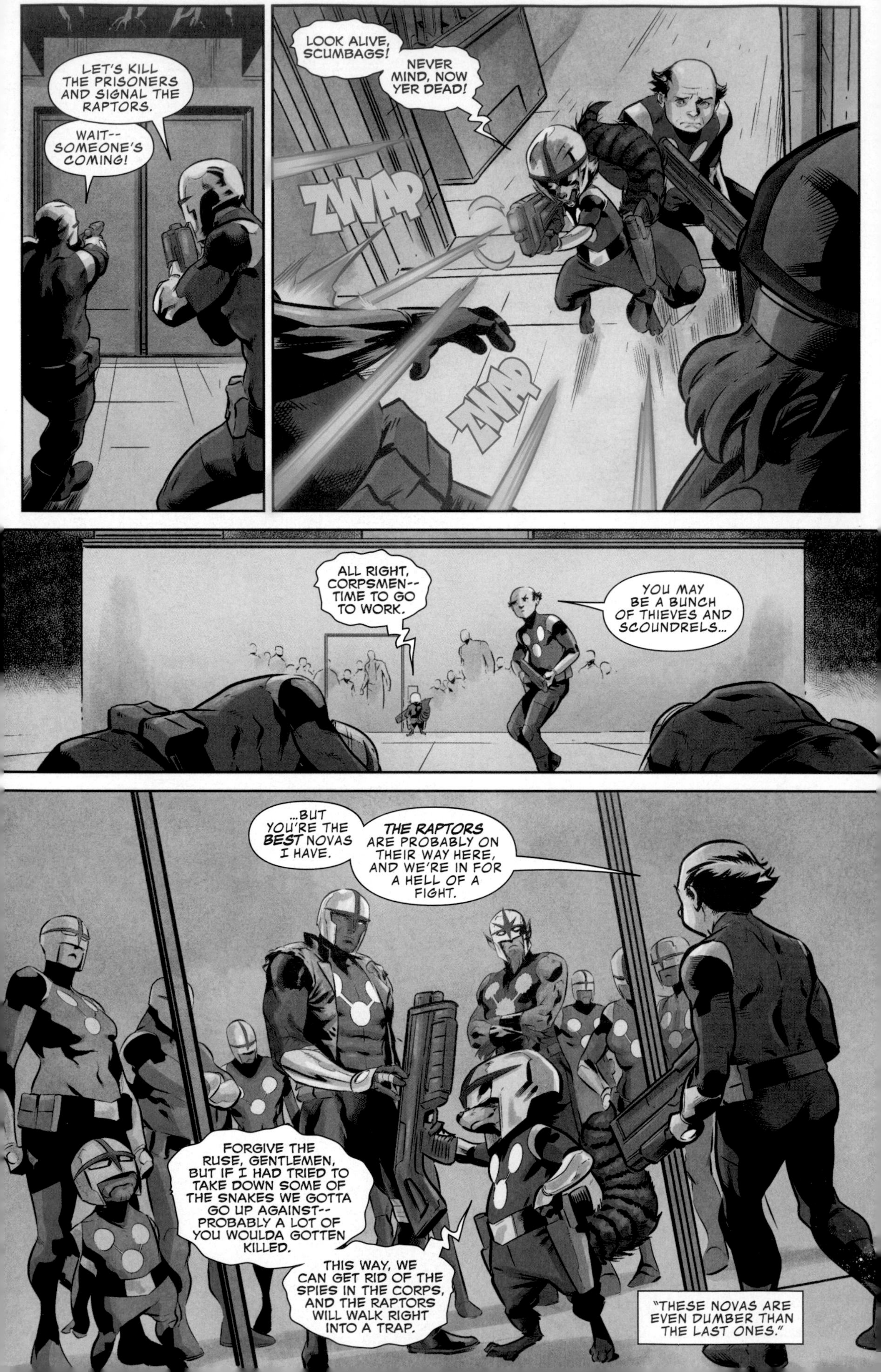
LET'S KILL THE PRISONERS AND SIGNAL THE RAPTORS.
WAIT-- SOMEONE'S COMING!
LOOK ALIVE, SCUMBAGS!
NEVER MIND, NOW YER DEAD!
ZWAP
ZWAP
ALL RIGHT, CORPSMEN-- TIME TO GO TO WORK.
YOU MAY BE A BUNCH OF THIEVES AND SCOUNDRELS...
...BUT YOU'RE THE BEST NOVAS I HAVE.
THE RAPTORS ARE PROBABLY ON THEIR WAY HERE, AND WE'RE IN FOR A HELL OF A FIGHT.
FORGIVE THE RUSE, GENTLEMEN, BUT IF I HAD TRIED TO TAKE DOWN SOME OF THE SNAKES WE GOTTA GO UP AGAINST-- PROBABLY A LOT OF YOU WOULDA GOTTEN KILLED.
THIS WAY, WE CAN GET RID OF THE SPIES IN THE CORPS, AND THE RAPTORS WILL WALK RIGHT INTO A TRAP.
"THESE NOVAS ARE EVEN DUMBER THAN THE LAST ONES."

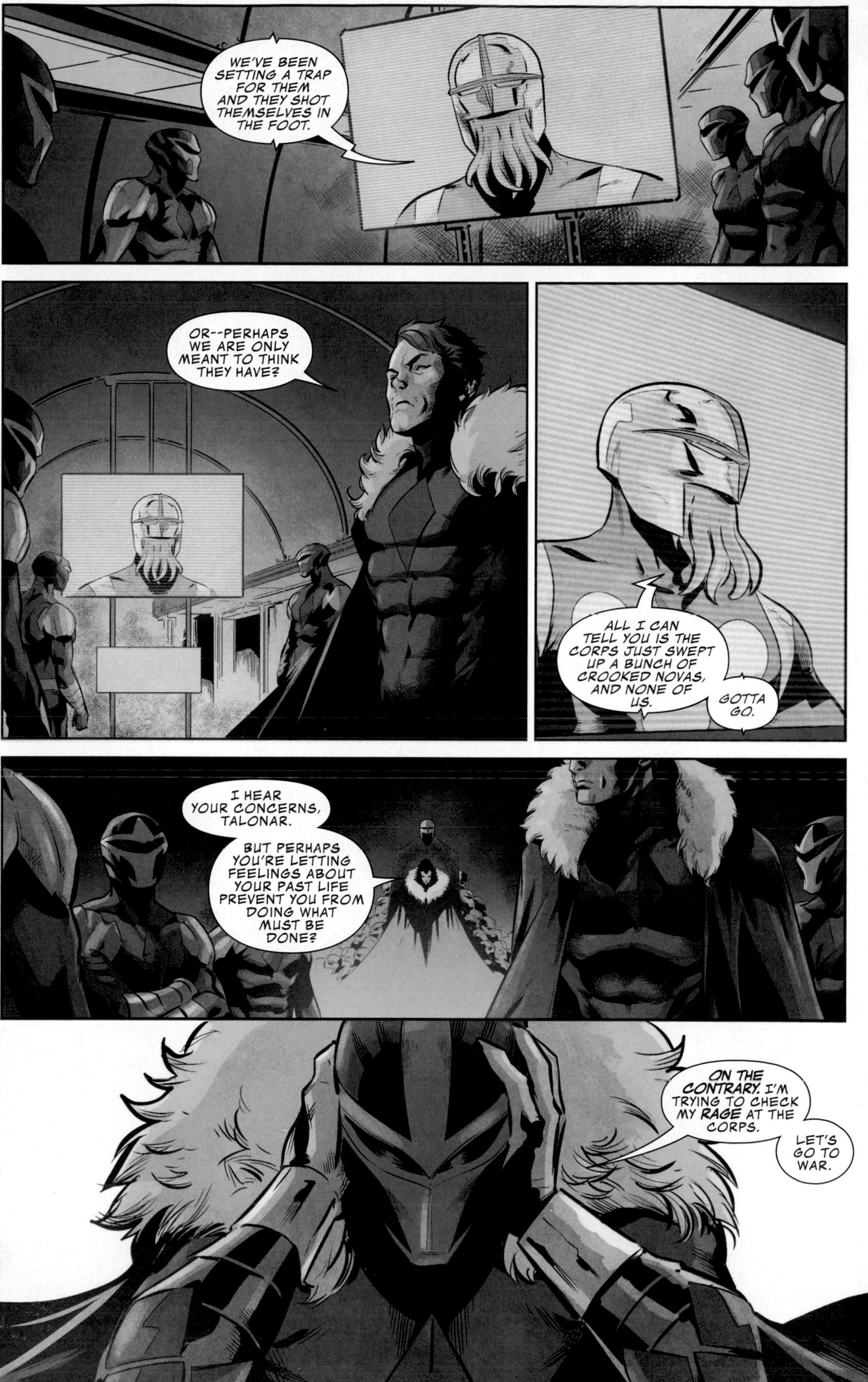
WE'VE BEEN SETTING A TRAP FOR THEM AND THEY SHOT THEMSELVES IN THE FOOT.
OR--PERHAPS WE ARE ONLY MEANT TO THINK THEY HAVE?
ALL I CAN TELL YOU IS THE CORPS JUST SWEPT UP A BUNCH OF CROOKED NOVAS, AND NONE OF US.
GOTTA GO.
I HEAR YOUR CONCERNS, TALONAR.
BUT PERHAPS YOU'RE LETTING FEELINGS ABOUT YOUR PAST LIFE PREVENT YOU FROM DOING WHAT MUST BE DONE?
ON THE CONTRARY. I'M TRYING TO CHECK MY RAGE AT THE CORPS.
LET'S GO TO WAR.

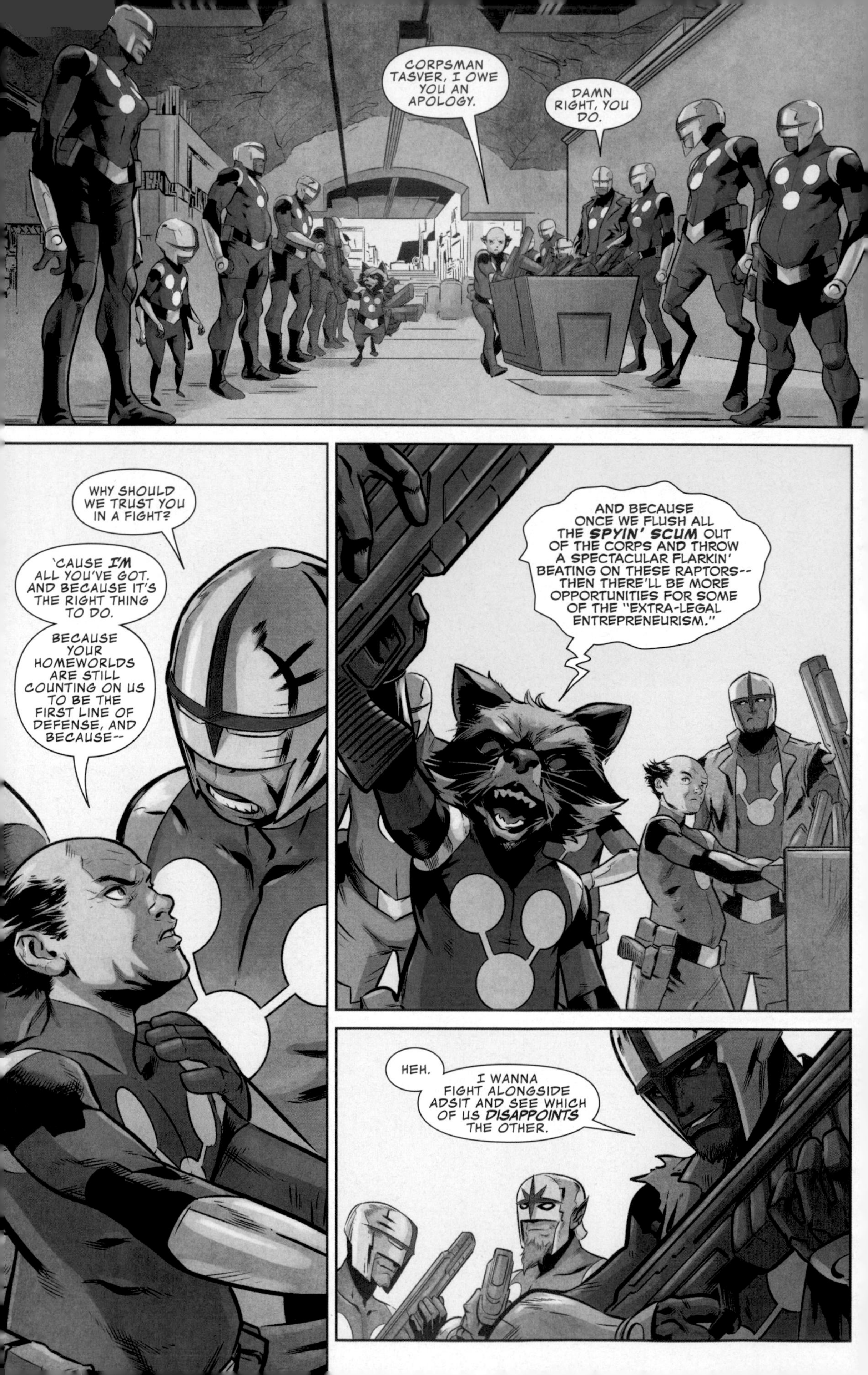
CORPSMAN TASVER, I OWE YOU AN APOLOGY.
DAMN RIGHT, YOU DO.
WHY SHOULD WE TRUST YOU IN A FIGHT?
'CAUSE *I'M* ALL YOU'VE GOT. AND BECAUSE IT'S THE RIGHT THING TO DO.
BECAUSE YOUR HOMEWORLDS ARE STILL COUNTING ON US TO BE THE FIRST LINE OF DEFENSE, AND BECAUSE--
AND BECAUSE ONCE WE FLUSH ALL THE **SPYIN' SCUM** OUT OF THE CORPS AND THROW A SPECTACULAR FLARKIN' BEATING ON THESE RAPTORS-- THEN THERE'LL BE MORE OPPORTUNITIES FOR SOME OF THE "EXTRA-LEGAL ENTREPRENEURISM."
HEH.
I WANNA FIGHT ALONGSIDE ADSIT AND SEE WHICH OF US *DISAPPOINTS* THE OTHER.

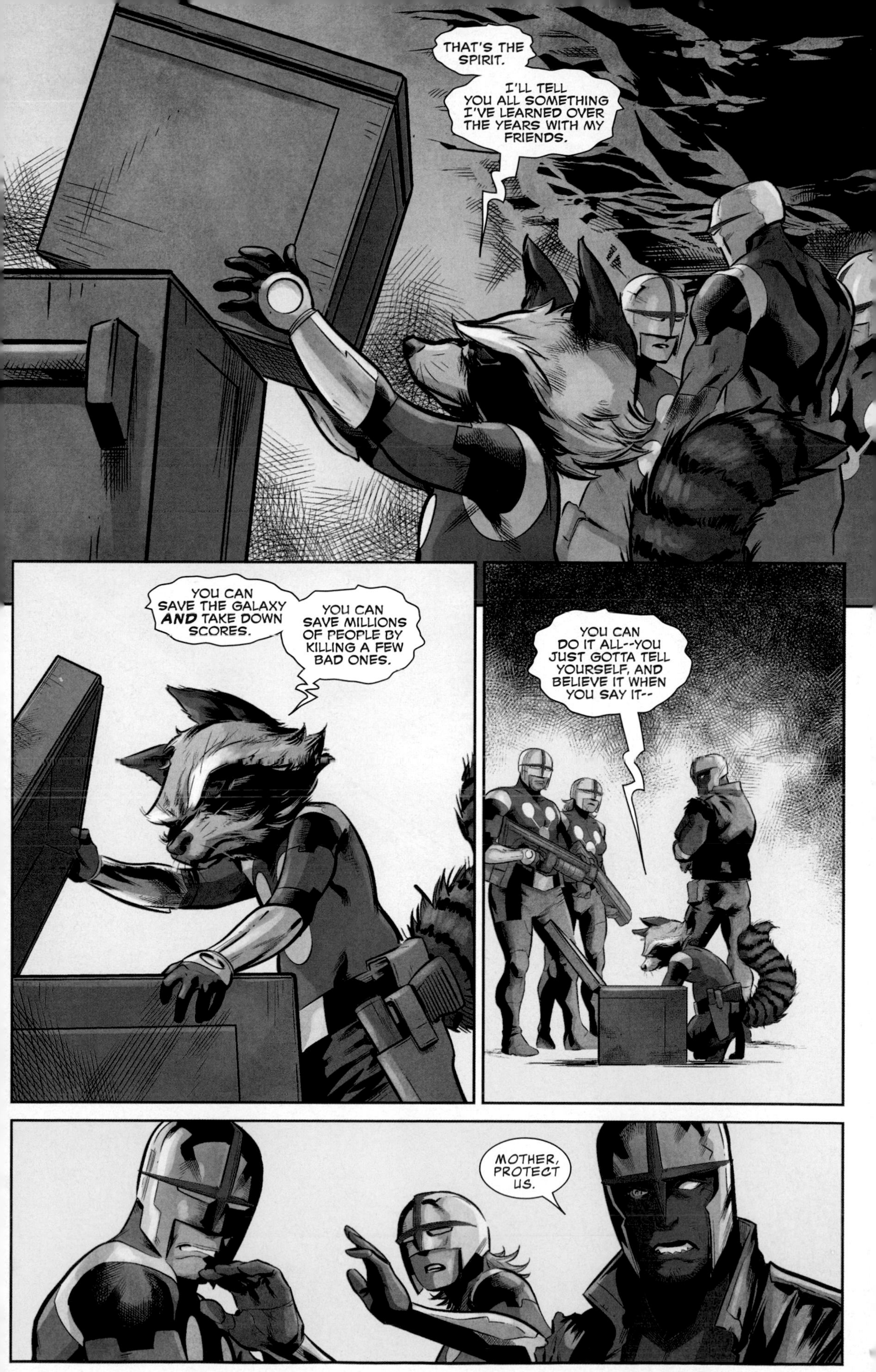
THAT'S THE SPIRIT.
I'LL TELL YOU ALL SOMETHING I'VE LEARNED OVER THE YEARS WITH MY FRIENDS.
YOU CAN SAVE THE GALAXY **AND** TAKE DOWN SCORES.
YOU CAN SAVE MILLIONS OF PEOPLE BY KILLING A FEW BAD ONES.
YOU CAN DO IT ALL--YOU JUST GOTTA TELL YOURSELF, AND BELIEVE IT WHEN YOU SAY IT--
MOTHER, PROTECT US.

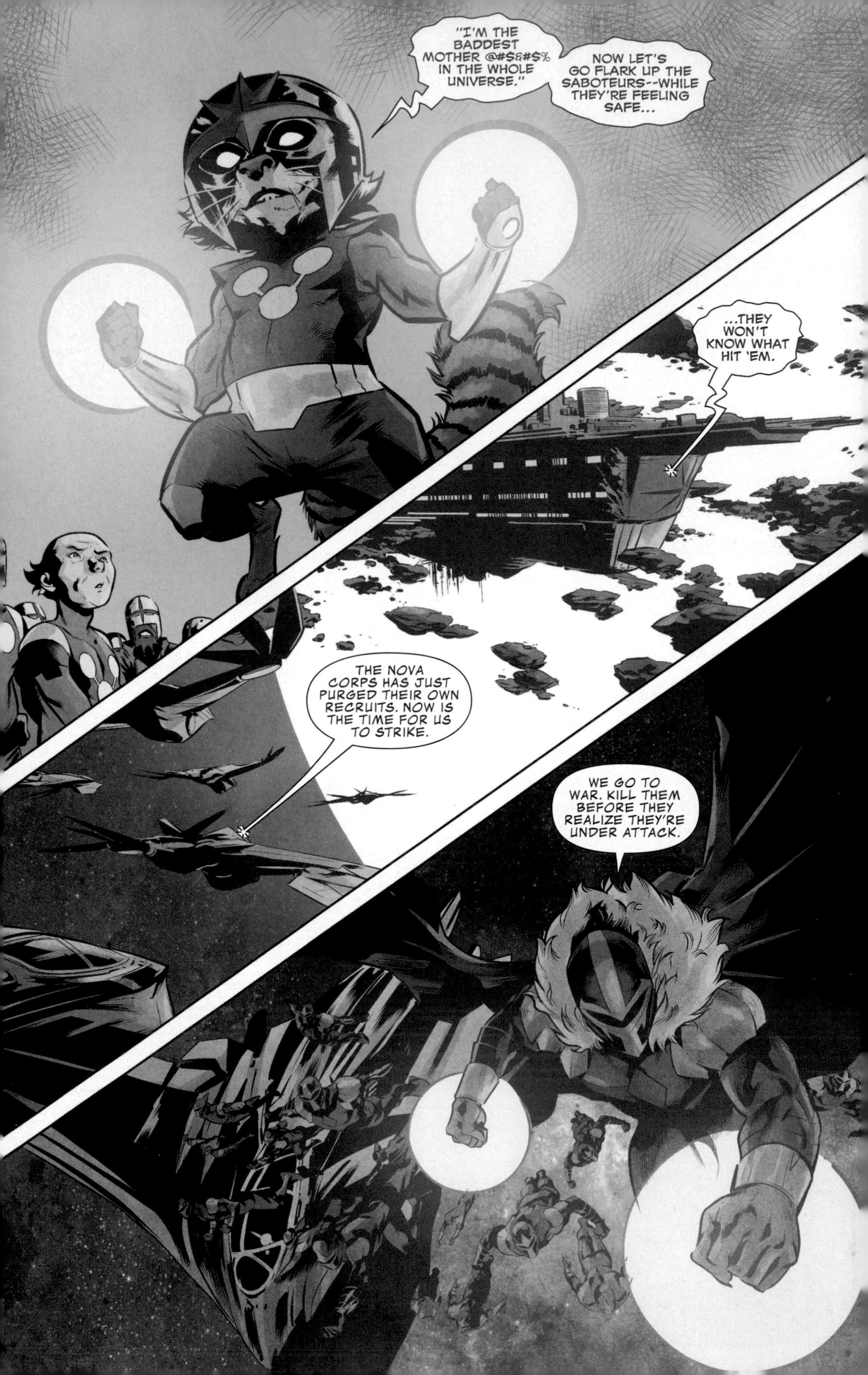
"I'M THE BADDEST MOTHER @#$&#$% IN THE WHOLE UNIVERSE."
NOW LET'S GO FLARK UP THE SABOTEURS--WHILE THEY'RE FEELING SAFE...
...THEY WON'T KNOW WHAT HIT 'EM.
THE NOVA CORPS HAS JUST PURGED THEIR OWN RECRUITS. NOW IS THE TIME FOR US TO STRIKE.
WE GO TO WAR. KILL THEM BEFORE THEY REALIZE THEY'RE UNDER ATTACK.

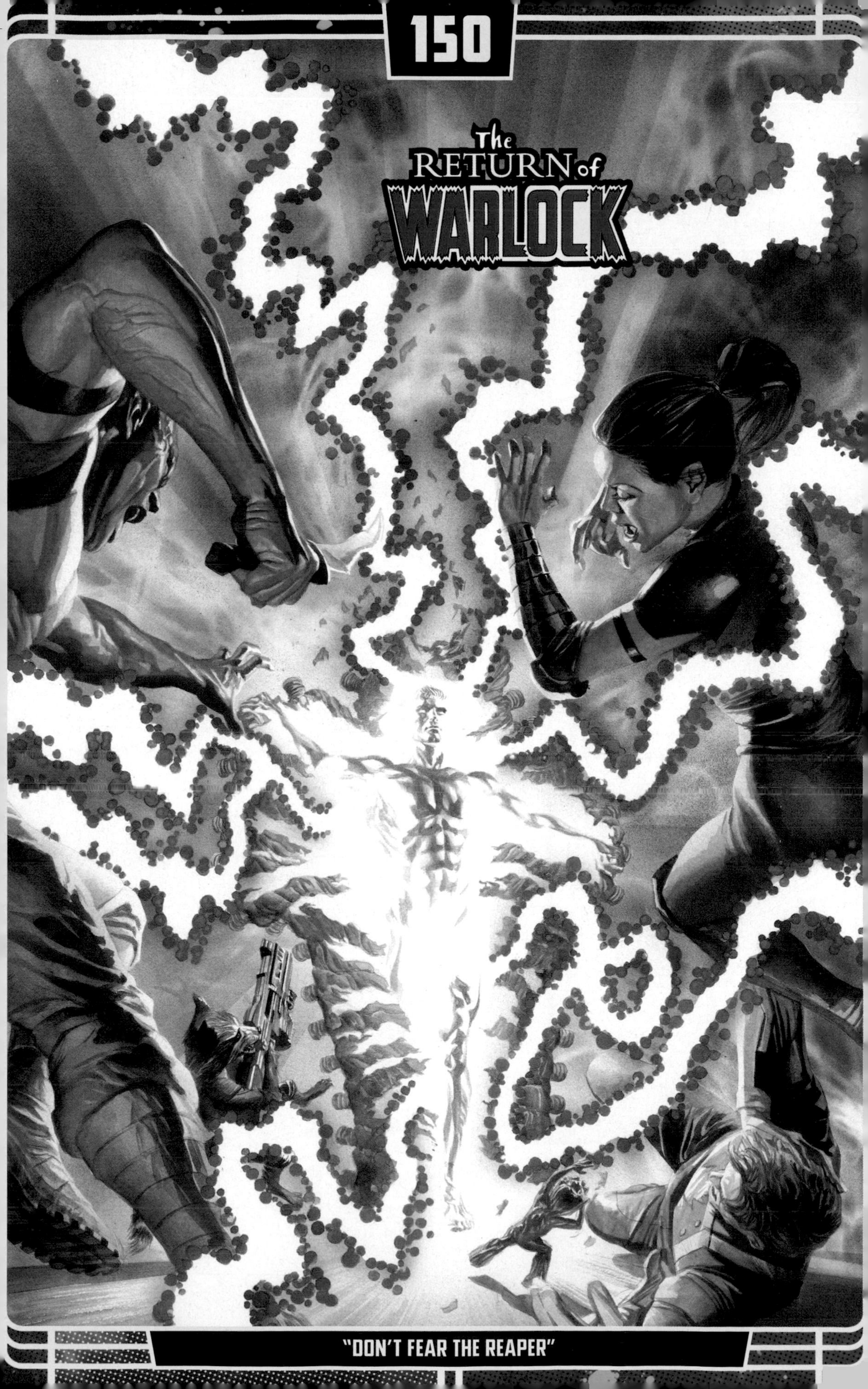
150
The RETURN of WARLOCK
"DON'T FEAR THE REAPER"

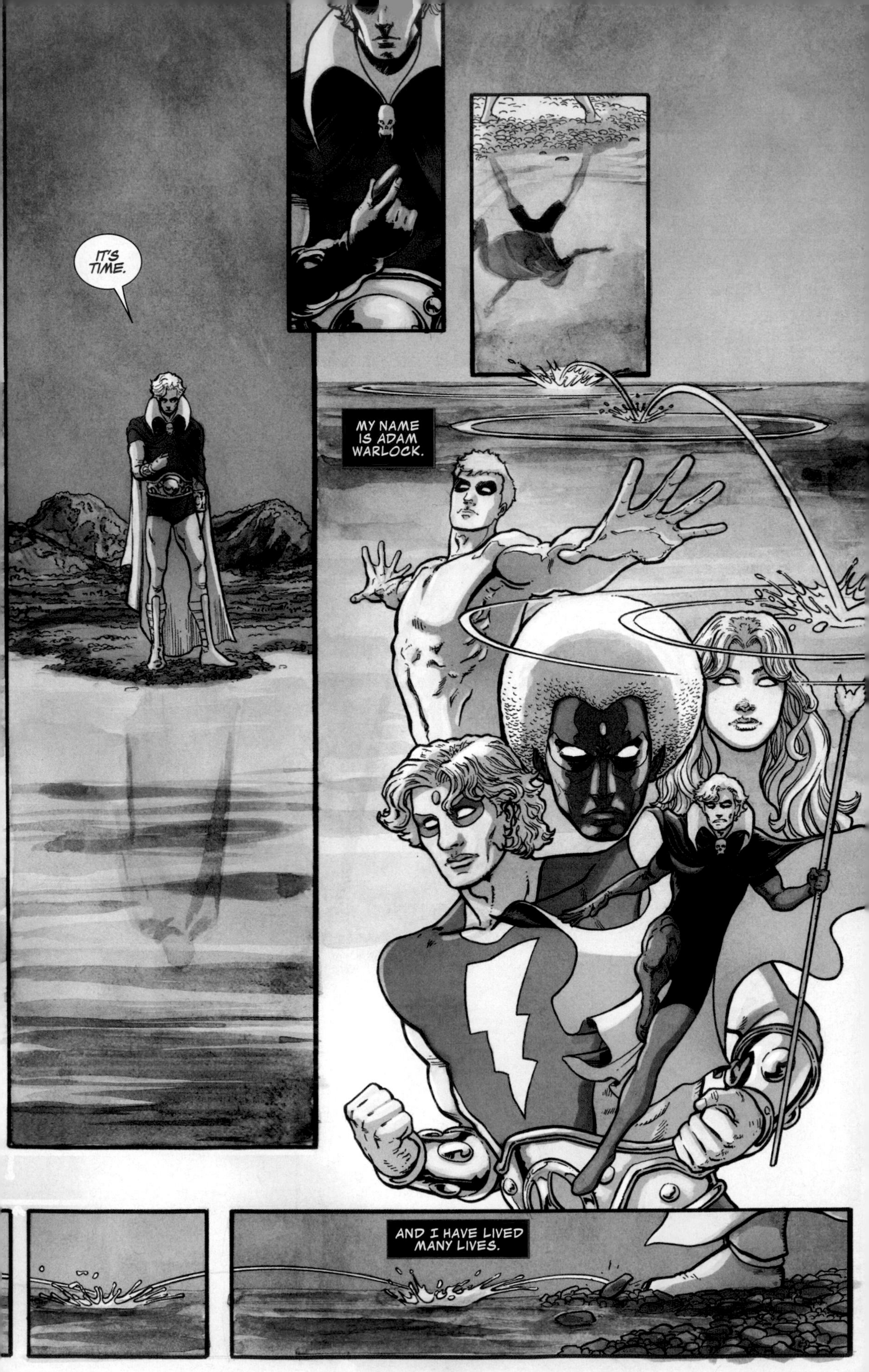
IT'S TIME.
MY NAME IS ADAM WARLOCK.
AND I HAVE LIVED MANY LIVES.

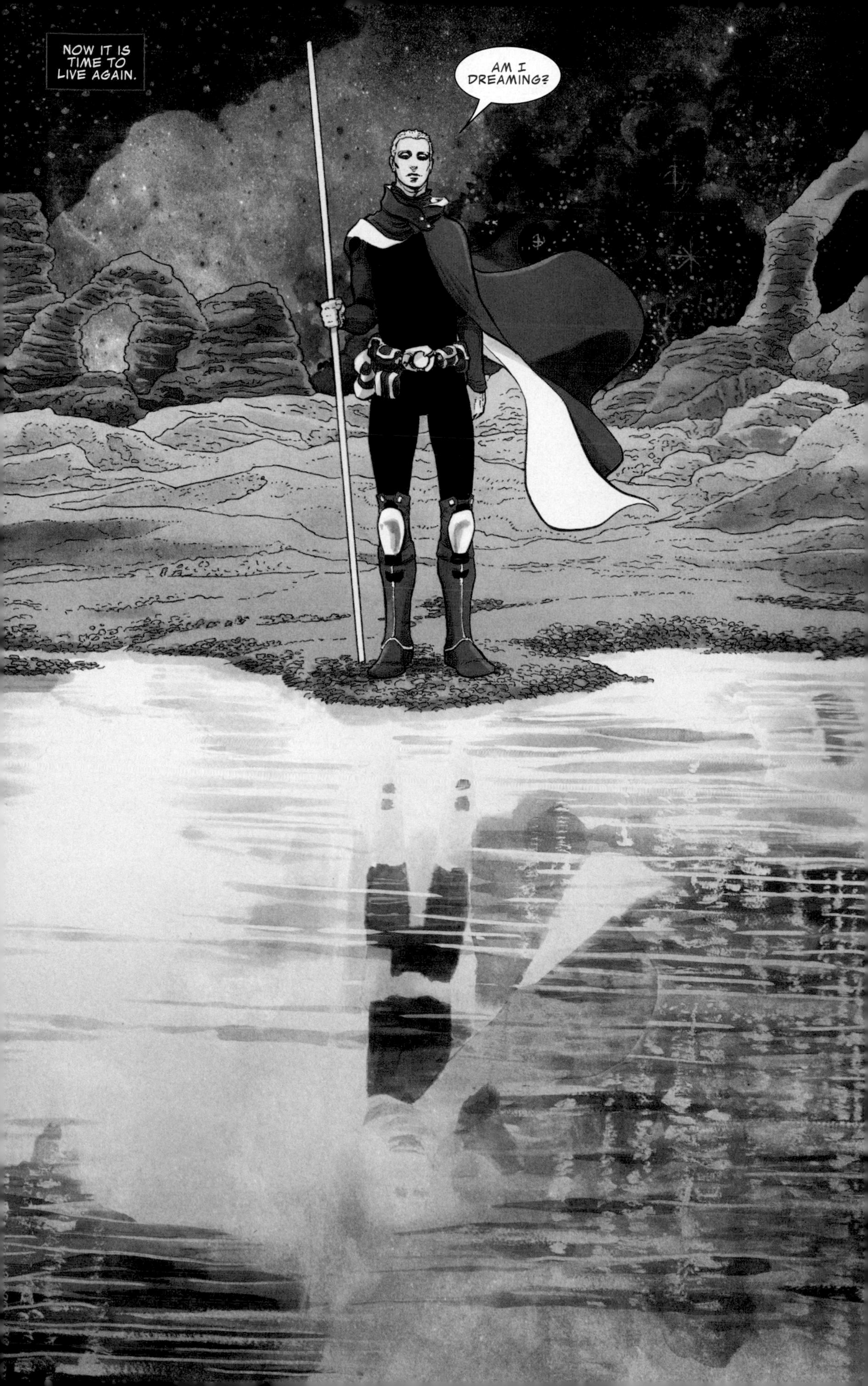
NOW IT IS TIME TO LIVE AGAIN.
AM I DREAMING?

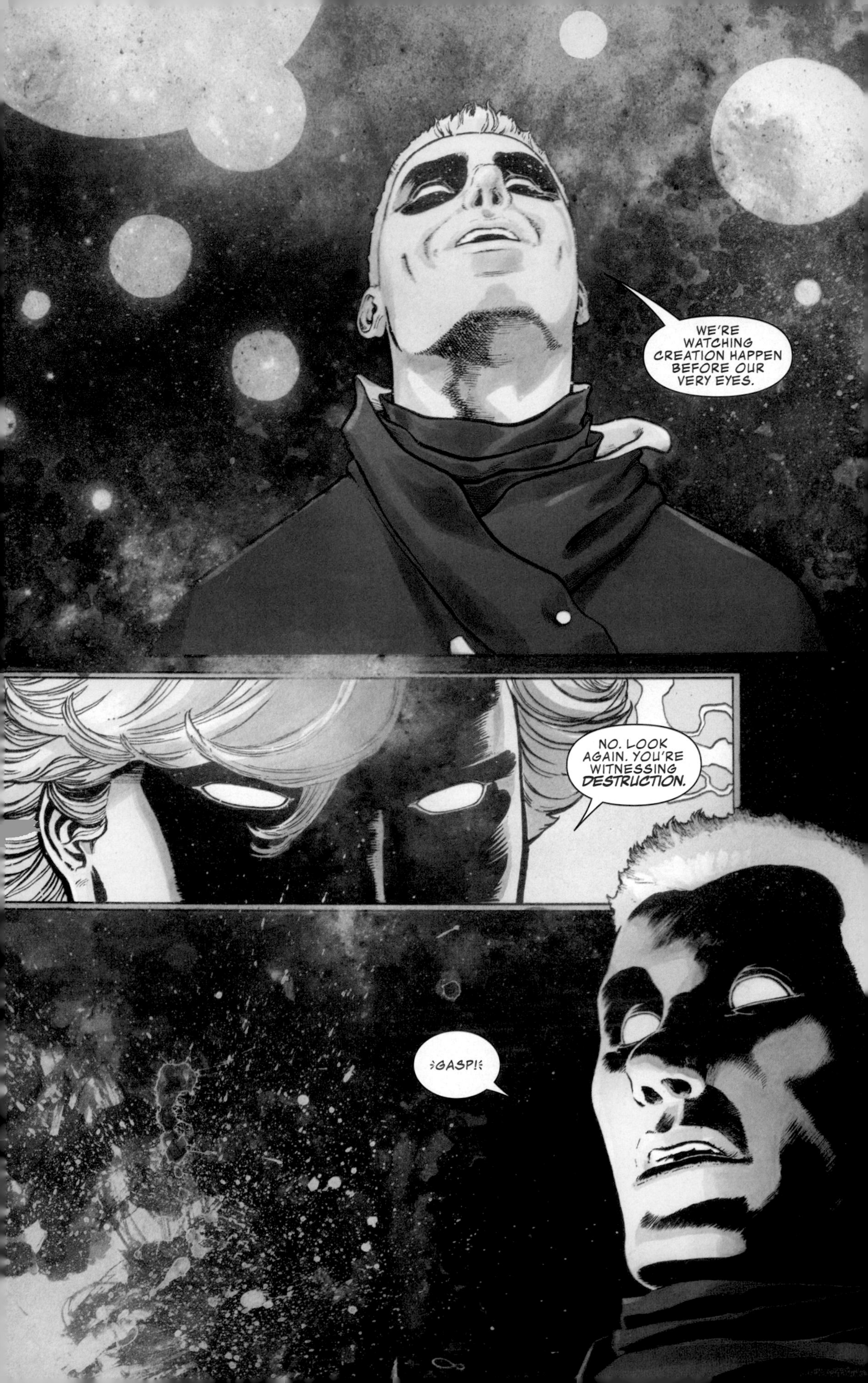
WE'RE WATCHING CREATION HAPPEN BEFORE OUR VERY EYES.
NO. LOOK AGAIN. YOU'RE WITNESSING ***DESTRUCTION.***
GASP!

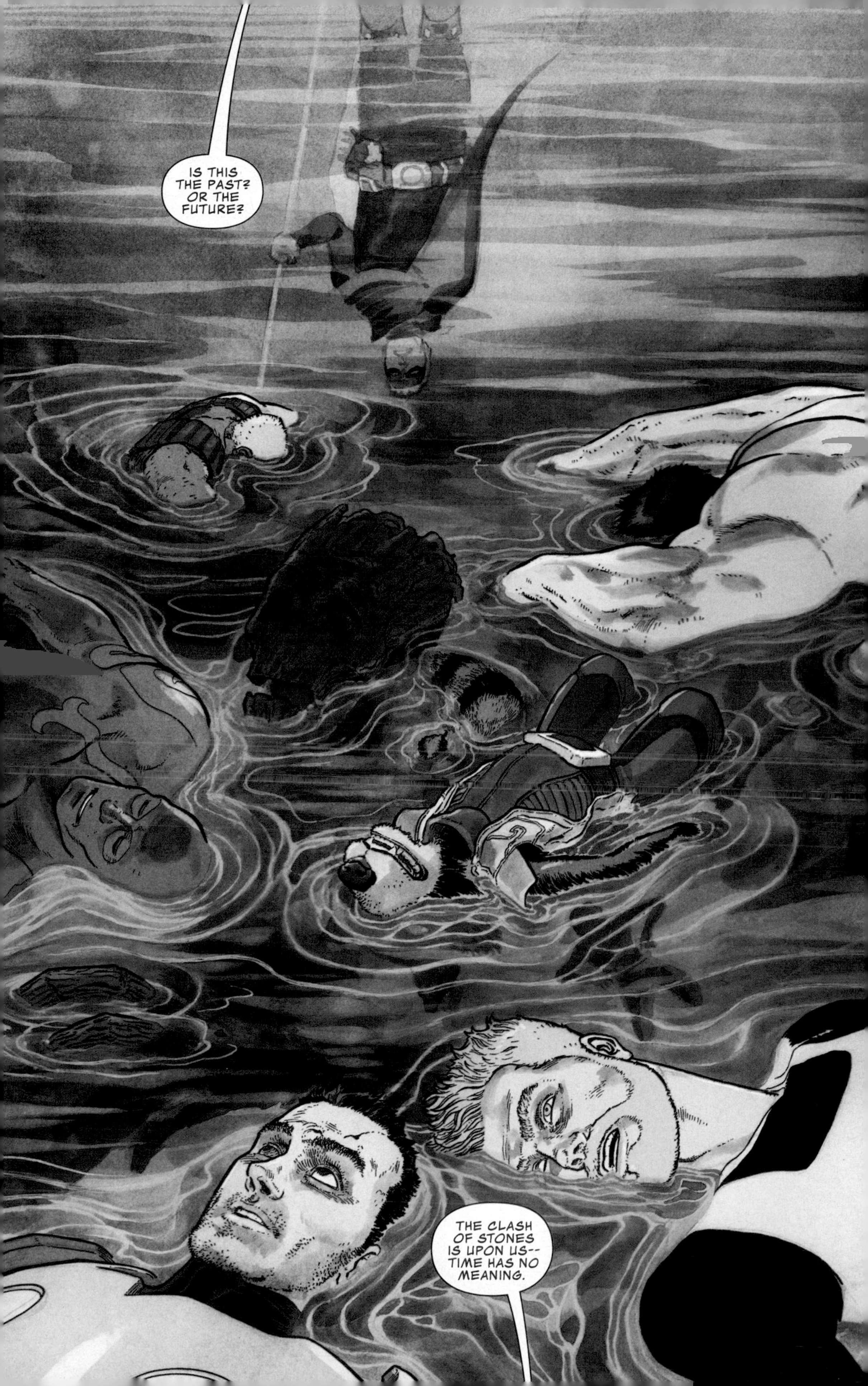
IS THIS THE PAST? OR THE FUTURE?
THE CLASH OF STONES IS UPON US-- TIME HAS NO MEANING.

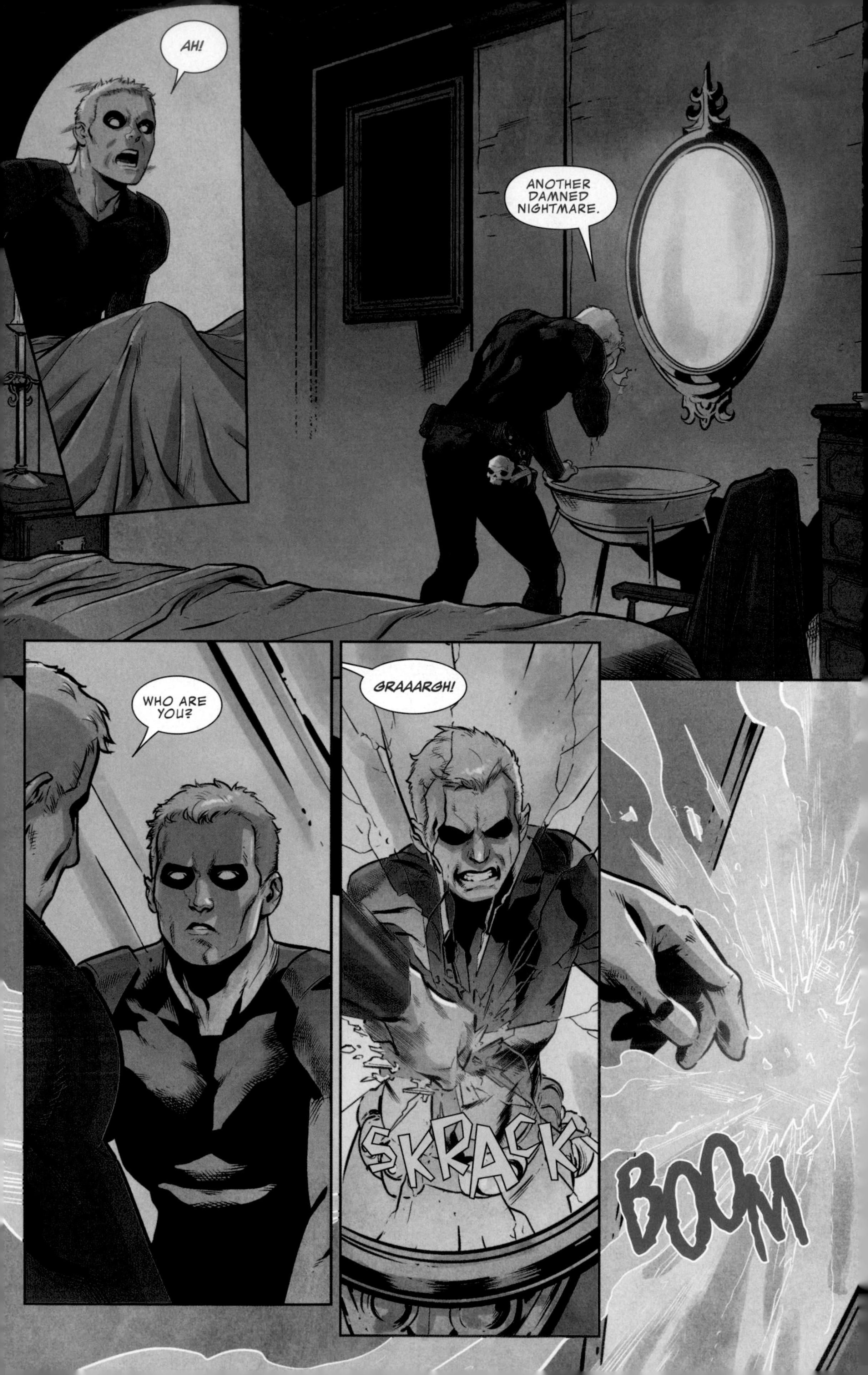
AH!
ANOTHER DAMNED NIGHTMARE.
WHO ARE YOU?
GRAAARGH!
SKRACK
BOOM

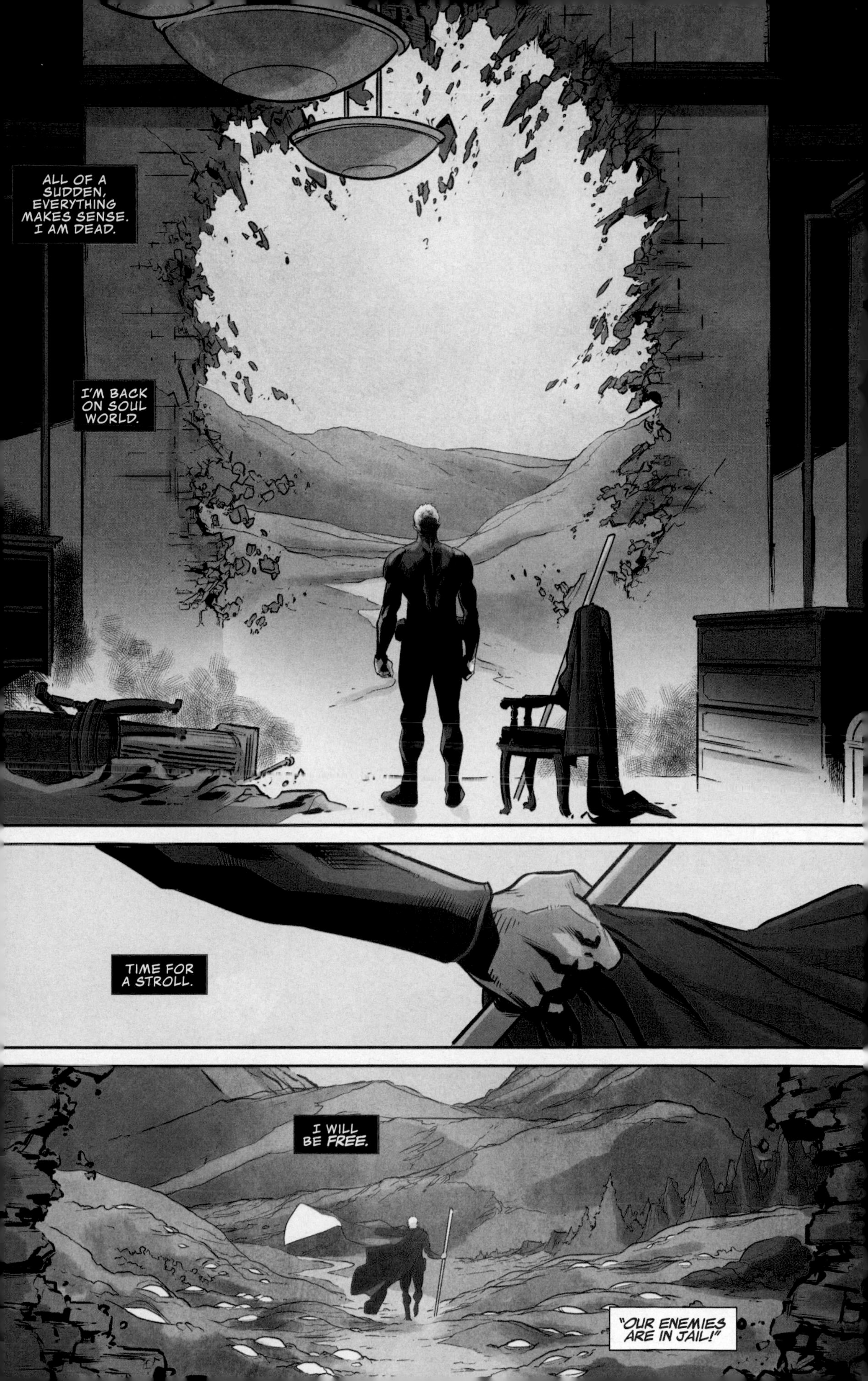
ALL OF A SUDDEN, EVERYTHING MAKES SENSE. I AM DEAD.
I'M BACK ON SOUL WORLD.
TIME FOR A STROLL.
I WILL BE FREE.
"OUR ENEMIES ARE IN JAIL!"

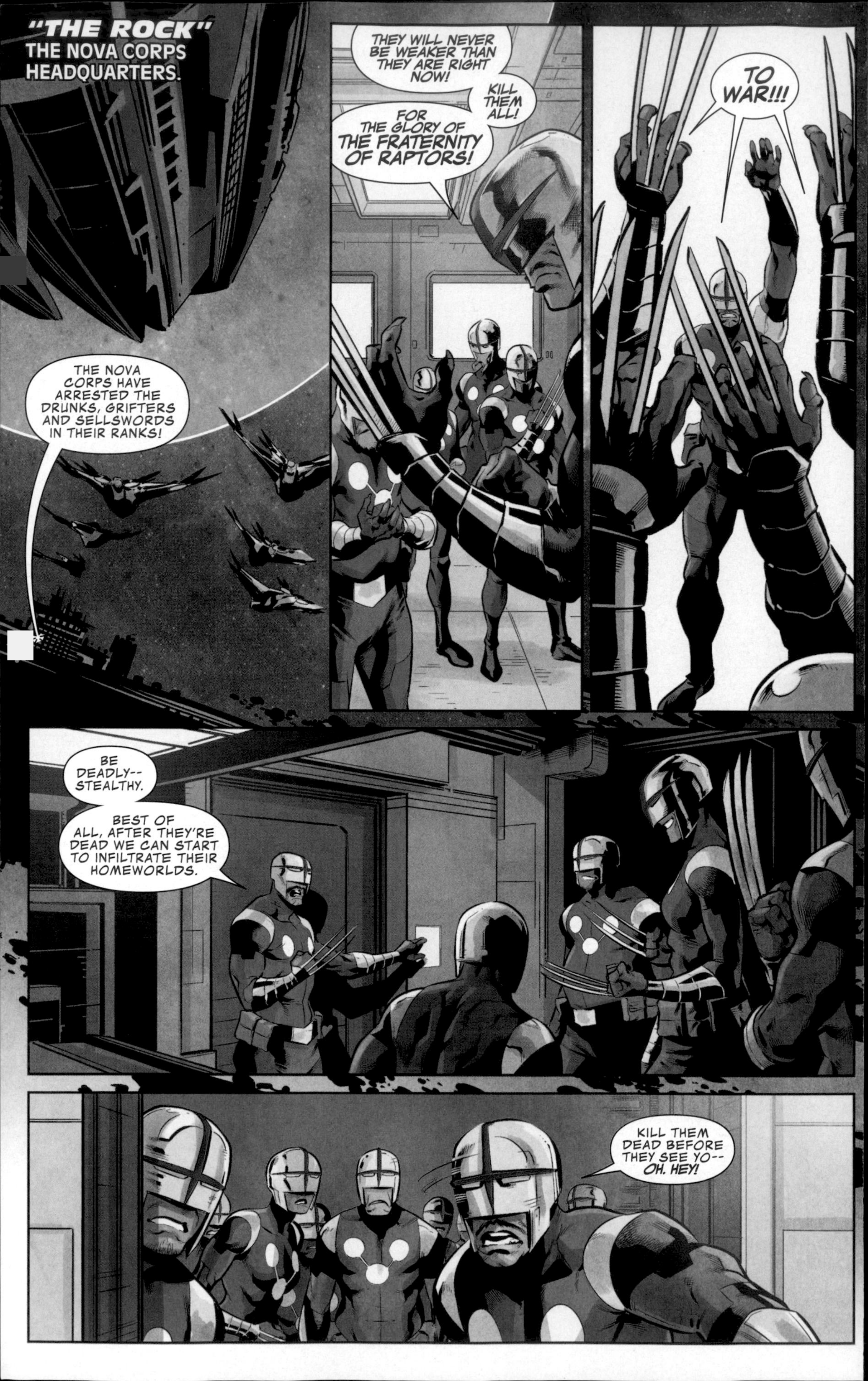
"THE ROCK"
THE NOVA CORPS HEADQUARTERS.
THE NOVA CORPS HAVE ARRESTED THE DRUNKS, GRIFTERS AND SELLSWORDS IN THEIR RANKS!
THEY WILL NEVER BE WEAKER THAN THEY ARE RIGHT NOW!
KILL THEM ALL!
FOR THE GLORY OF THE FRATERNITY OF RAPTORS!
TO WAR!!!
BE DEADLY-- STEALTHY.
BEST OF ALL, AFTER THEY'RE DEAD WE CAN START TO INFILTRATE THEIR HOMEWORLDS.
KILL THEM DEAD BEFORE THEY SEE YO-- OH. HEY!

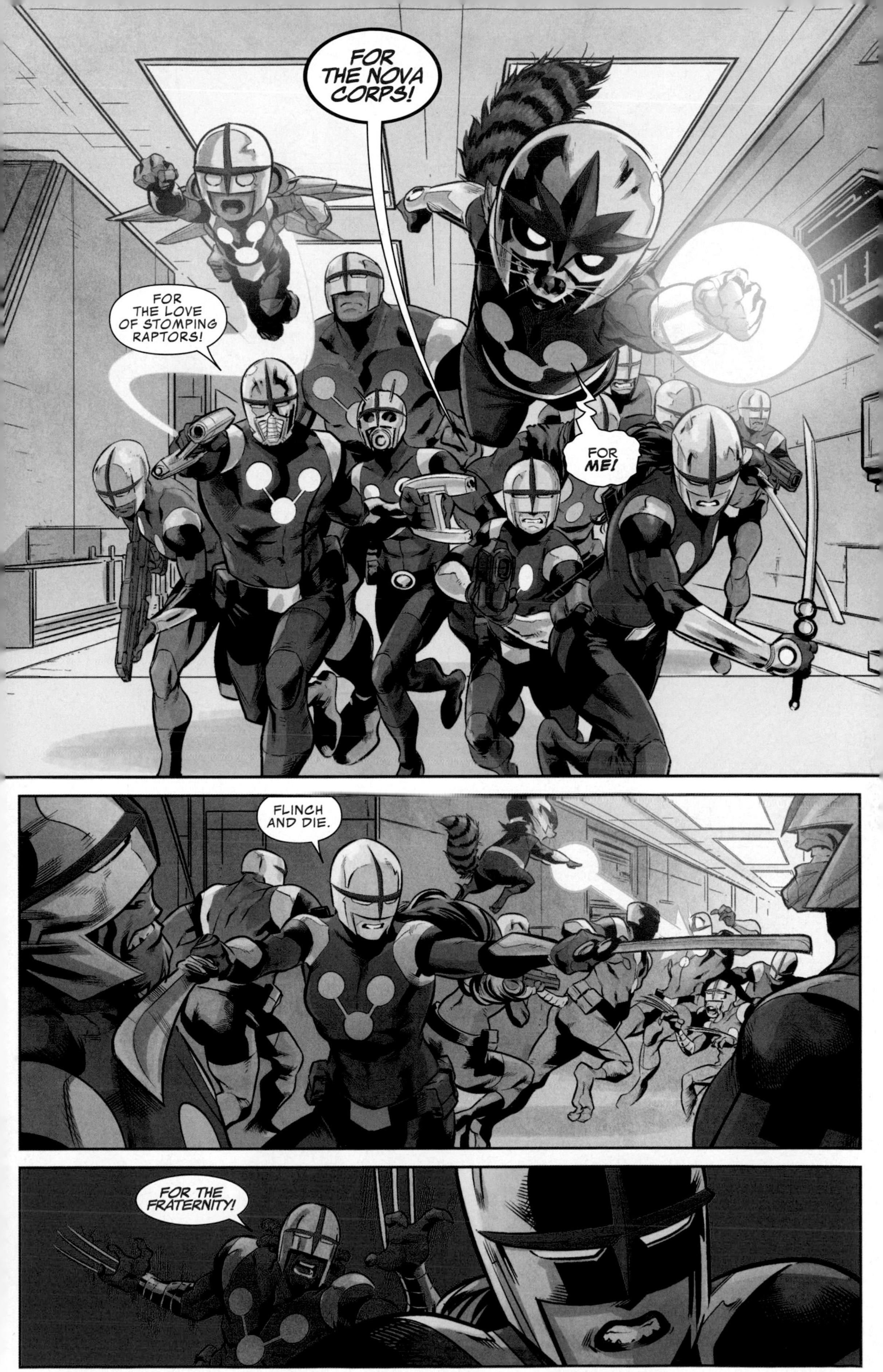
FOR THE NOVA CORPS!
FOR THE LOVE OF STOMPING RAPTORS!
FOR ME!
FLINCH AND DIE.
FOR THE FRATERNITY!

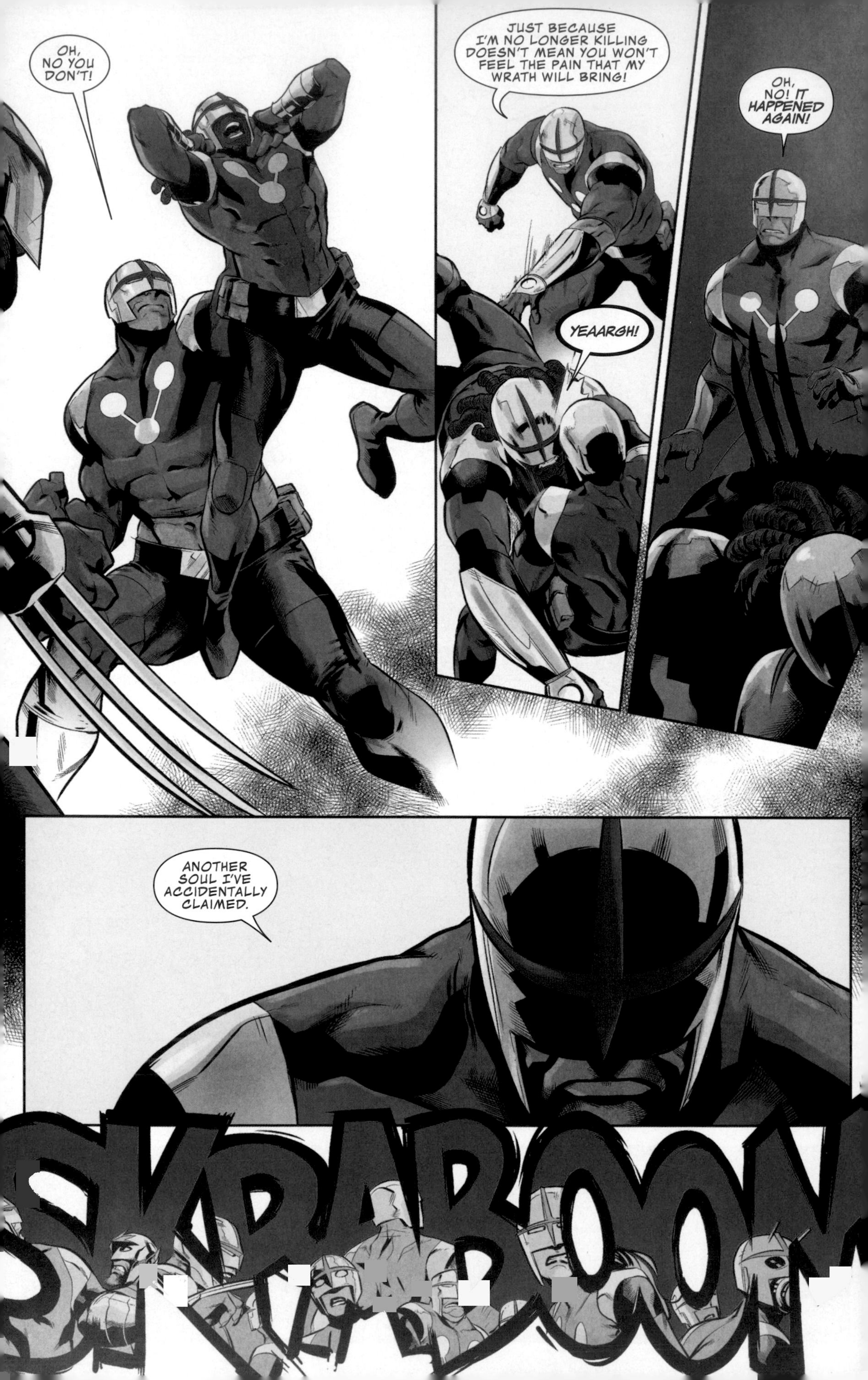
OH, NO YOU DON'T!
JUST BECAUSE I'M NO LONGER KILLING DOESN'T MEAN YOU WON'T FEEL THE PAIN THAT MY WRATH WILL BRING!
YEAARGH!
OH, NO! IT HAPPENED AGAIN!
ANOTHER SOUL I'VE ACCIDENTALLY CLAIMED.
SKRABOOOM

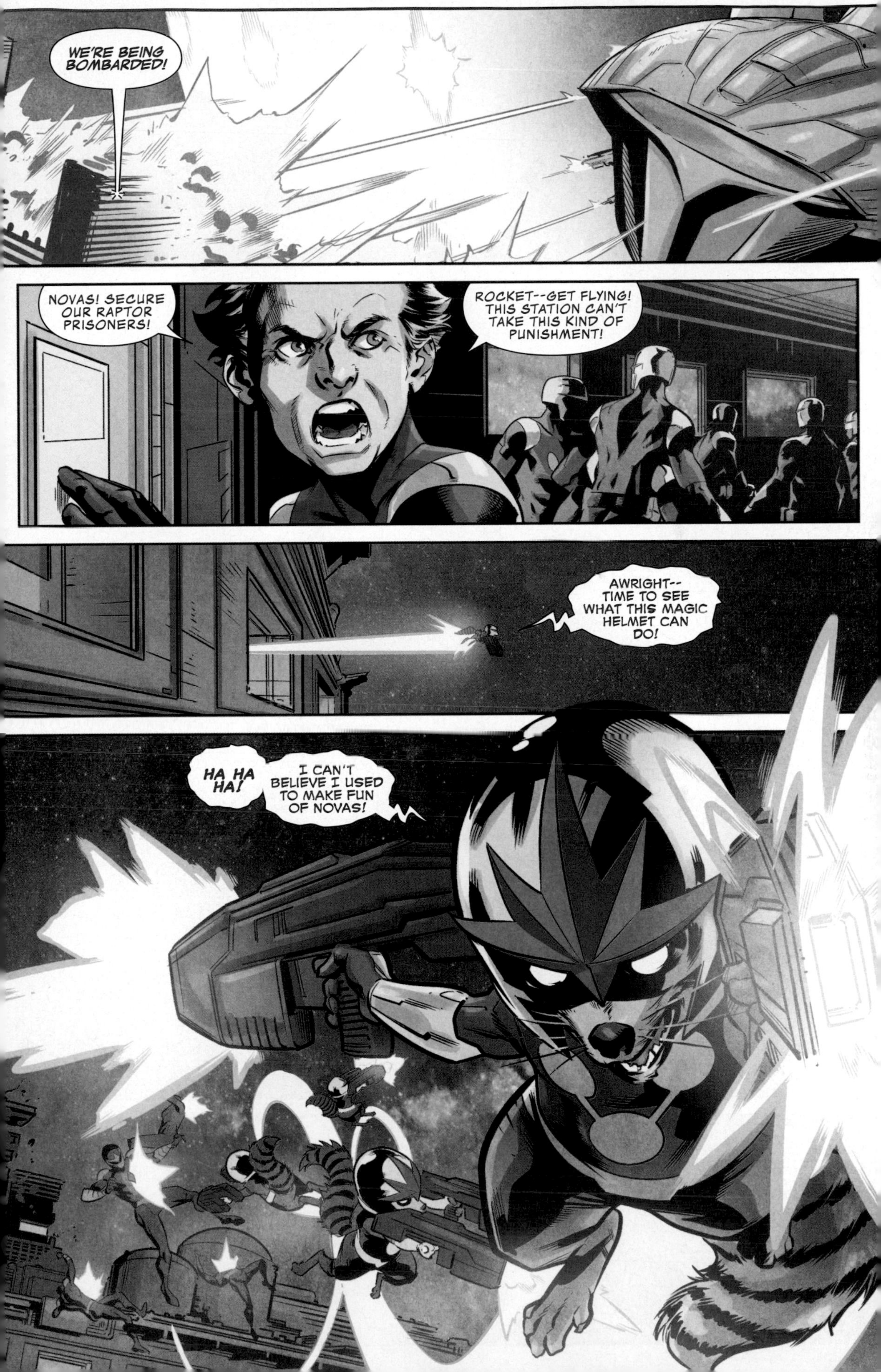
WE'RE BEING BOMBARDED!
NOVAS! SECURE OUR RAPTOR PRISONERS!
ROCKET--GET FLYING! THIS STATION CAN'T TAKE THIS KIND OF PUNISHMENT!
AWRIGHT-- TIME TO SEE WHAT THIS MAGIC HELMET CAN DO!
HA HA HA!
I CAN'T BELIEVE I USED TO MAKE FUN OF NOVAS!

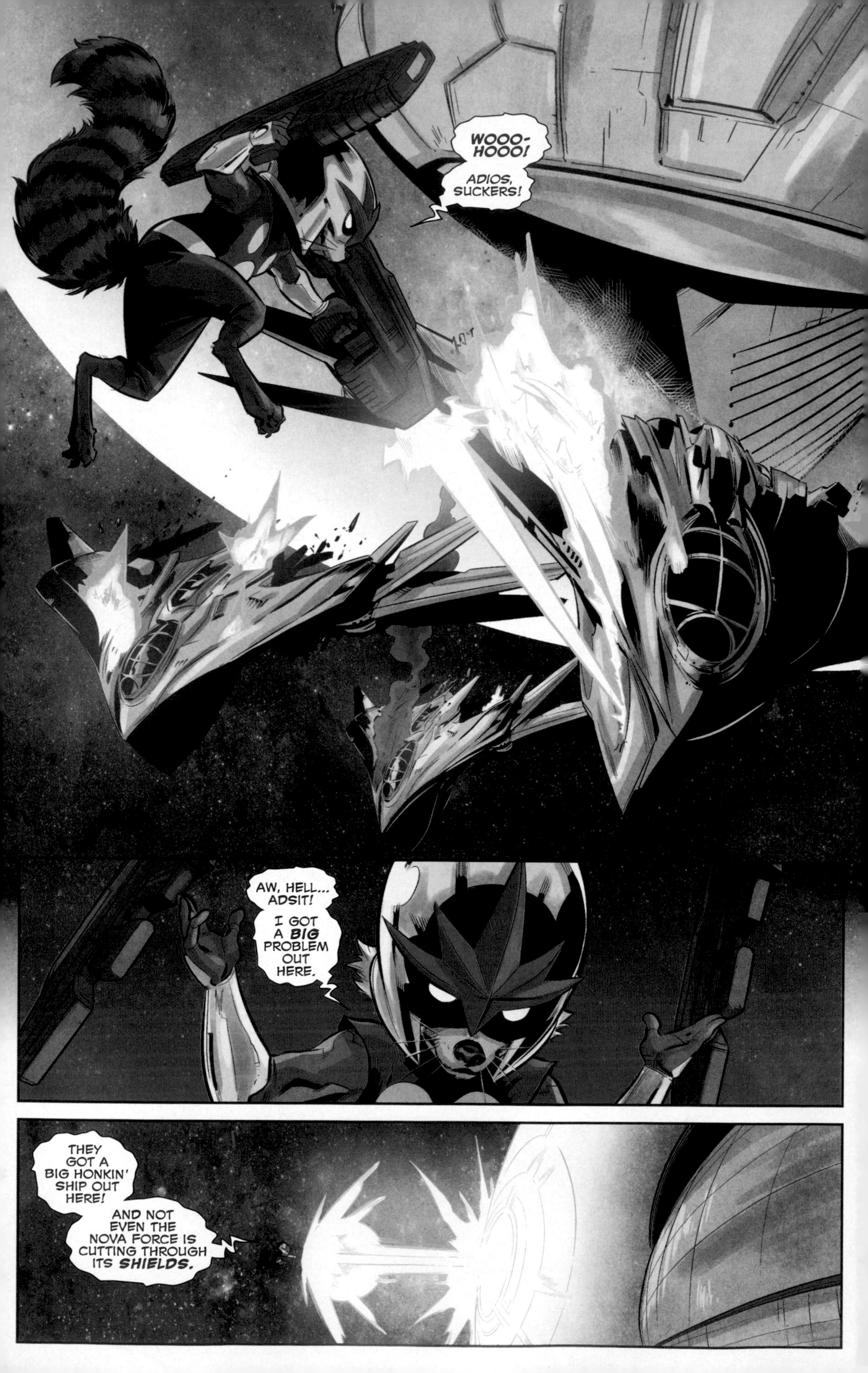
WOOO-HOOO!
ADIOS, SUCKERS!
AW, HELL... ADSIT!
I GOT A BIG PROBLEM OUT HERE.
THEY GOT A BIG HONKIN' SHIP OUT HERE!
AND NOT EVEN THE NOVA FORCE IS CUTTING THROUGH ITS SHIELDS.

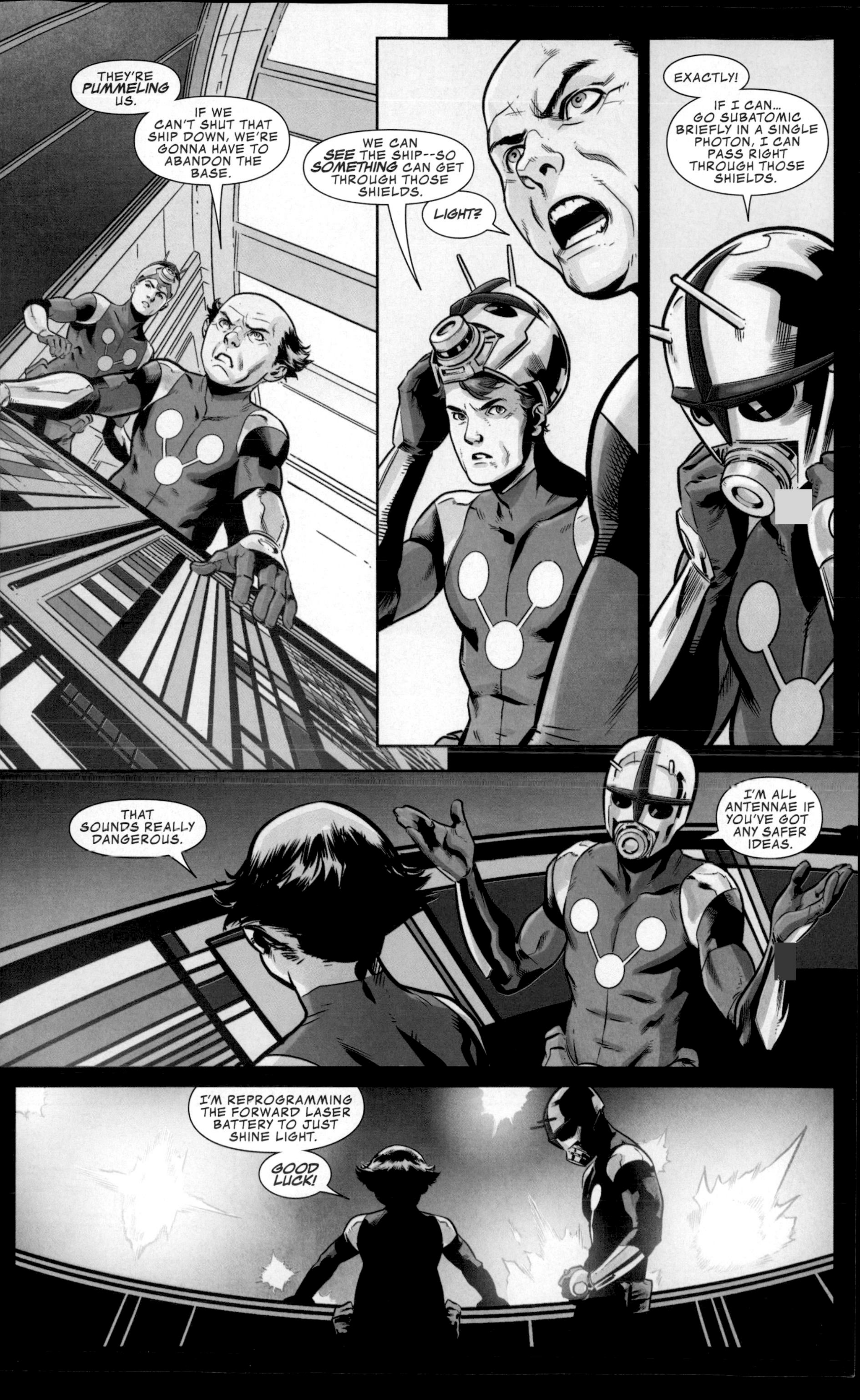
THEY'RE *PUMMELING* US.
IF WE CAN'T SHUT THAT SHIP DOWN, WE'RE GONNA HAVE TO ABANDON THE BASE.
WE CAN *SEE* THE SHIP--SO *SOMETHING* CAN GET THROUGH THOSE SHIELDS.
LIGHT?
EXACTLY!
IF I CAN... GO SUBATOMIC BRIEFLY IN A SINGLE PHOTON, I CAN PASS RIGHT THROUGH THOSE SHIELDS.
THAT SOUNDS REALLY DANGEROUS.
I'M ALL ANTENNAE IF YOU'VE GOT ANY SAFER IDEAS.
I'M REPROGRAMMING THE FORWARD LASER BATTERY TO JUST SHINE LIGHT.
GOOD LUCK!

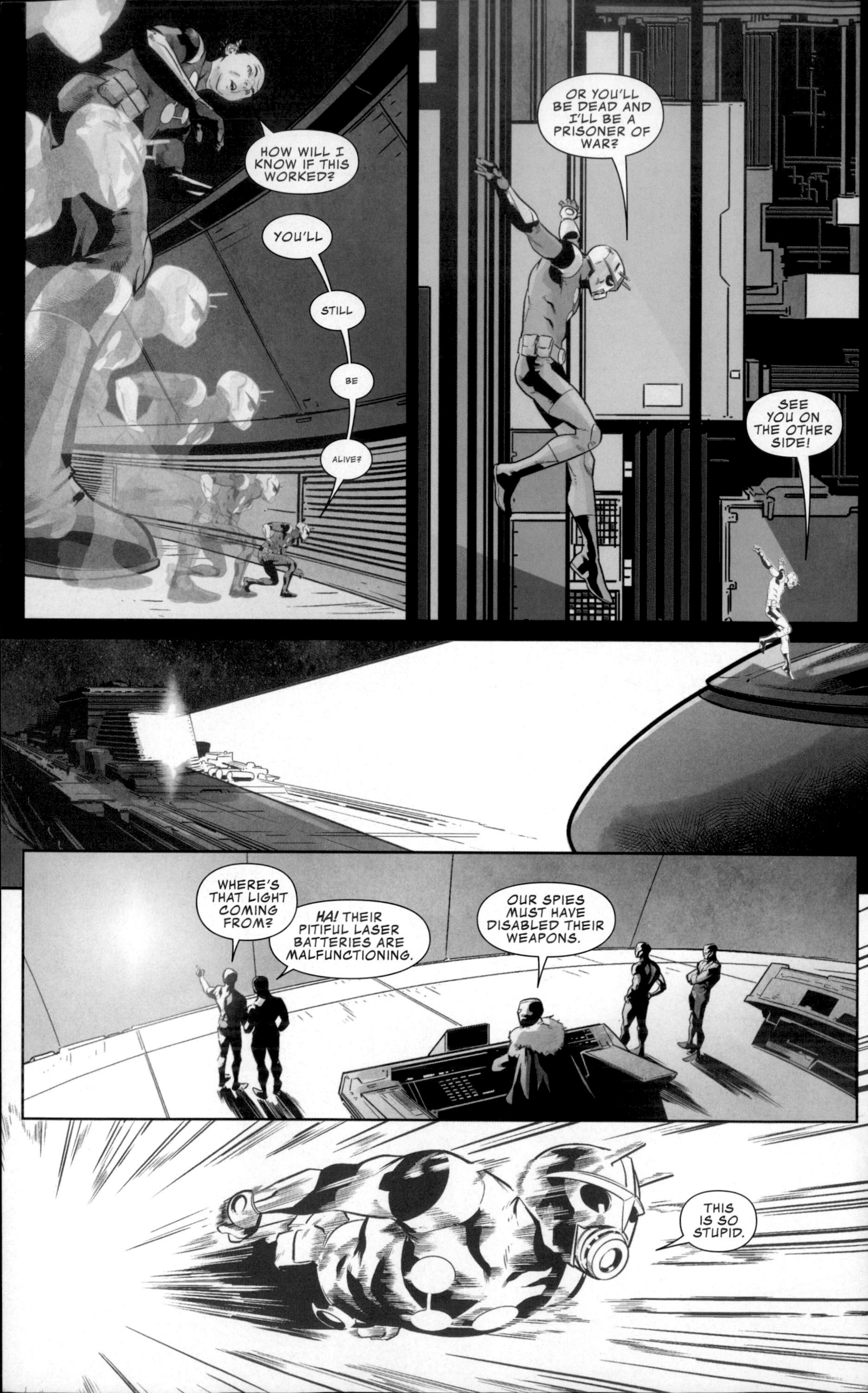
HOW WILL I KNOW IF THIS WORKED?
YOU'LL
STILL
BE
ALIVE?
OR YOU'LL BE DEAD AND I'LL BE A PRISONER OF WAR?
SEE YOU ON THE OTHER SIDE!
WHERE'S THAT LIGHT COMING FROM?
HA! THEIR PITIFUL LASER BATTERIES ARE MALFUNCTIONING.
OUR SPIES MUST HAVE DISABLED THEIR WEAPONS.
THIS IS SO STUPID.

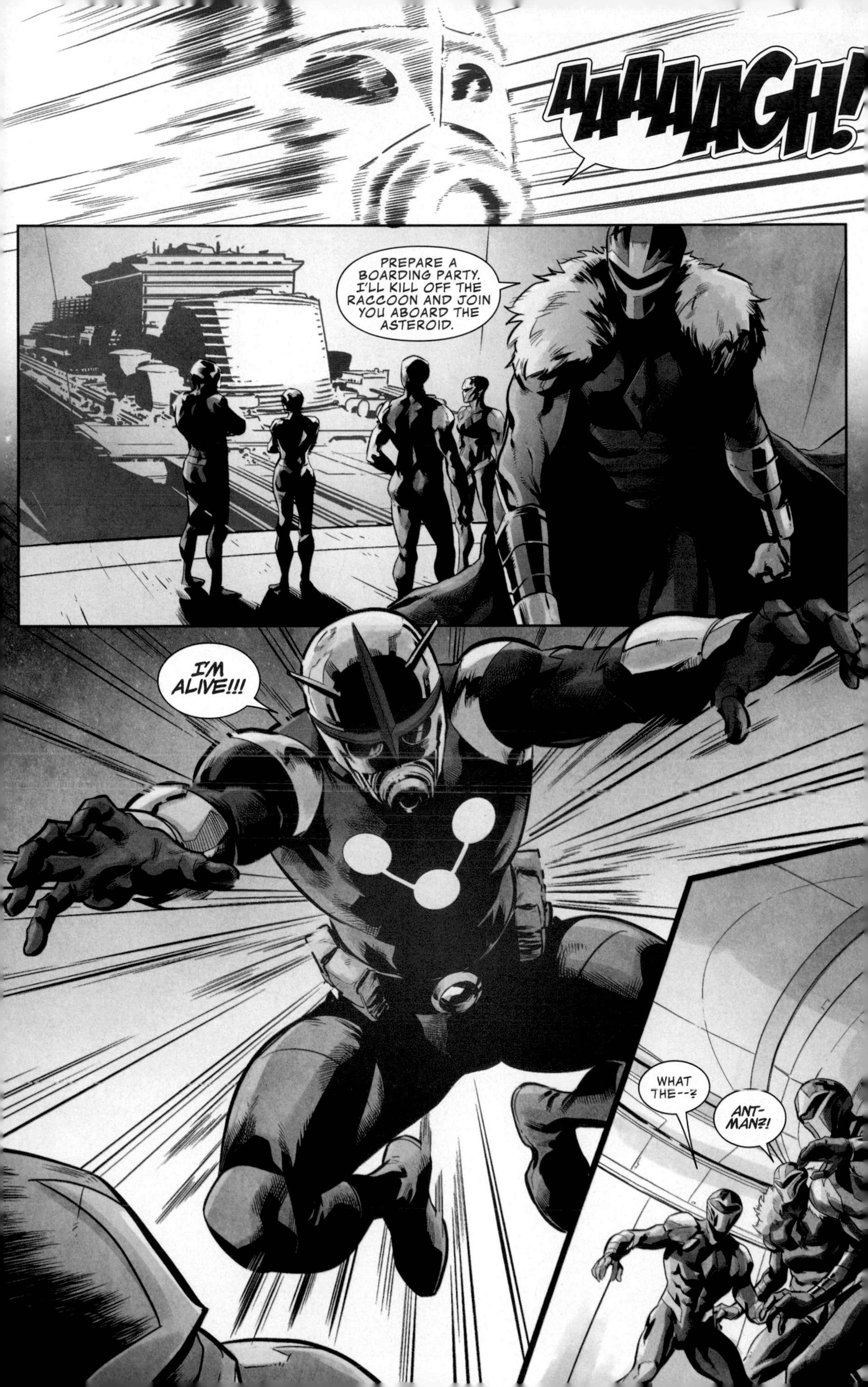
AAAAAGH!
PREPARE A BOARDING PARTY. I'LL KILL OFF THE RACCOON AND JOIN YOU ABOARD THE ASTEROID.
I'M ALIVE!!!
WHAT THE--?
ANT-MAN?!

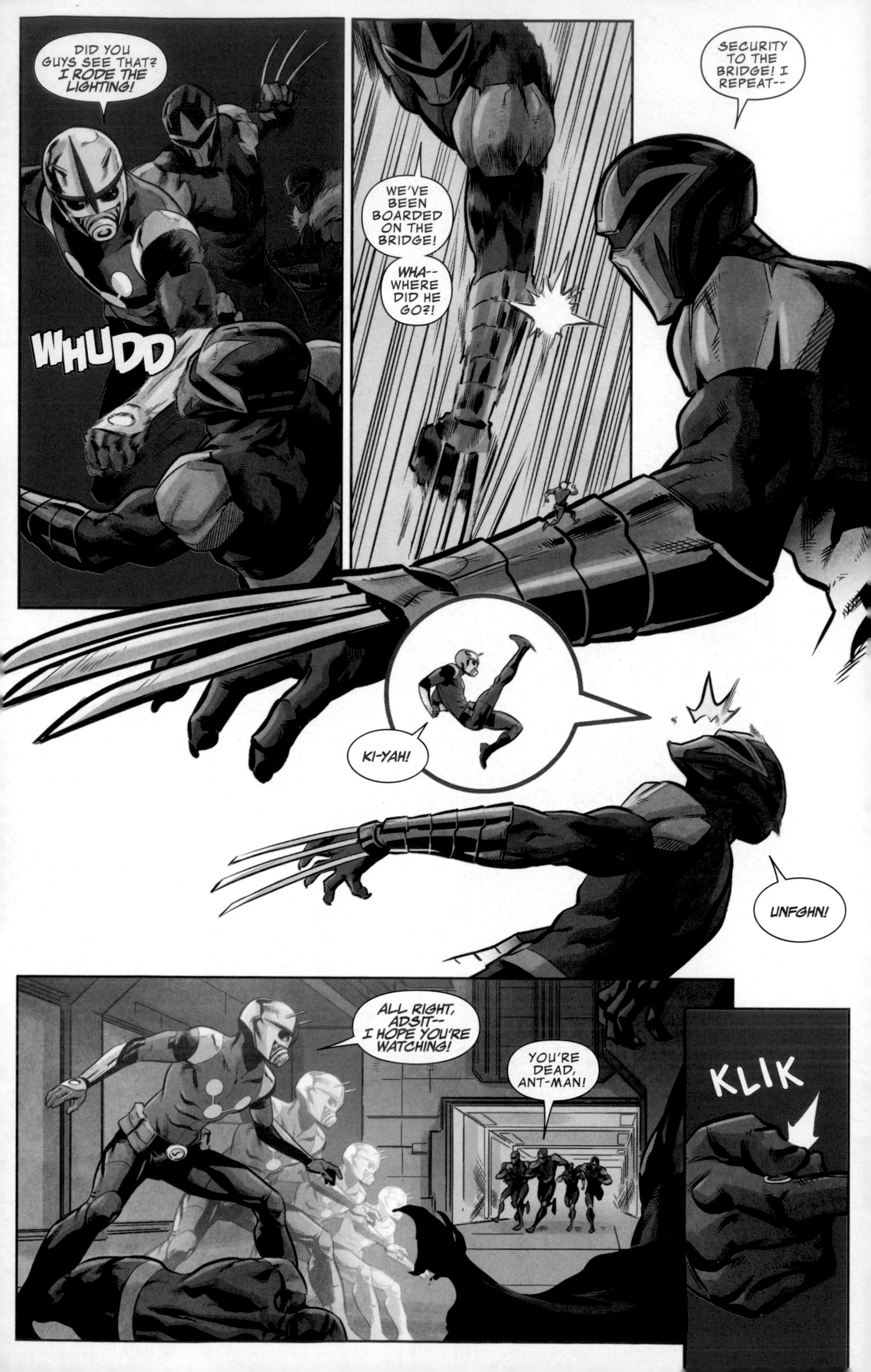
DID YOU GUYS SEE THAT? I RODE THE LIGHTING!
WHUDD
SECURITY TO THE BRIDGE! I REPEAT--
WE'VE BEEN BOARDED ON THE BRIDGE!
WHA-- WHERE DID HE GO?!
KI-YAH!
UNFGHN!
ALL RIGHT, ADSIT-- I HOPE YOU'RE WATCHING!
YOU'RE DEAD, ANT-MAN!
KLIK

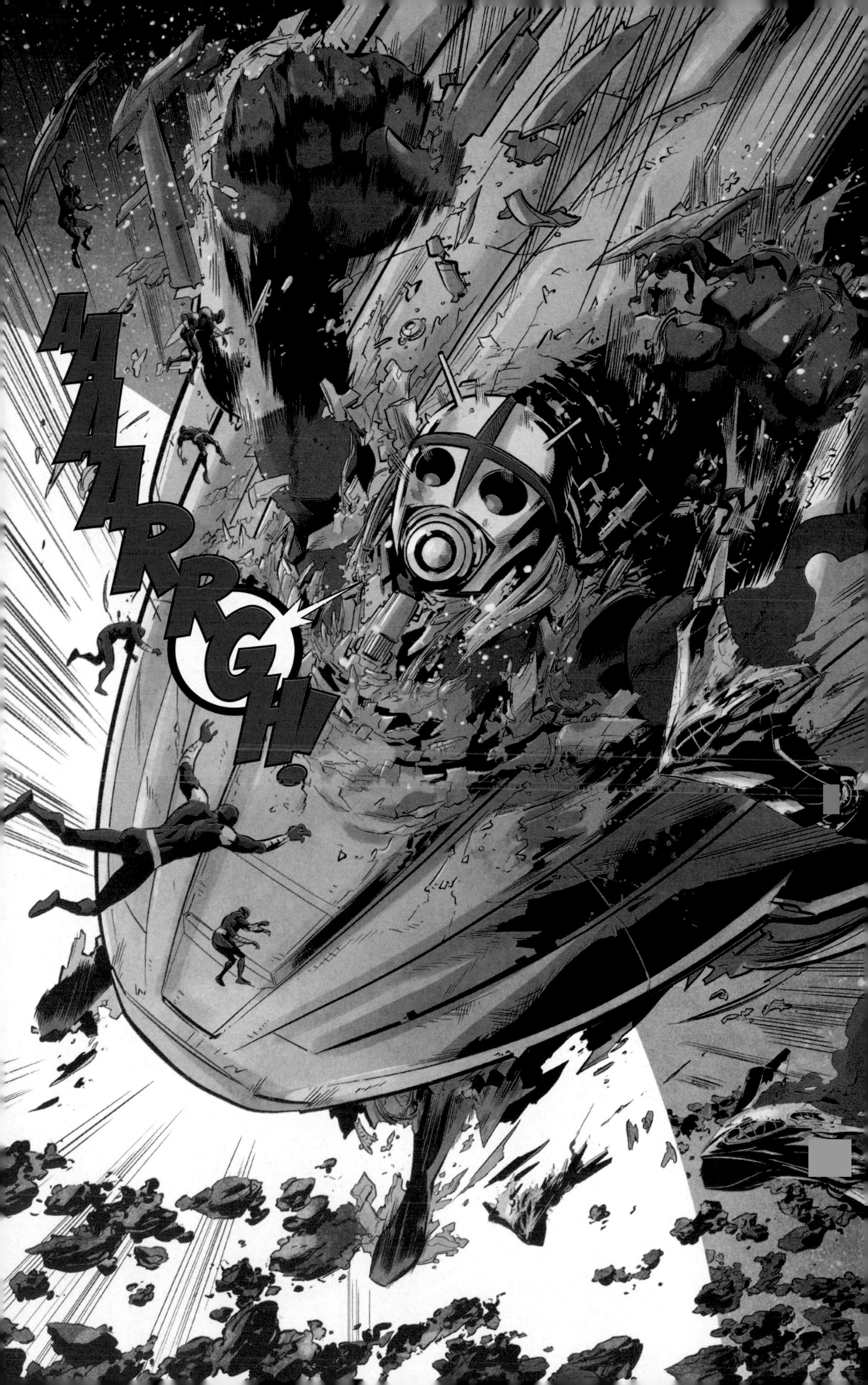
AAARRGH!

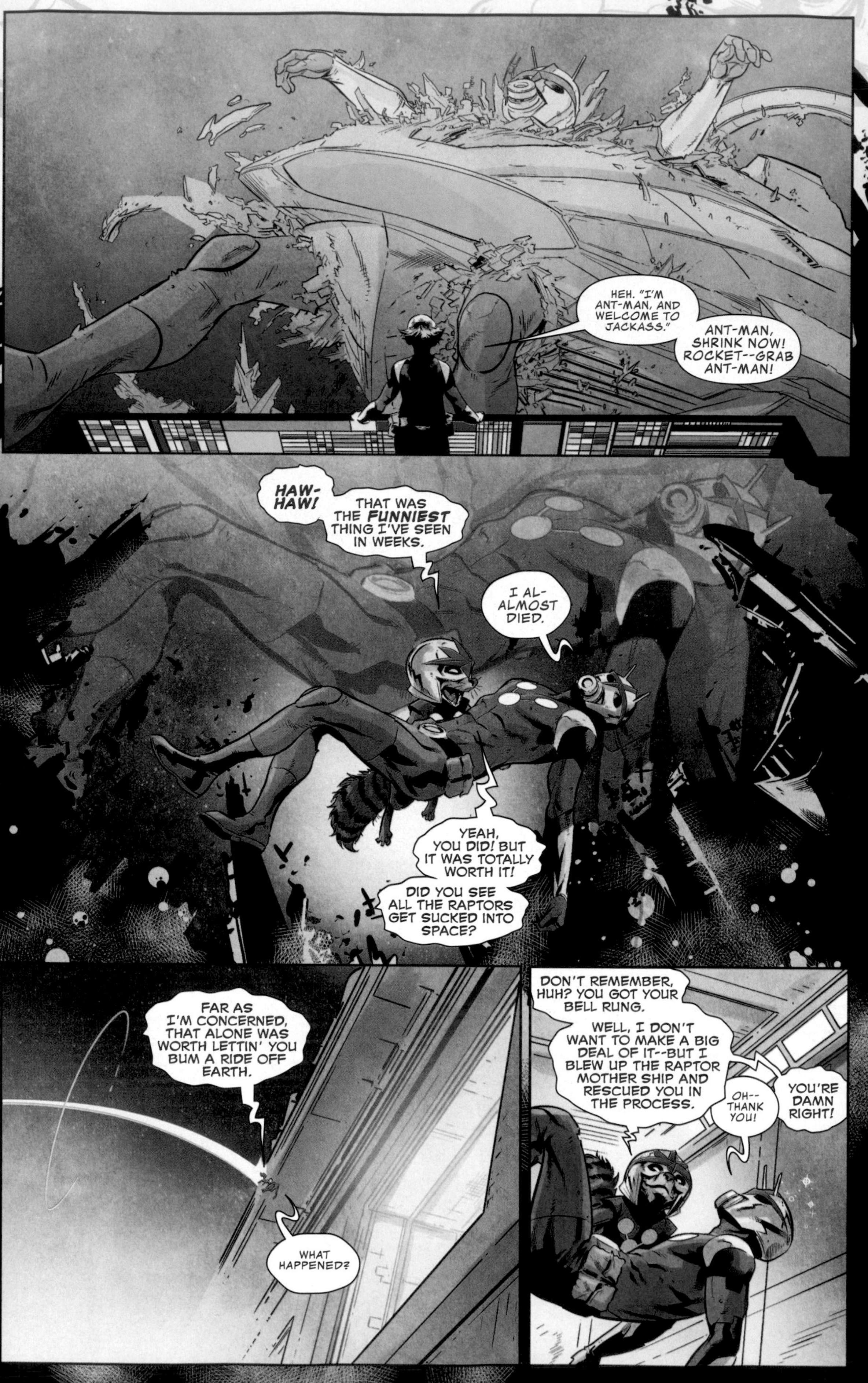
HEH. "I'M ANT-MAN, AND WELCOME TO JACKASS."
ANT-MAN, SHRINK NOW! ROCKET--GRAB ANT-MAN!
HAW-HAW!
THAT WAS THE FUNNIEST THING I'VE SEEN IN WEEKS.
I AL- ALMOST DIED.
YEAH, YOU DID! BUT IT WAS TOTALLY WORTH IT!
DID YOU SEE ALL THE RAPTORS GET SUCKED INTO SPACE?
FAR AS I'M CONCERNED, THAT ALONE WAS WORTH LETTIN' YOU BUM A RIDE OFF EARTH.
WHAT HAPPENED?
DON'T REMEMBER, HUH? YOU GOT YOUR BELL RUNG.
WELL, I DON'T WANT TO MAKE A BIG DEAL OF IT--BUT I BLEW UP THE RAPTOR MOTHER SHIP AND RESCUED YOU IN THE PROCESS.
OH-- THANK YOU!
YOU'RE DAMN RIGHT!

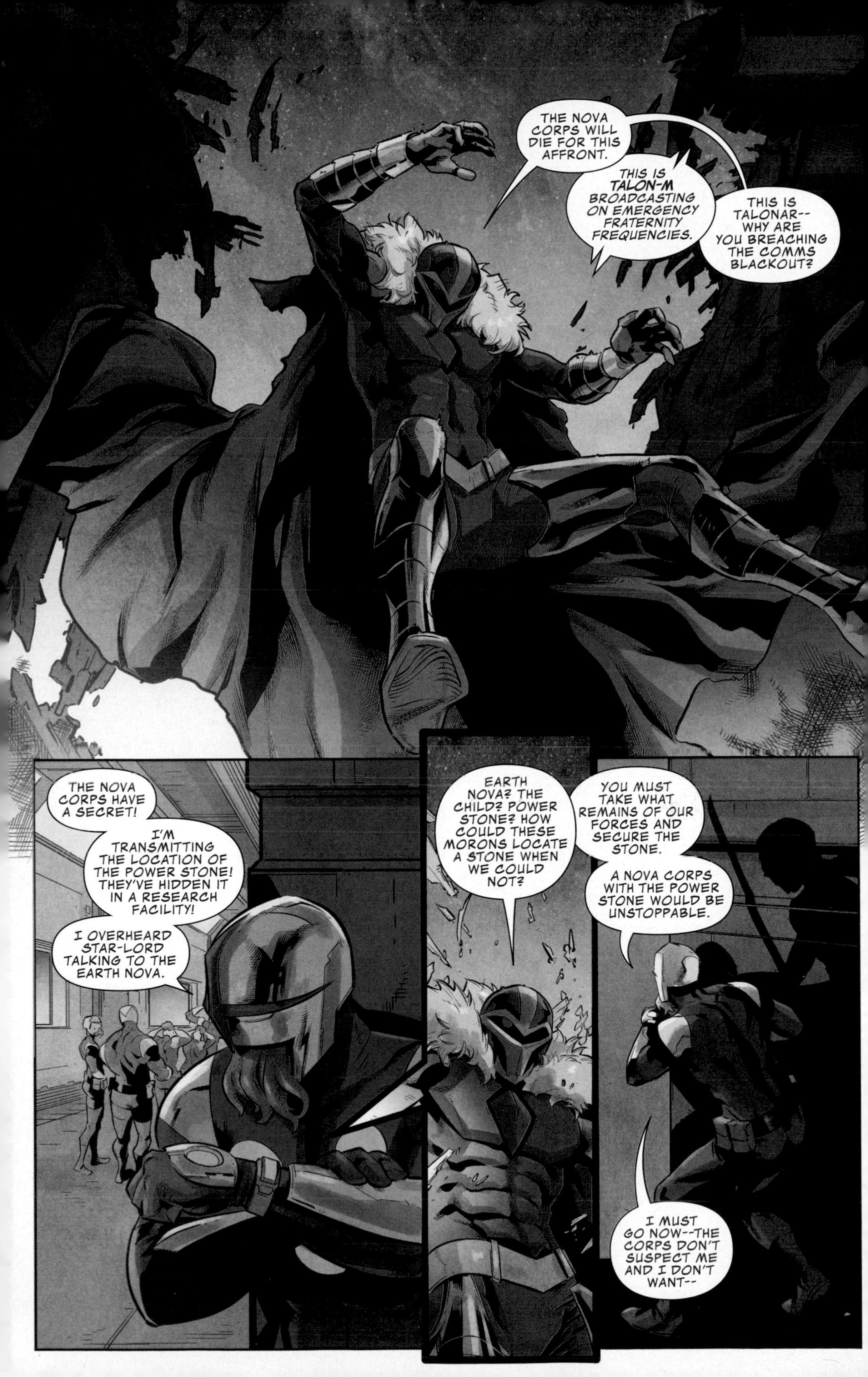
THE NOVA CORPS WILL DIE FOR THIS AFFRONT.
THIS IS TALON-M BROADCASTING ON EMERGENCY FRATERNITY FREQUENCIES.
THIS IS TALONAR-- WHY ARE YOU BREACHING THE COMMS BLACKOUT?
THE NOVA CORPS HAVE A SECRET!
I'M TRANSMITTING THE LOCATION OF THE POWER STONE! THEY'VE HIDDEN IT IN A RESEARCH FACILITY!
I OVERHEARD STAR-LORD TALKING TO THE EARTH NOVA.
EARTH NOVA? THE CHILD? POWER STONE? HOW COULD THESE MORONS LOCATE A STONE WHEN WE COULD NOT?
YOU MUST TAKE WHAT REMAINS OF OUR FORCES AND SECURE THE STONE.
A NOVA CORPS WITH THE POWER STONE WOULD BE UNSTOPPABLE.
I MUST GO NOW--THE CORPS DON'T SUSPECT ME AND I DON'T WANT--

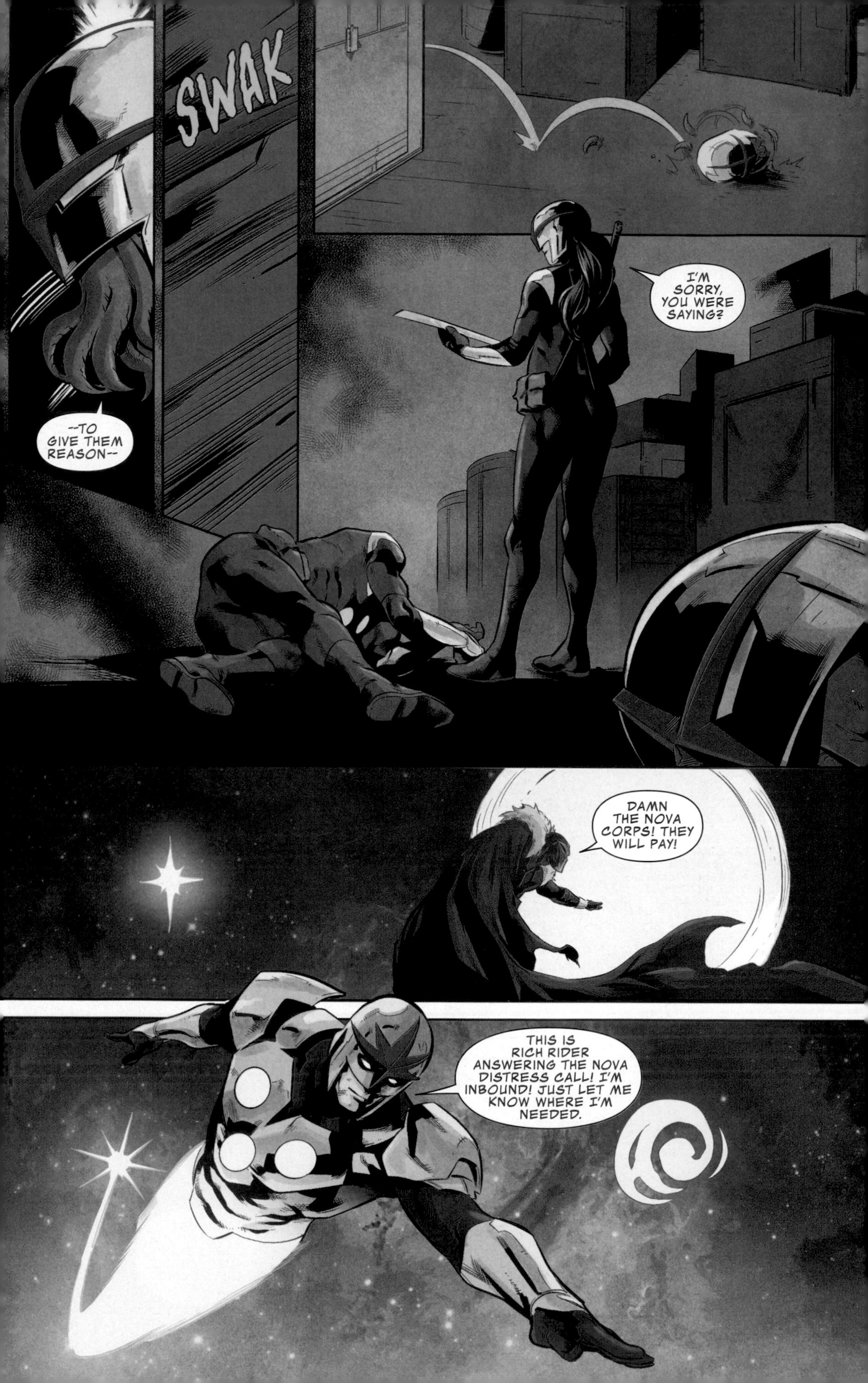
SWAK
--TO GIVE THEM REASON--
I'M SORRY, YOU WERE SAYING?
DAMN THE NOVA CORPS! THEY WILL PAY!
THIS IS RICH RIDER ANSWERING THE NOVA DISTRESS CALL! I'M INBOUND! JUST LET ME KNOW WHERE I'M NEEDED.

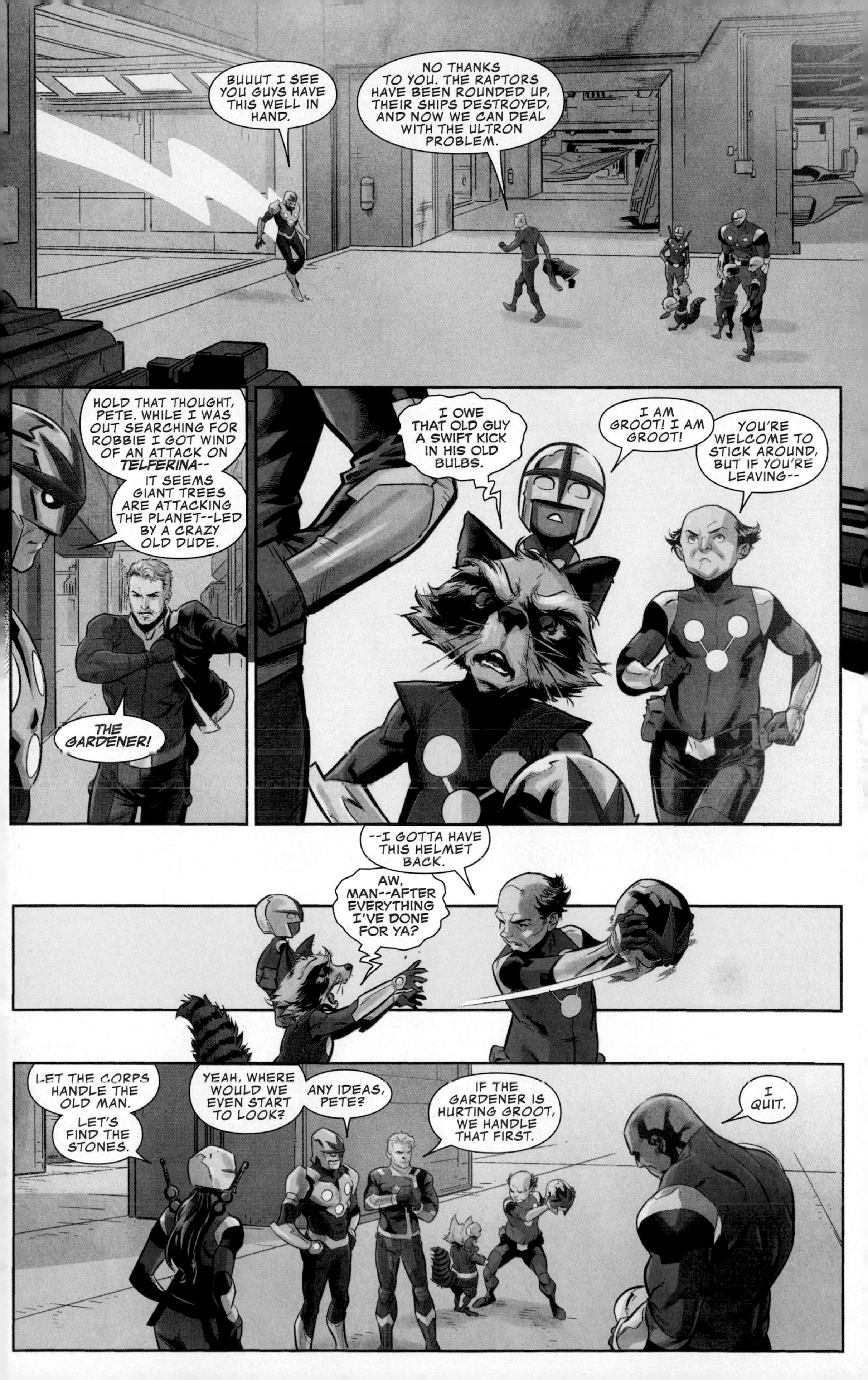
BUUUT I SEE YOU GUYS HAVE THIS WELL IN HAND.
NO THANKS TO YOU. THE RAPTORS HAVE BEEN ROUNDED UP, THEIR SHIPS DESTROYED, AND NOW WE CAN DEAL WITH THE ULTRON PROBLEM.
HOLD THAT THOUGHT, PETE. WHILE I WAS OUT SEARCHING FOR ROBBIE I GOT WIND OF AN ATTACK ON TELFERINA--
IT SEEMS GIANT TREES ARE ATTACKING THE PLANET--LED BY A CRAZY OLD DUDE.
THE GARDENER!
I OWE THAT OLD GUY A SWIFT KICK IN HIS OLD BULBS.
I AM GROOT! I AM GROOT!
YOU'RE WELCOME TO STICK AROUND, BUT IF YOU'RE LEAVING--
--I GOTTA HAVE THIS HELMET BACK.
AW, MAN--AFTER EVERYTHING I'VE DONE FOR YA?
LET THE CORPS HANDLE THE OLD MAN.
LET'S FIND THE STONES.
YEAH, WHERE WOULD WE EVEN START TO LOOK?
ANY IDEAS, PETE?
IF THE GARDENER IS HURTING GROOT, WE HANDLE THAT FIRST.
I QUIT.

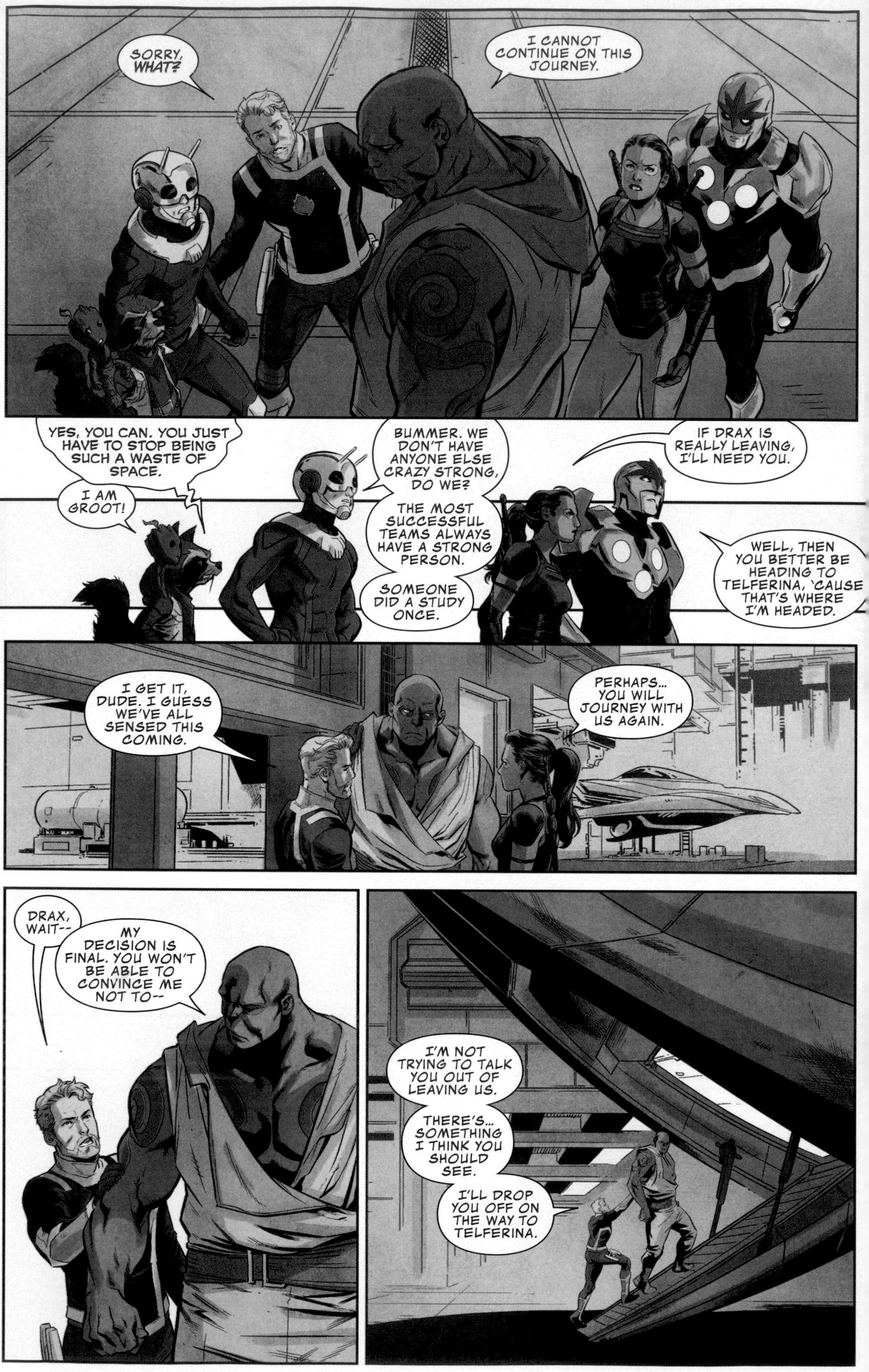
SORRY, WHAT?
I CANNOT CONTINUE ON THIS JOURNEY.
YES, YOU CAN. YOU JUST HAVE TO STOP BEING SUCH A WASTE OF SPACE.
I AM GROOT!
BUMMER. WE DON'T HAVE ANYONE ELSE CRAZY STRONG, DO WE?
THE MOST SUCCESSFUL TEAMS ALWAYS HAVE A STRONG PERSON.
SOMEONE DID A STUDY ONCE.
IF DRAX IS REALLY LEAVING, I'LL NEED YOU.
WELL, THEN YOU BETTER BE HEADING TO TELFERINA, 'CAUSE THAT'S WHERE I'M HEADED.
I GET IT, DUDE. I GUESS WE'VE ALL SENSED THIS COMING.
PERHAPS... YOU WILL JOURNEY WITH US AGAIN.
DRAX, WAIT--
MY DECISION IS FINAL. YOU WON'T BE ABLE TO CONVINCE ME NOT TO--
I'M NOT TRYING TO TALK YOU OUT OF LEAVING US.
THERE'S... SOMETHING I THINK YOU SHOULD SEE.
I'LL DROP YOU OFF ON THE WAY TO TELFERINA.

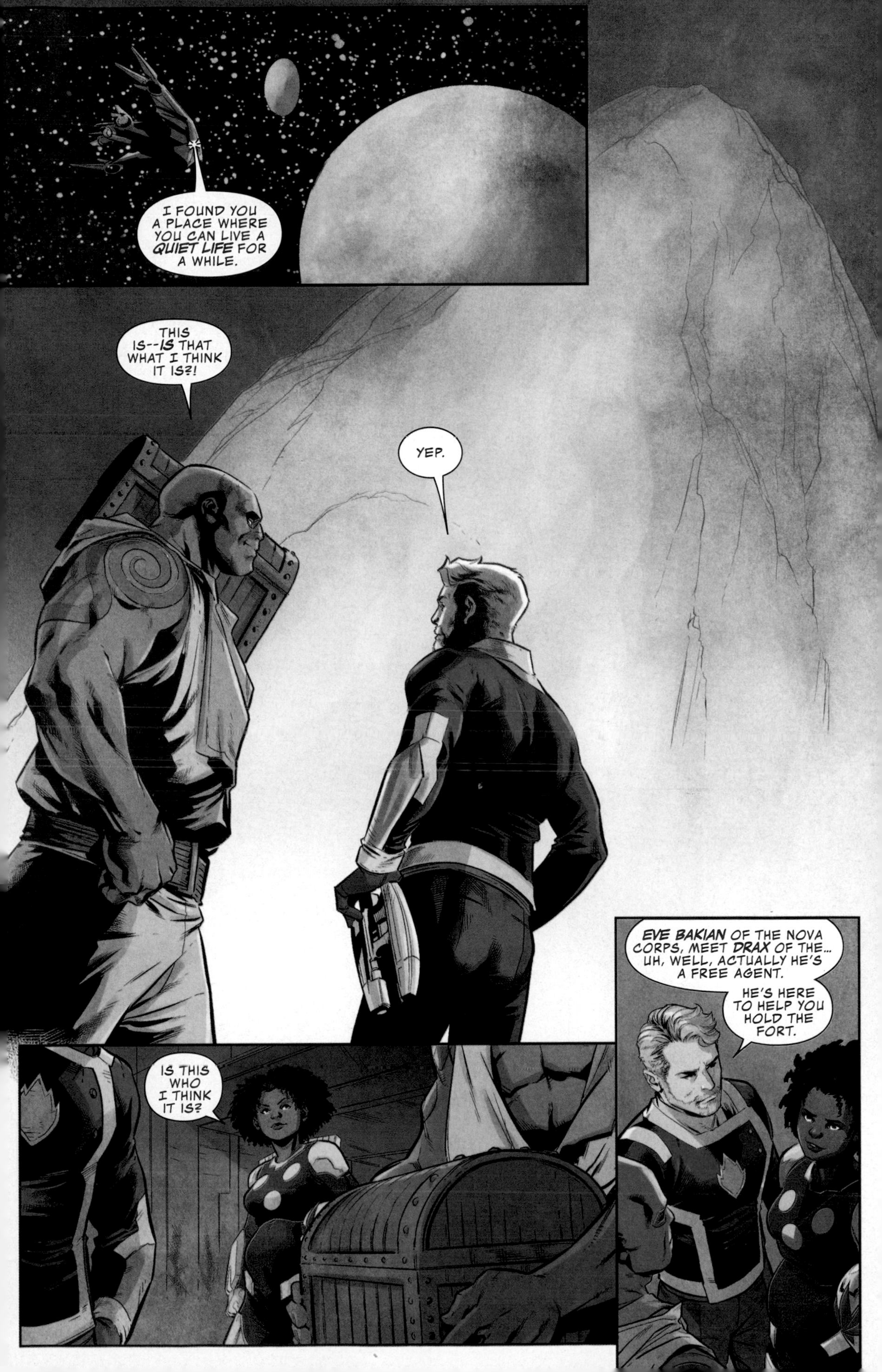
I FOUND YOU A PLACE WHERE YOU CAN LIVE A QUIET LIFE FOR A WHILE.
THIS IS--IS THAT WHAT I THINK IT IS?!
YEP.
IS THIS WHO I THINK IT IS?
EVE BAKIAN OF THE NOVA CORPS, MEET DRAX OF THE... UH, WELL, ACTUALLY HE'S A FREE AGENT.
HE'S HERE TO HELP YOU HOLD THE FORT.

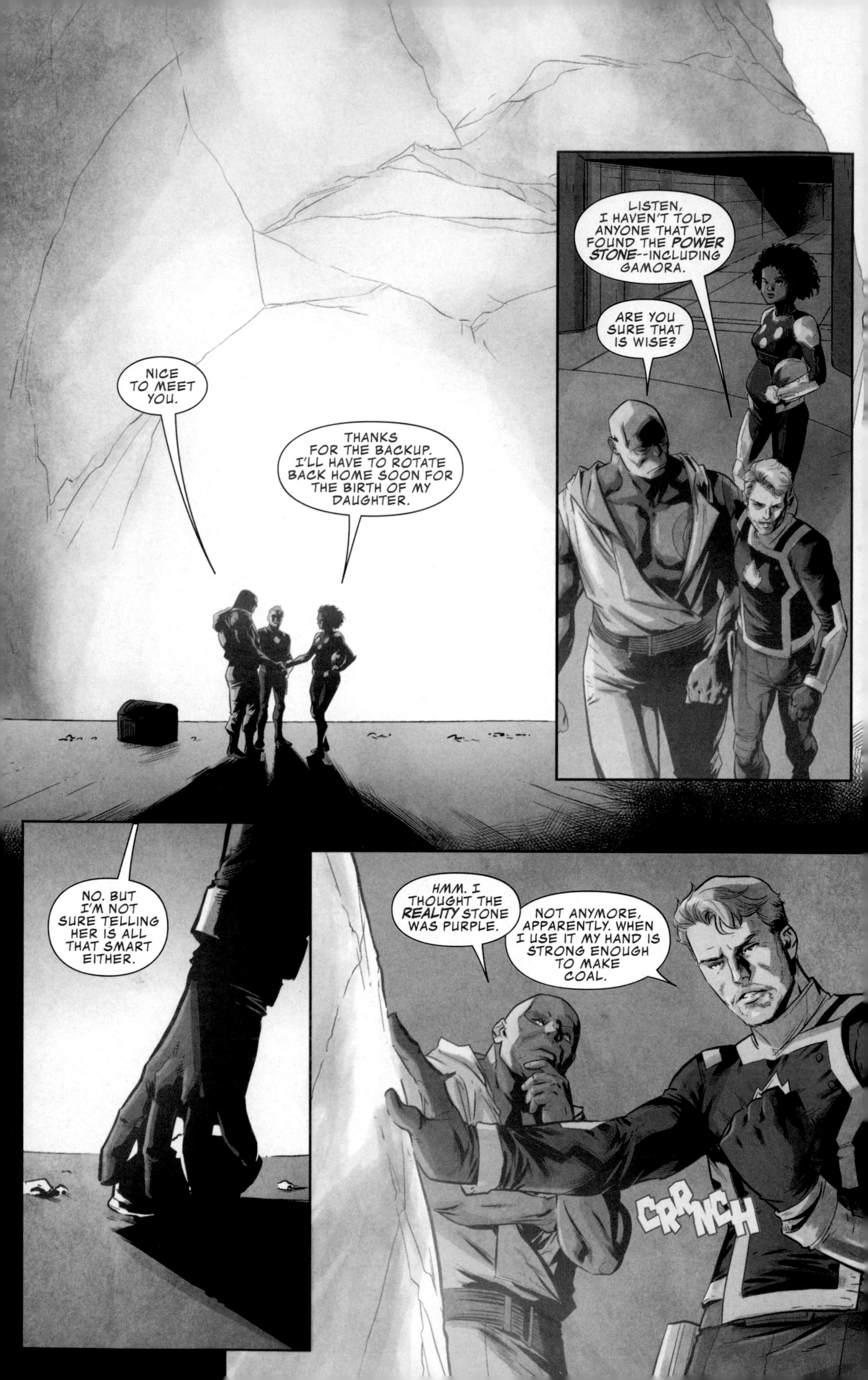
NICE TO MEET YOU.
THANKS FOR THE BACKUP. I'LL HAVE TO ROTATE BACK HOME SOON FOR THE BIRTH OF MY DAUGHTER.
LISTEN, I HAVEN'T TOLD ANYONE THAT WE FOUND THE POWER STONE--INCLUDING GAMORA.
ARE YOU SURE THAT IS WISE?
NO. BUT I'M NOT SURE TELLING HER IS ALL THAT SMART EITHER.
HMM. I THOUGHT THE REALITY STONE WAS PURPLE.
NOT ANYMORE, APPARENTLY. WHEN I USE IT MY HAND IS STRONG ENOUGH TO MAKE COAL.
CRRNCH

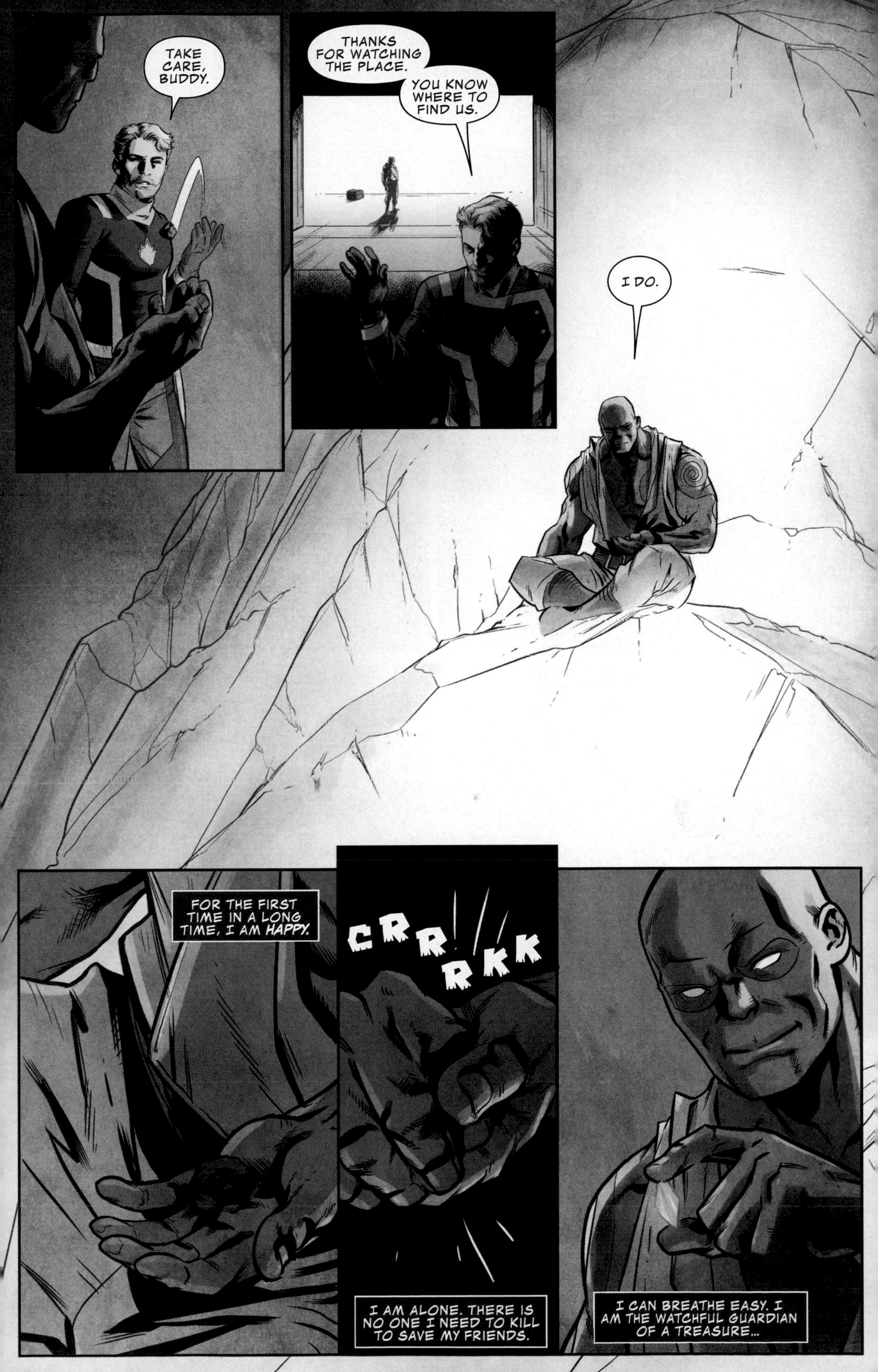
TAKE CARE, BUDDY.
THANKS FOR WATCHING THE PLACE.
YOU KNOW WHERE TO FIND US.
I DO.
FOR THE FIRST TIME IN A LONG TIME, I AM HAPPY.
CRRRKK
I AM ALONE. THERE IS NO ONE I NEED TO KILL TO SAVE MY FRIENDS.
I CAN BREATHE EASY. I AM THE WATCHFUL GUARDIAN OF A TREASURE...

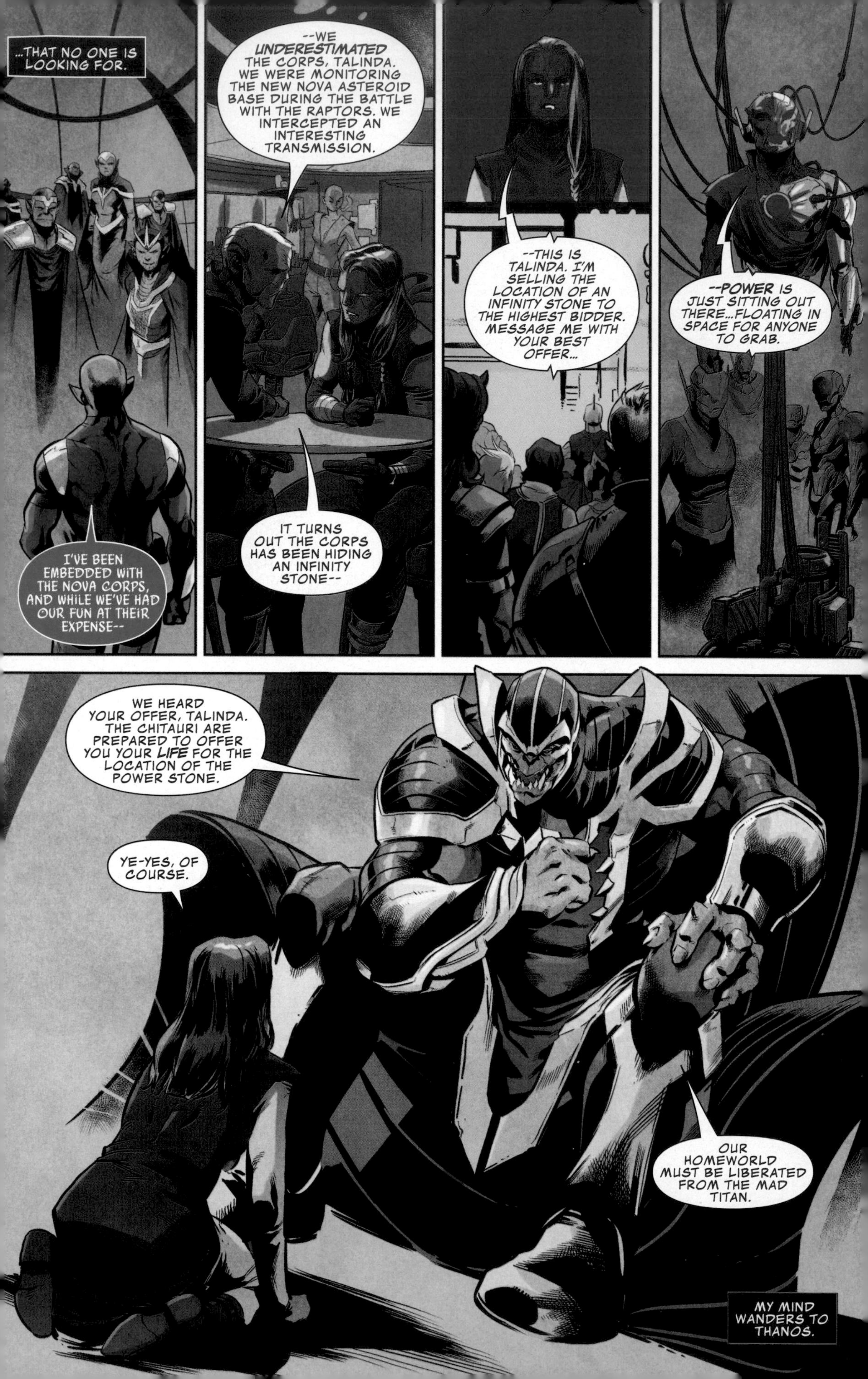
...THAT NO ONE IS LOOKING FOR.
I'VE BEEN EMBEDDED WITH THE NOVA CORPS, AND WHILE WE'VE HAD OUR FUN AT THEIR EXPENSE--
--WE UNDERESTIMATED THE CORPS, TALINDA. WE WERE MONITORING THE NEW NOVA ASTEROID BASE DURING THE BATTLE WITH THE RAPTORS. WE INTERCEPTED AN INTERESTING TRANSMISSION.
IT TURNS OUT THE CORPS HAS BEEN HIDING AN INFINITY STONE--
--THIS IS TALINDA. I'M SELLING THE LOCATION OF AN INFINITY STONE TO THE HIGHEST BIDDER. MESSAGE ME WITH YOUR BEST OFFER...
--POWER IS JUST SITTING OUT THERE...FLOATING IN SPACE FOR ANYONE TO GRAB.
WE HEARD YOUR OFFER, TALINDA. THE CHITAURI ARE PREPARED TO OFFER YOU YOUR LIFE FOR THE LOCATION OF THE POWER STONE.
YE-YES, OF COURSE.
OUR HOMEWORLD MUST BE LIBERATED FROM THE MAD TITAN.
MY MIND WANDERS TO THANOS.

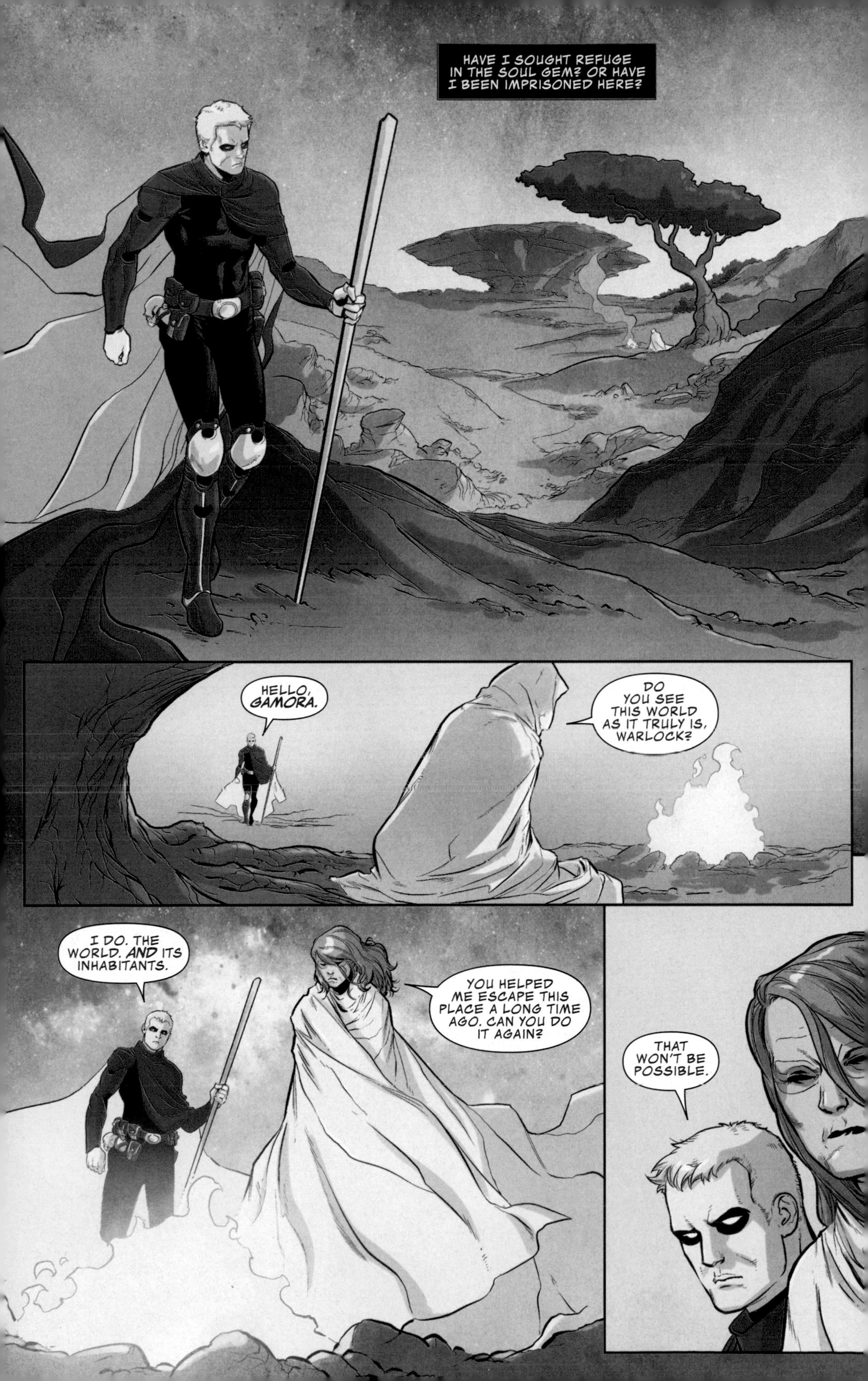
HAVE I SOUGHT REFUGE IN THE SOUL GEM? OR HAVE I BEEN IMPRISONED HERE?
HELLO, GAMORA.
DO YOU SEE THIS WORLD AS IT TRULY IS, WARLOCK?
I DO. THE WORLD. AND ITS INHABITANTS.
YOU HELPED ME ESCAPE THIS PLACE A LONG TIME AGO. CAN YOU DO IT AGAIN?
THAT WON'T BE POSSIBLE.

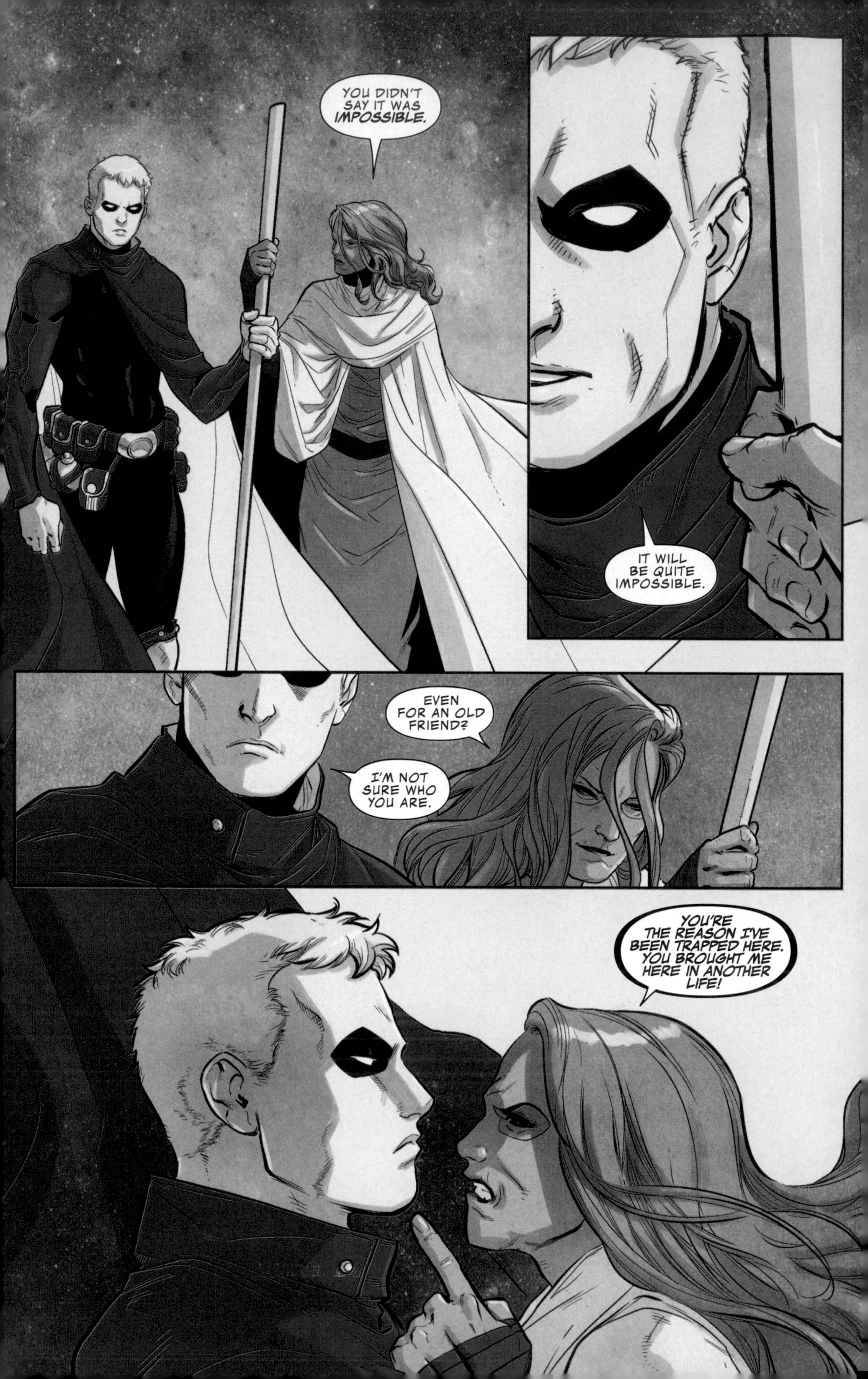
YOU DIDN'T SAY IT WAS IMPOSSIBLE.
IT WILL BE QUITE IMPOSSIBLE.
EVEN FOR AN OLD FRIEND?
I'M NOT SURE WHO YOU ARE.
YOU'RE THE REASON I'VE BEEN TRAPPED HERE. YOU BROUGHT ME HERE IN ANOTHER LIFE!

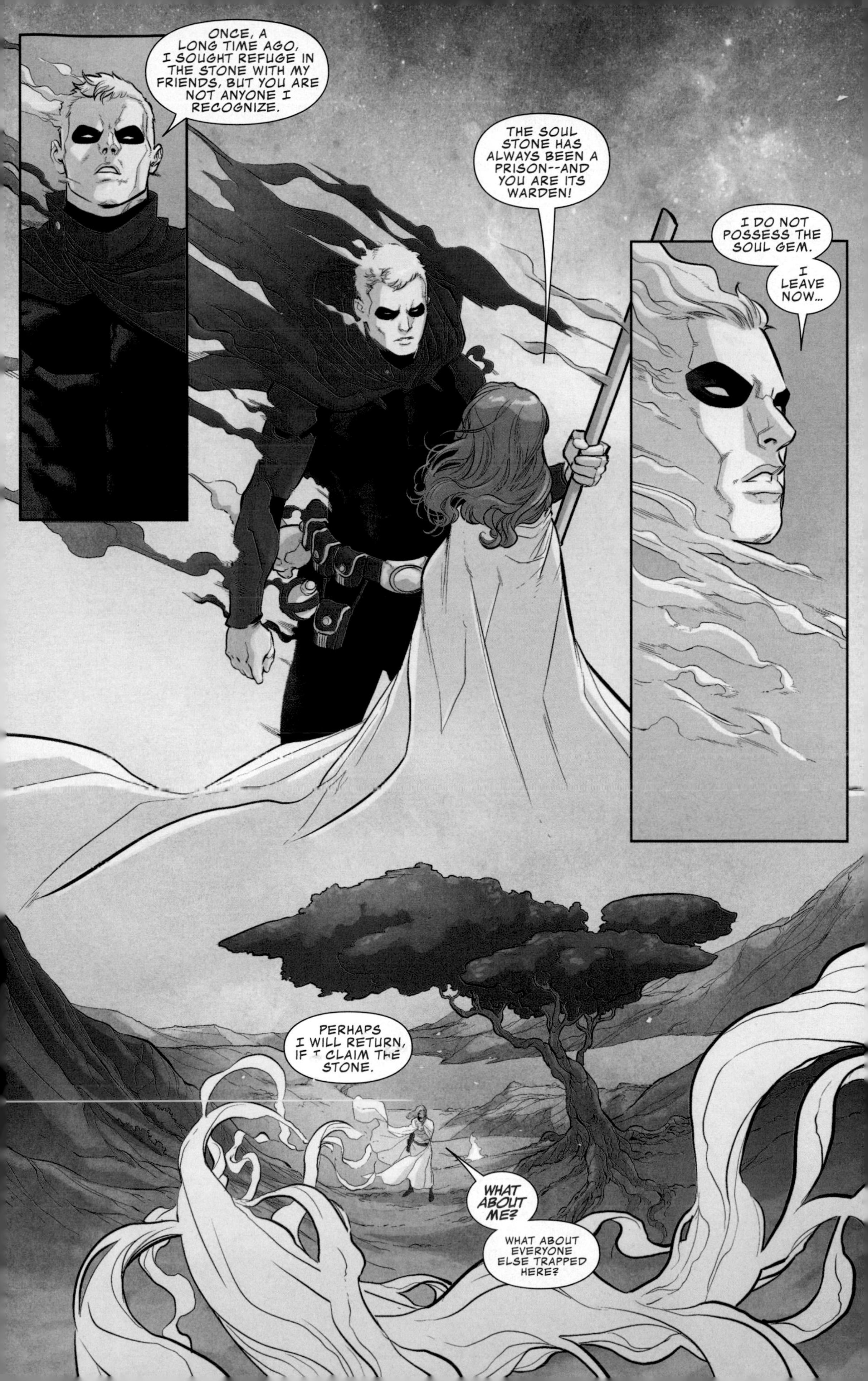
ONCE, A LONG TIME AGO, I SOUGHT REFUGE IN THE STONE WITH MY FRIENDS, BUT YOU ARE NOT ANYONE I RECOGNIZE.
THE SOUL STONE HAS ALWAYS BEEN A PRISON--AND YOU ARE ITS WARDEN!
I DO NOT POSSESS THE SOUL GEM.
I LEAVE NOW...
PERHAPS I WILL RETURN, IF I CLAIM THE STONE.
WHAT ABOUT ME?
WHAT ABOUT EVERYONE ELSE TRAPPED HERE?

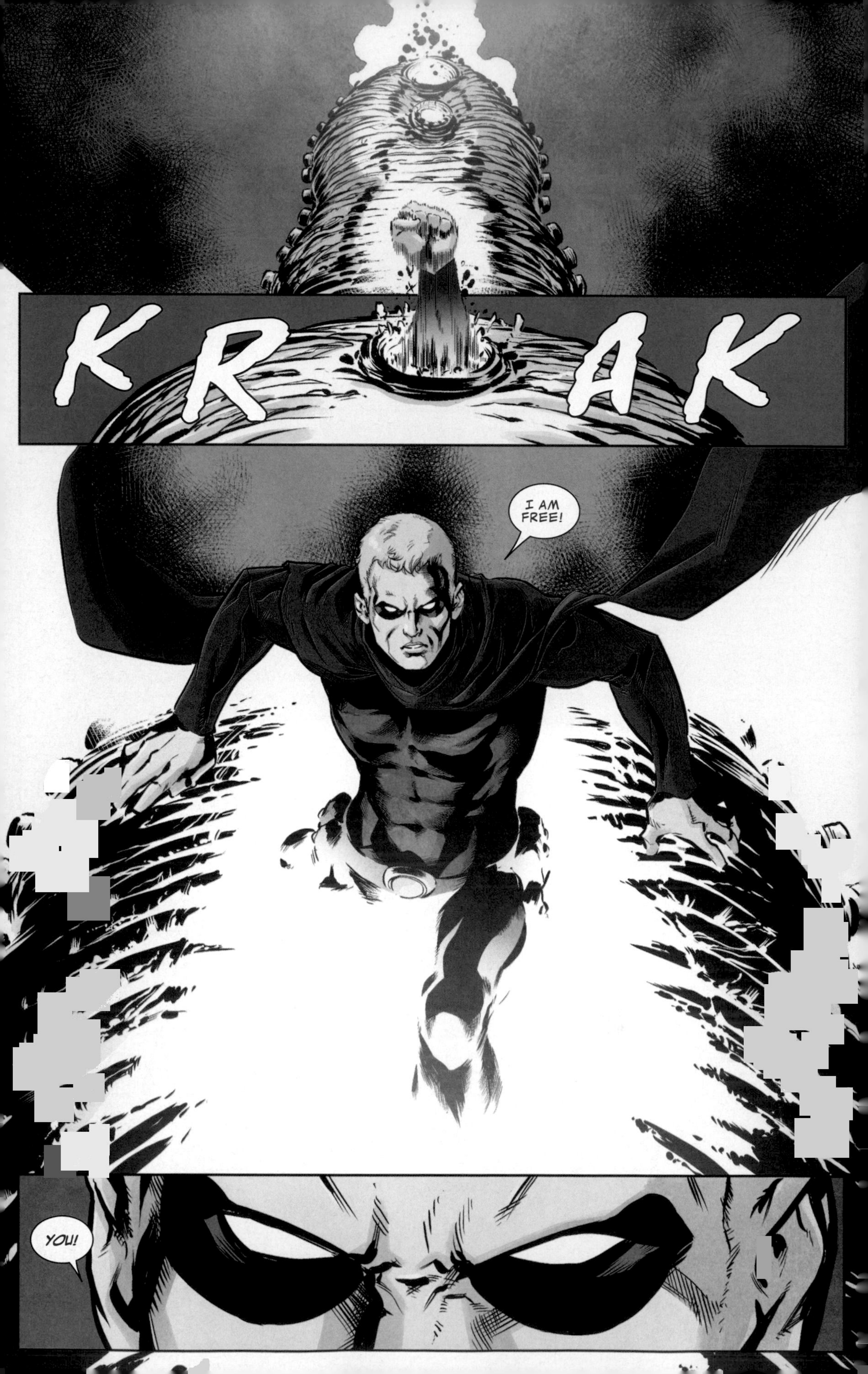
KRAK
I AM FREE!
YOU!

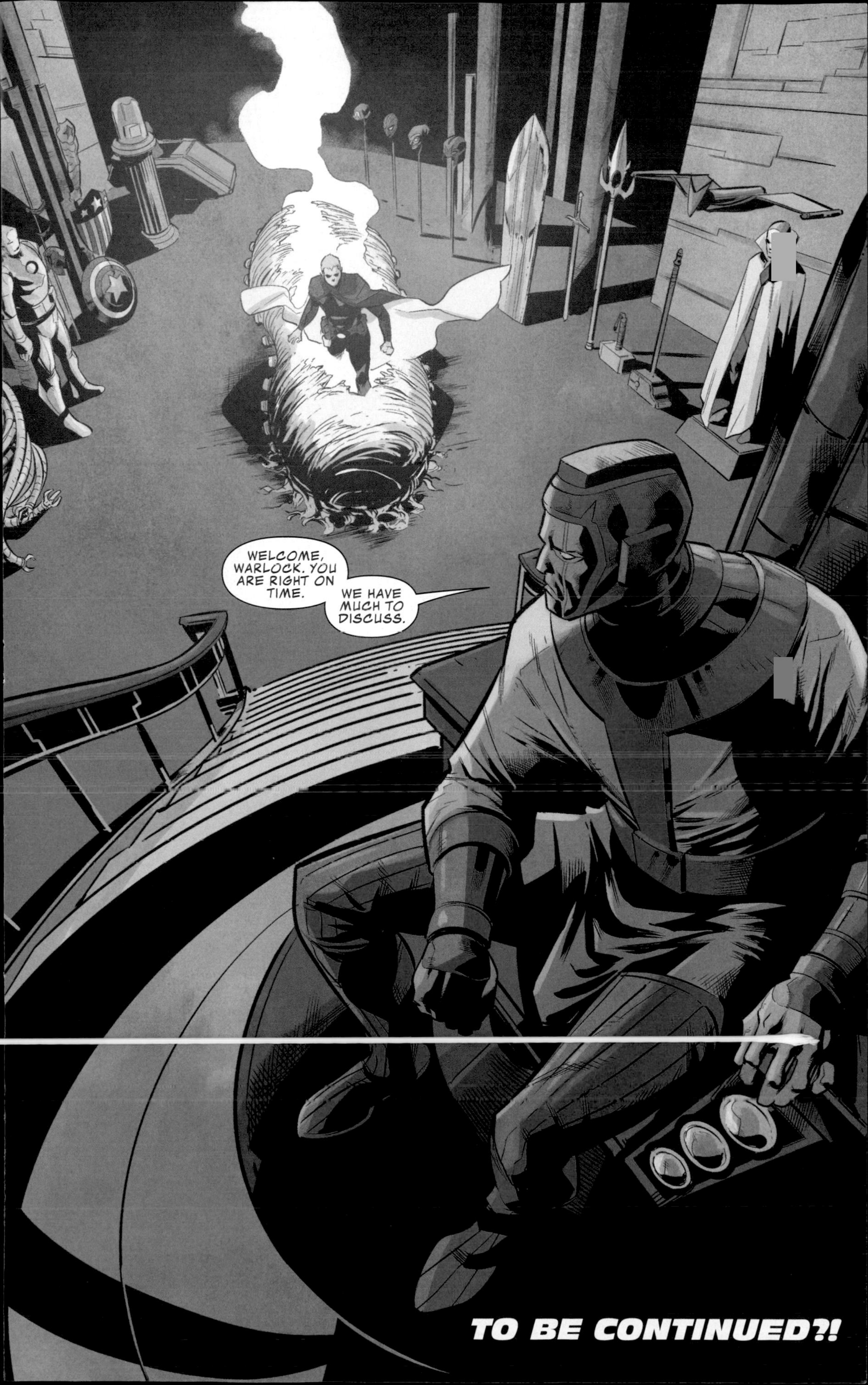
WELCOME, WARLOCK. YOU ARE RIGHT ON TIME.
WE HAVE MUCH TO DISCUSS.
TO BE CONTINUED?!

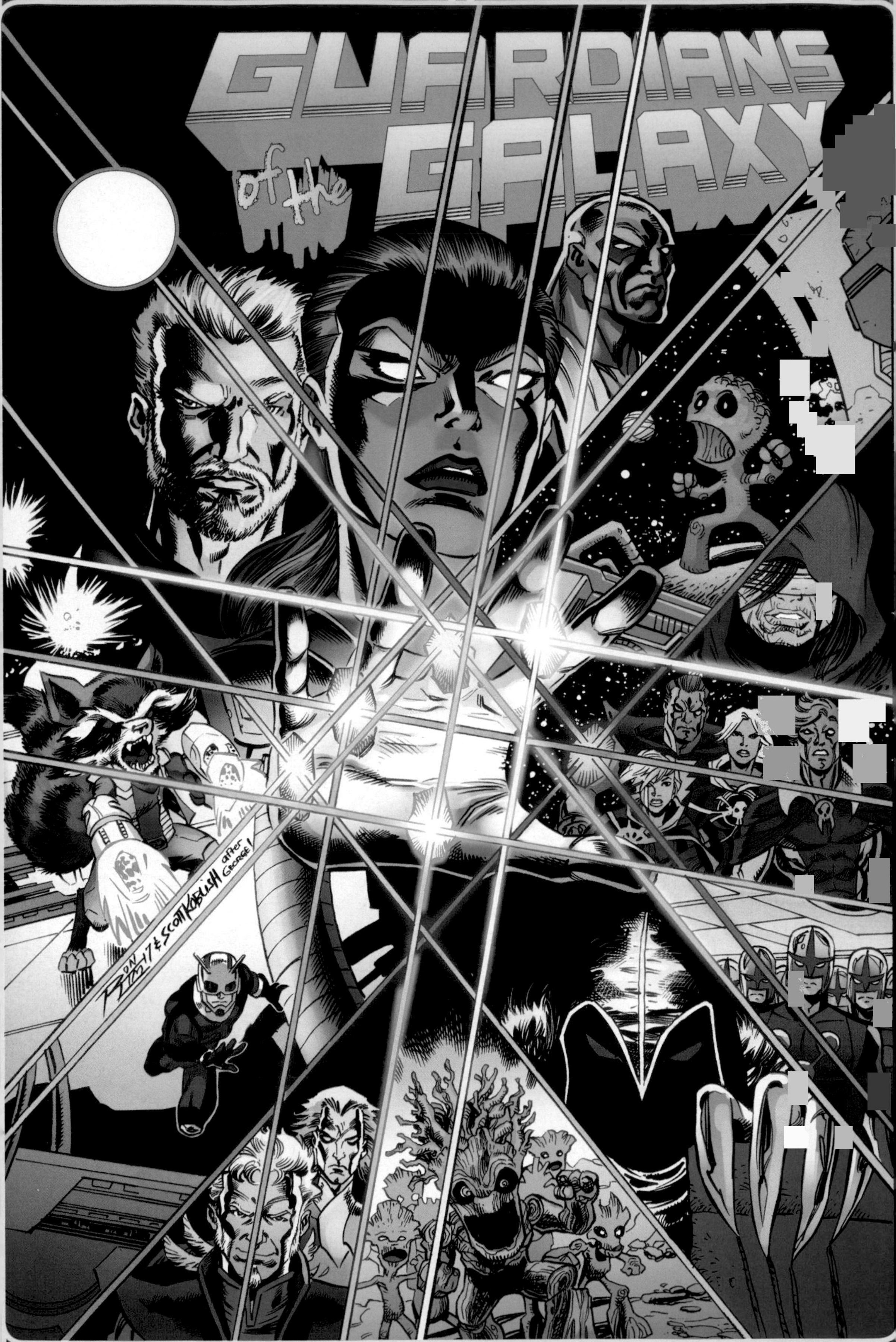
GUARDIANS of the GALAXY
RON LIM '17 & SCOTT KOBLISH after GEORGE!

#146 HOMAGE VARIANT BY RON LIM, SCOTT KOBLISH & RACHELLE ROSENBERG

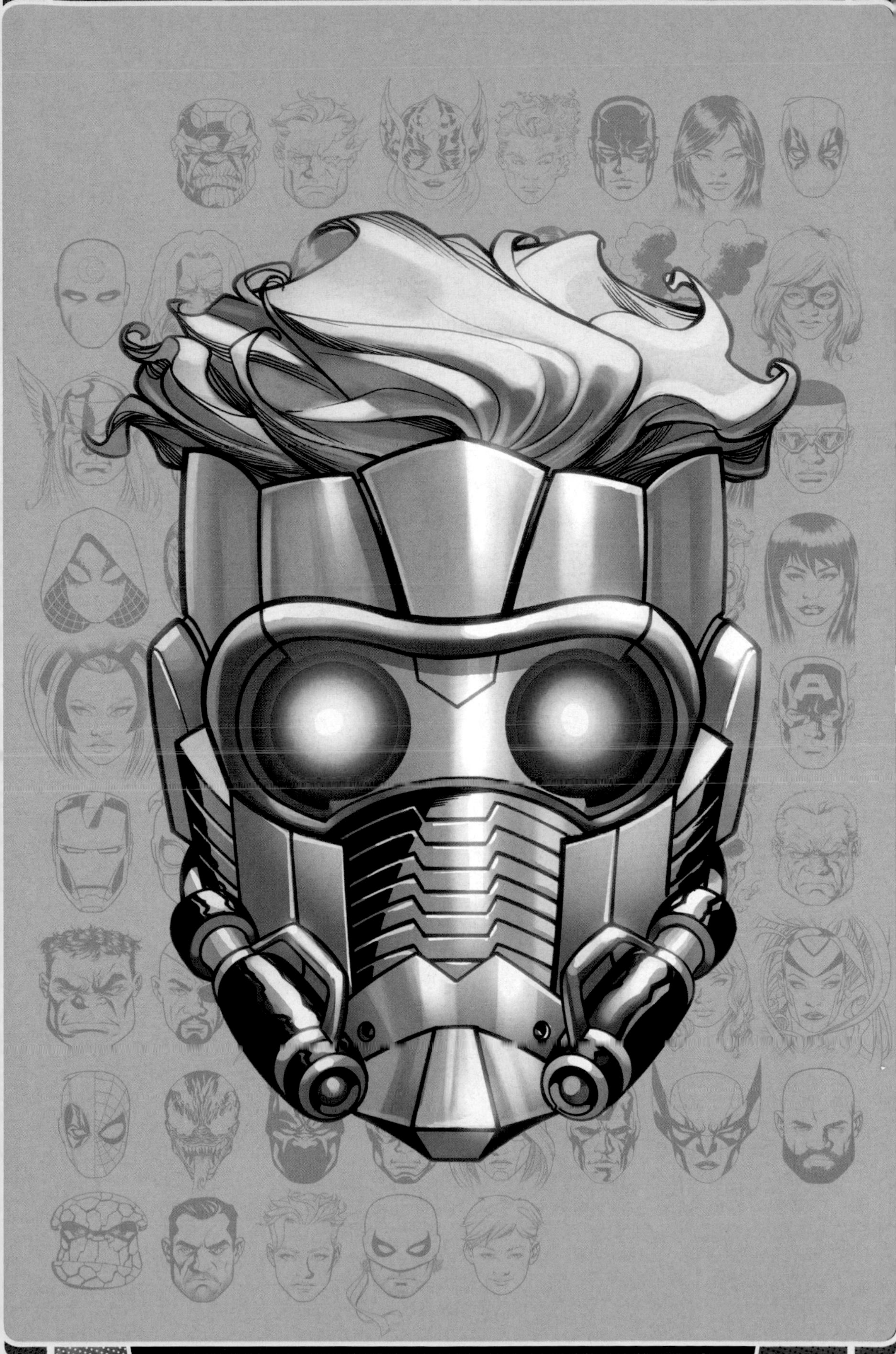

#146 LEGACY HEADSHOT VARIANT BY **MIKE McKONE & RACHELLE ROSENBERG**

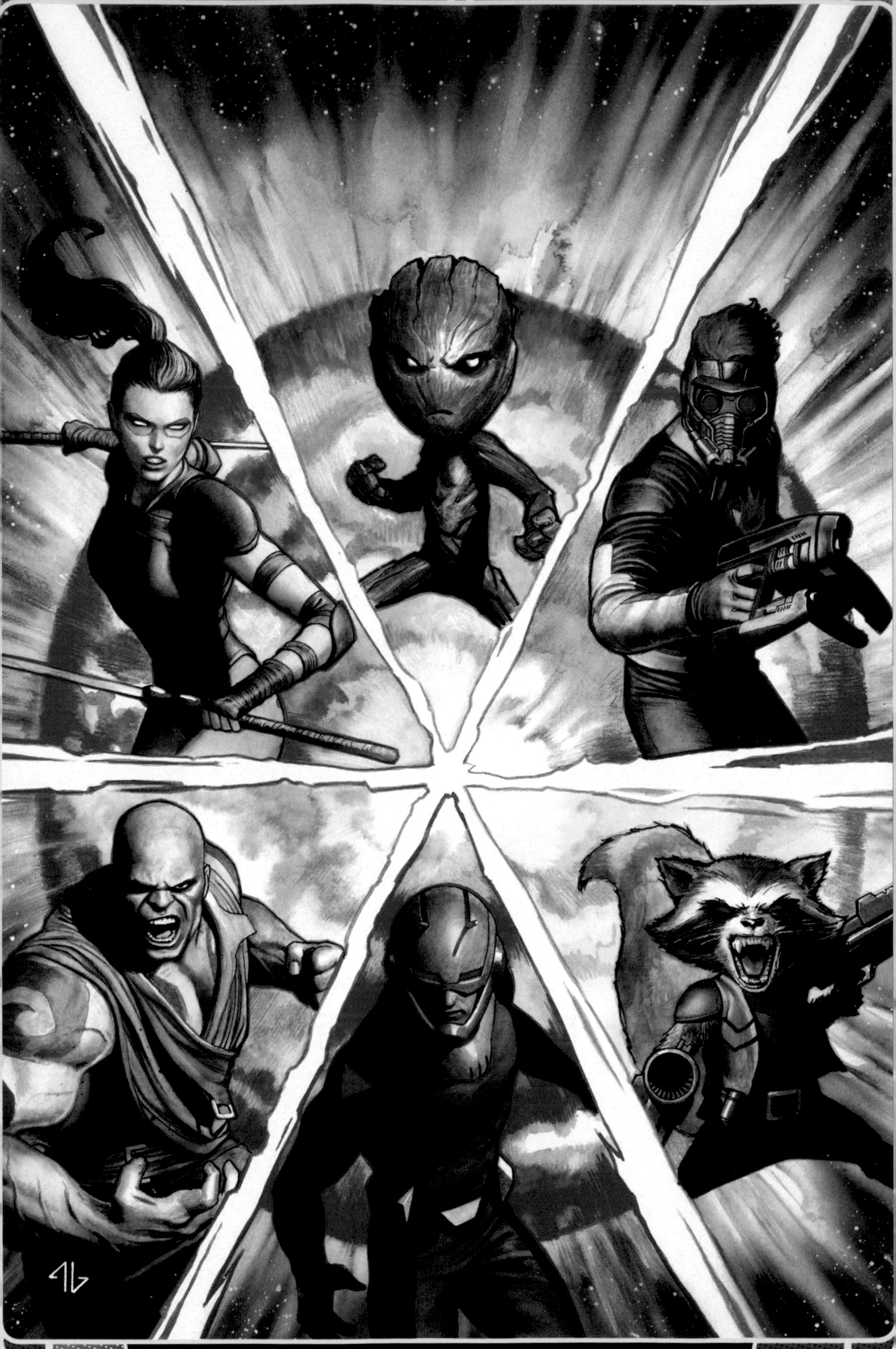

#146 VARIANT BY ADI GRANOV

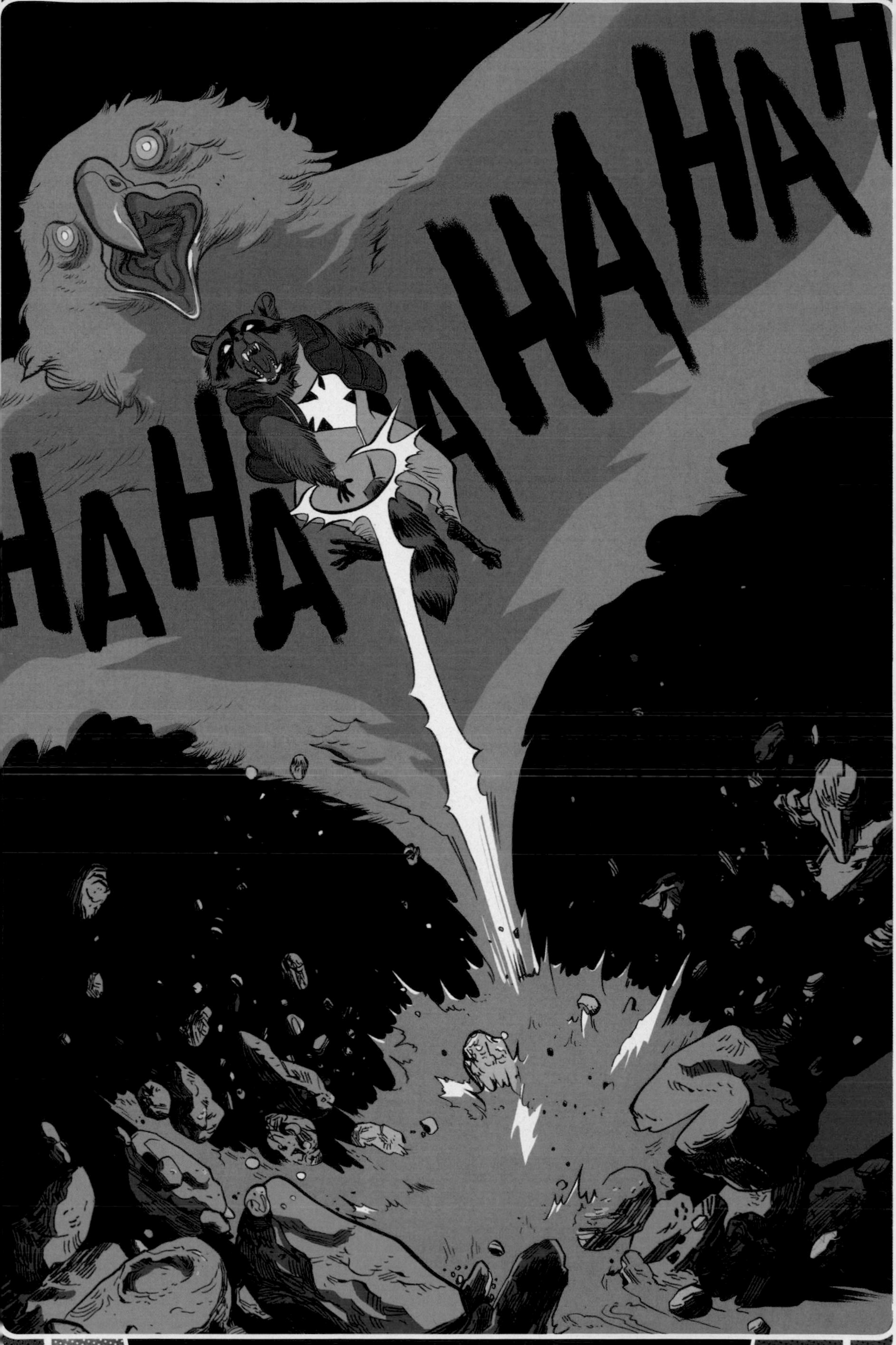
HAHAHAHAHAHA

#148 PHOENIX VARIANT BY ERICA HENDERSON

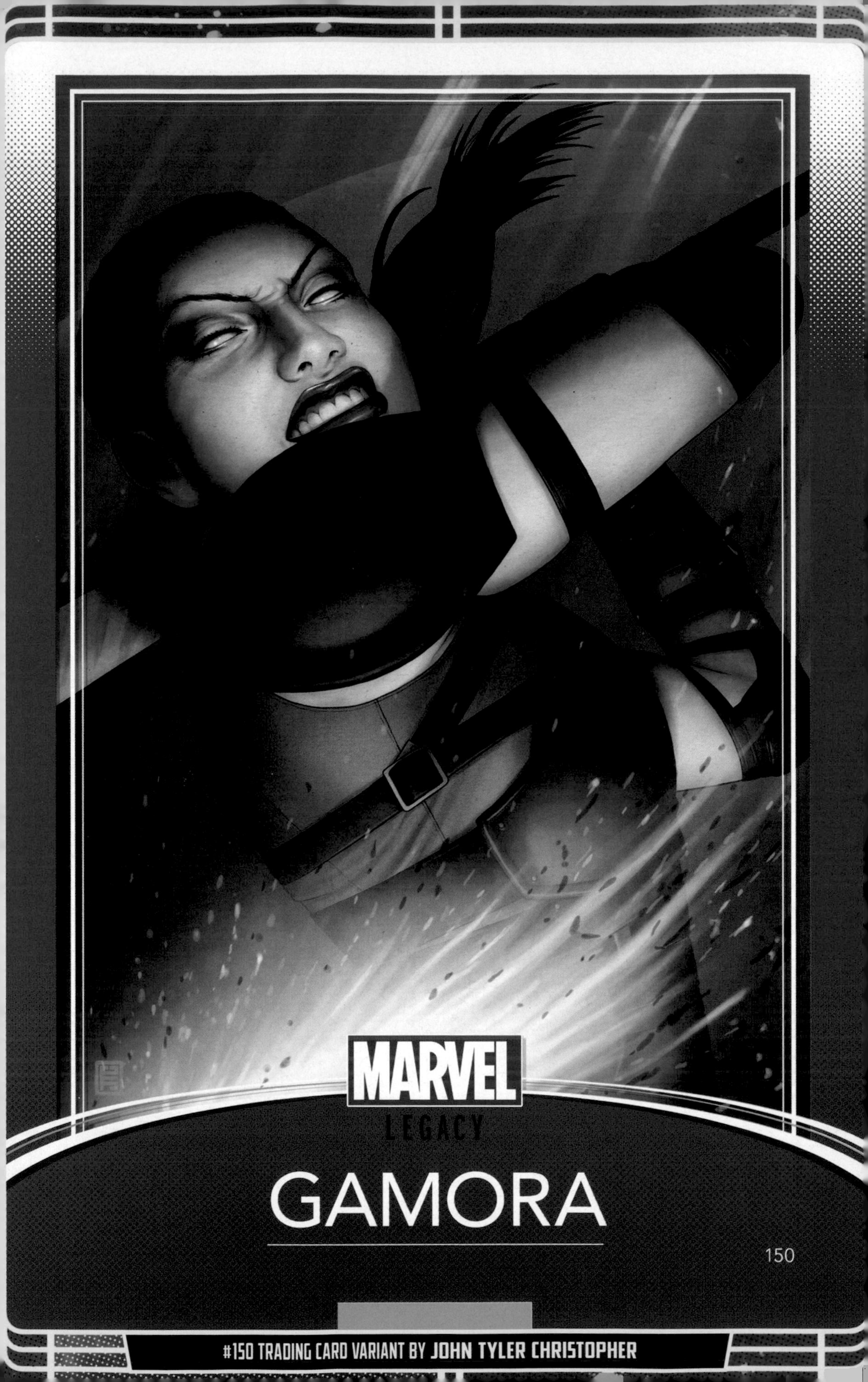

MARVEL
LEGACY
GAMORA
150
#150 TRADING CARD VARIANT BY JOHN TYLER CHRISTOPHER

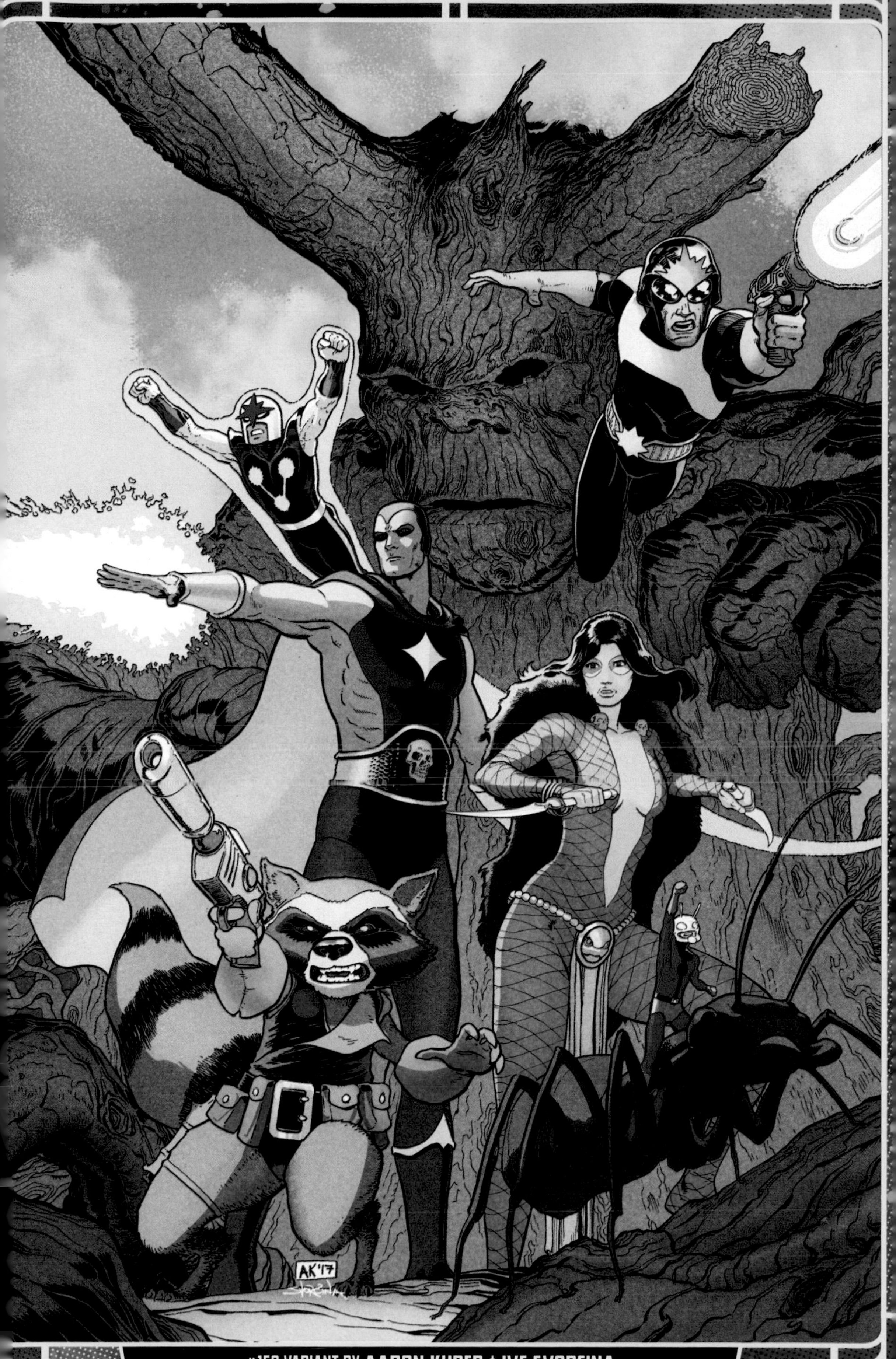
AK'17

#150 VARIANT BY AARON KUDER & IVE SVORCINA

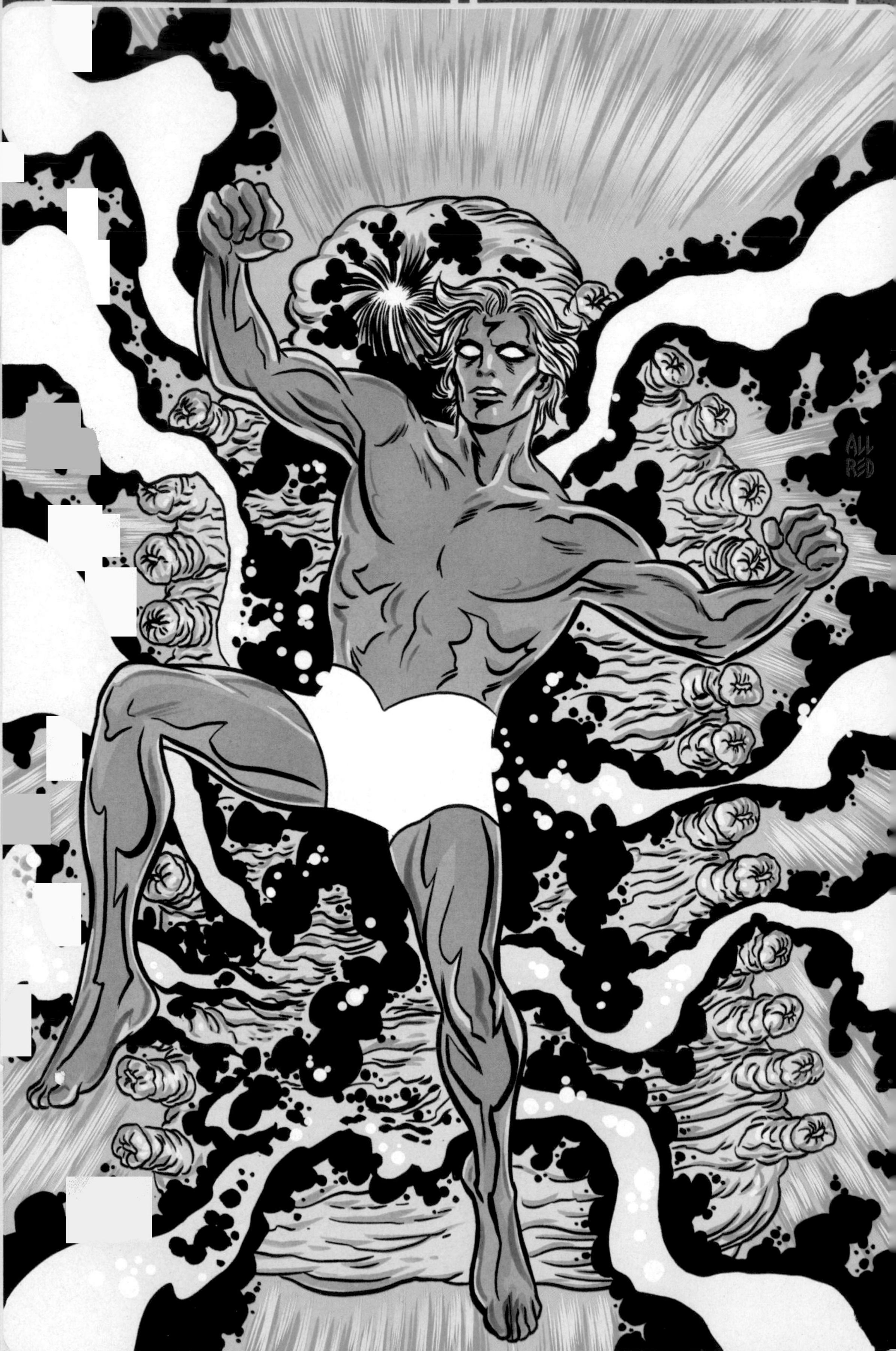
ALLRED

#150 VARIANT BY MICHAEL ALLRED & LAURA ALLRED

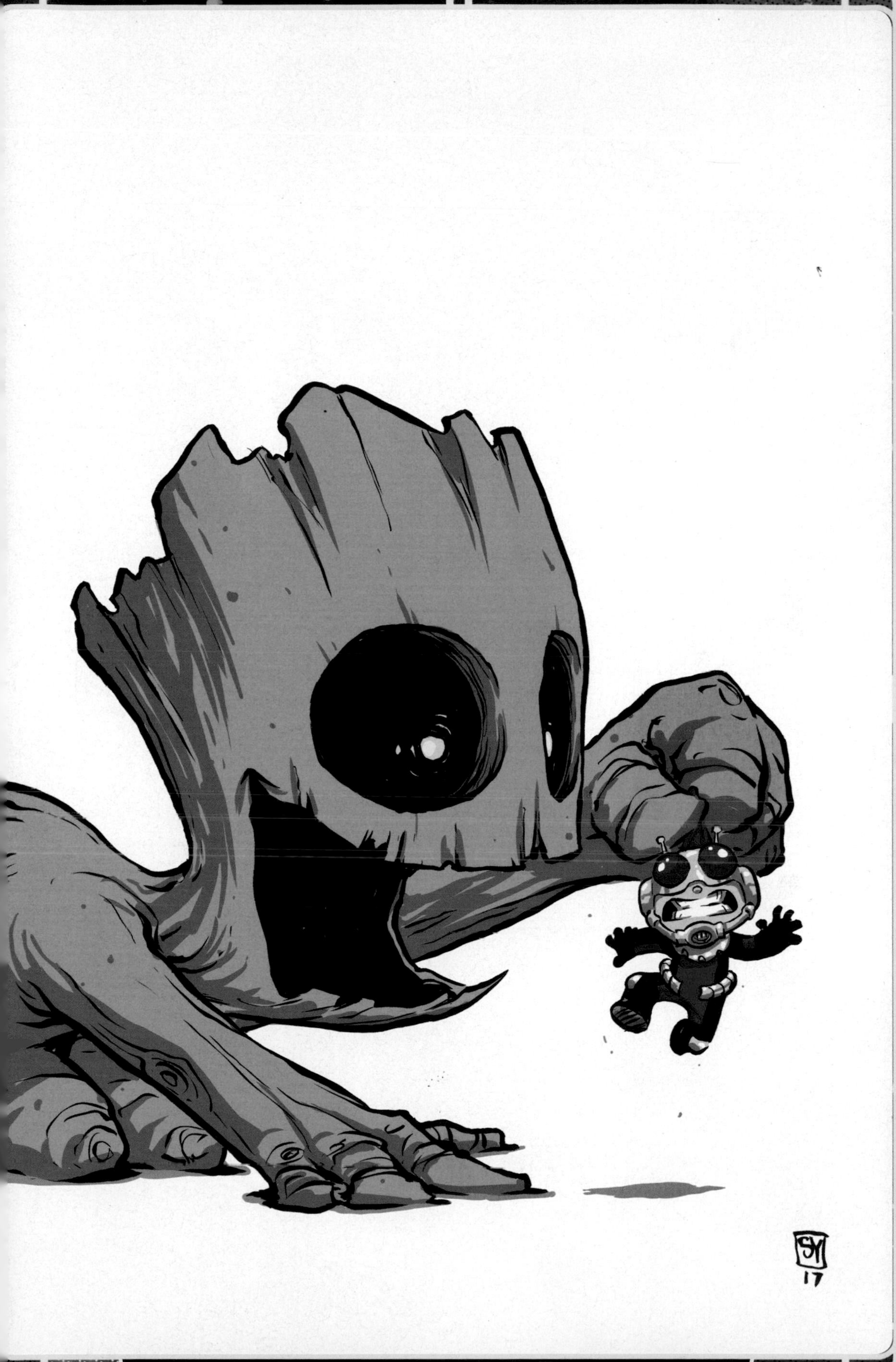
SY
17

#150 VARIANT BY SCOTTIE YOUNG

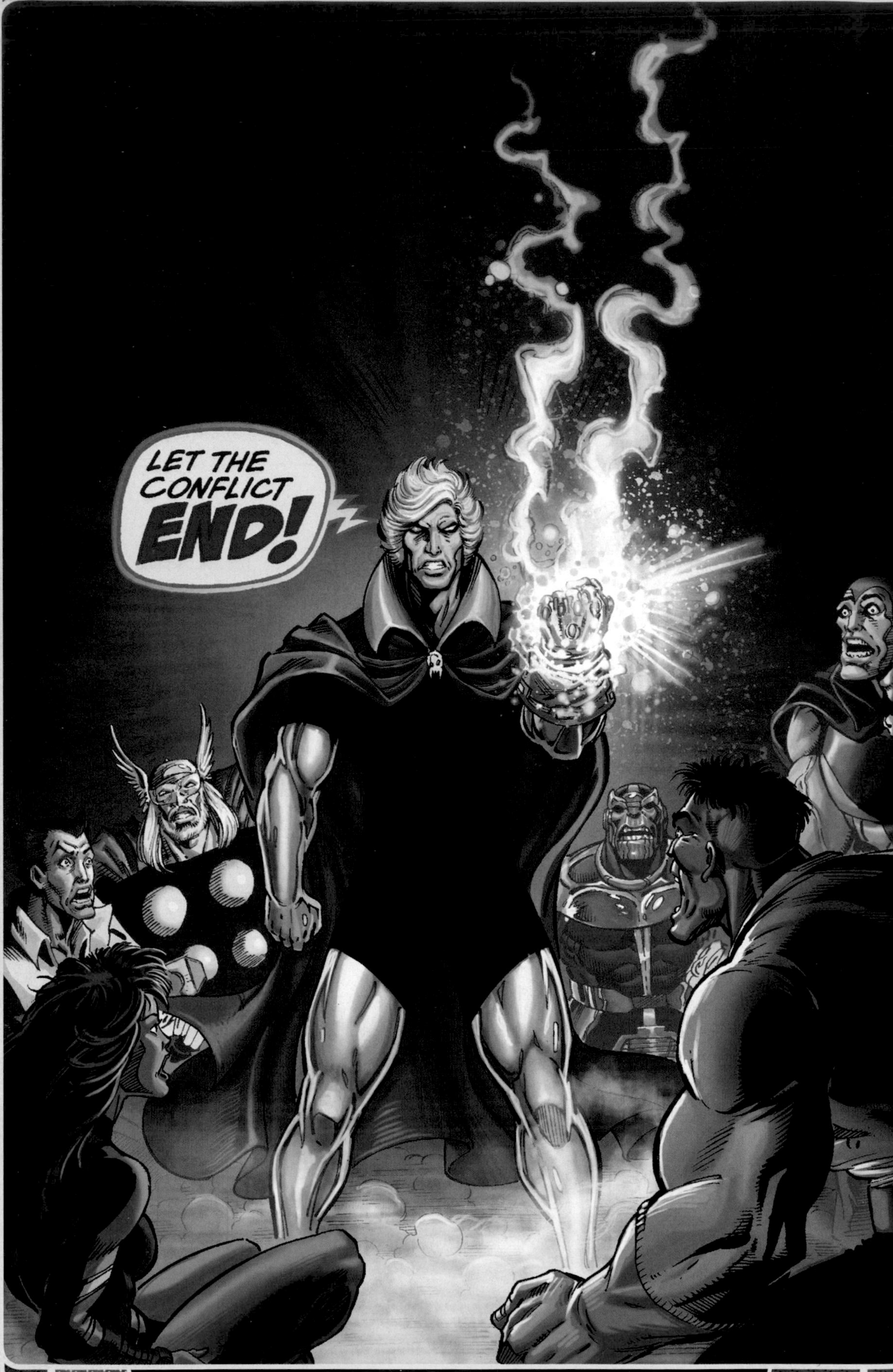
LET THE CONFLICT END!

#150 REMASTERED VARIANT BY **RON LIM, JOSEF RUBINSTEIN & DEAN WHITE**